Collection Evaluation in Academic Libraries

PRACTICAL GUIDES FOR LIBRARIANS

About the Series

This innovative series written and edited for librarians by librarians provides authoritative, practical information and guidance on a wide spectrum of library processes and operations.

Books in the series are focused, describing practical and innovative solutions to a problem facing today's librarian and delivering step-by-step guidance for planning, creating, implementing, managing, and evaluating a wide range of services and programs.

The books are aimed at beginning and intermediate librarians needing basic instruction/ guidance in a specific subject and at experienced librarians who need to gain knowledge in a new area or guidance in implementing a new program/service.

About the Series Editor

The **Practical Guides for Librarians** series was conceived by and is edited by M. Sandra Wood, MLS, MBA, AHIP, FMLA, Librarian Emerita, Penn State University Libraries.

M. Sandra Wood was a librarian at the George T. Harrell Library, The Milton S. Hershey Medical Center, College of Medicine, Pennsylvania State University, Hershey, PA, for over 35 years, specializing in reference, educational, and database services. Ms. Wood worked for several years as a Development Editor for Neal-Schuman Publishers.

Ms. Wood received a MLS from Indiana University and a MBA from the University of Maryland. She is a Fellow of the Medical Library Association and served as a member of MLA's Board of Directors from 1991 to 1995. Ms. Wood is founding and current editor of *Medical Reference Services Quarterly*, now in its 35th volume. She also was founding editor of the *Journal of Consumer Health on the Internet* and the *Journal of Electronic Resources in Medical Libraries* and served as editor/co-editor of both journals through 2011.

Titles in the Series

1. *How to Teach: A Practical Guide for Librarians* by Beverley E. Crane
2. *Implementing an Inclusive Staffing Model for Today's Reference Services* by Julia K. Nims, Paula Storm, and Robert Stevens
3. *Managing Digital Audiovisual Resources: A Practical Guide for Librarians* by Matthew C. Mariner
4. *Outsourcing Technology: A Practical Guide for Librarians* by Robin Hastings
5. *Making the Library Accessible for All: A Practical Guide for Librarians* by Jane Vincent
6. *Discovering and Using Historical Geographical Resources on the Web: A Practical Guide for Librarians* by Eva H. Dodsworth and L. W. Laliberté
7. *Digitization and Digital Archiving: A Practical Guide for Librarians* by Elizabeth R. Leggett
8. *Makerspaces: A Practical Guide for Librarians* by John J. Burke
9. *Implementing Web-Scale Discovery Services: A Practical Guide for Librarians* by JoLinda Thompson
10. *Using iPhones and iPads: A Practical Guide for Librarians* by Matthew Connolly and Tony Cosgrave
11. *Usability Testing: A Practical Guide for Librarians* by Rebecca Blakiston
12. *Mobile Devices: A Practical Guide for Librarians* by Ben Rawlins
13. *Going Beyond Loaning Books to Loaning Technologies: A Practical Guide for Librarians* by Janelle Sander, Lori S. Mestre, and Eric Kurt
14. *Children's Services Today: A Practical Guide for Librarians* by Jeanette Larson
15. *Genealogy: A Practical Guide for Librarians* by Katherine Pennavaria
16. *Collection Evaluation in Academic Libraries: A Practical Guide for Librarians* by Karen C. Kohn

Collection Evaluation
in Academic Libraries

A Practical Guide
for Librarians

Karen C. Kohn

PRACTICAL GUIDES FOR LIBRARIANS, NO. 16

ROWMAN & LITTLEFIELD
Lanham • Boulder • New York • London

Published by Rowman & Littlefield
A wholly owned subsidiary of The Rowman & Littlefield Publishing Group, Inc.
4501 Forbes Boulevard, Suite 200, Lanham, Maryland 20706
www.rowman.com

Unit A, Whitacre Mews, 26-34 Stannary Street, London SE11 4AB

British Library Cataloguing in Publication Information Available

Library of Congress Cataloging-in-Publication Data

Kohn, Karen C., 1978–
    Collection evaluation in academic libraries : a practical guide for librarians / Karen C. Kohn.
        pages cm. — (Practical guides for librarians ; no. 16)
    Includes bibliographical references and index.
    ISBN 978-1-4422-3859-6 (hardcover : alk. paper) — ISBN 978-1-4422-3860-2 (pbk. : alk.
paper) — ISBN 978-1-4422-5065-9 (ebook)
    1. Academic libraries—Collection development. 2. Collection development (Libraries)—
Evaluation. I. Title.
    Z675.U5K765 2015
    025.2'1877—dc23   2015004170

∞™ The paper used in this publication meets the minimum requirements of American
National Standard for Information Sciences—Permanence of Paper for Printed Library
Materials, ANSI/NISO Z39.48-1992.

Printed in the United States of America

Contents

Illustrations

Figures

Tables

Textboxes

Preface

If you work in an academic library, you've probably been hearing talk about assessment. Academic librarians are getting the message from university administrators and from our professional associations that we need to find ways to quantify how our collections and services are benefiting our institutions. In 2009, the Association of College and Research Libraries published a white paper calling for "librarians to learn how to initiate and design assessment that demonstrates the library's contribution to institutional mission and strategic goals" (Brown and Malenfant, 2012: 13). Assessment is becoming especially important in the area of collection development due to tighter budgets. When you can't afford to purchase as much as you used to, a responsible approach is to try to figure out in some objective way which materials are most relevant and useful so you can cut out the rest. On the other hand, you might want data that can help you make a case that you need to continue purchasing at the same level in order to remain competitive. Whether your motivation for doing a collection evaluation is coming from your own desire to make informed decisions or is driven by your institution's culture of assessment, you'll need to figure out what assessment or evaluation involves and how to do it.

Collection evaluation is the process of systematically gathering data and using it to learn about the quality or value of your collection. This data can come from your catalog and circulation records, interlibrary loan requests, expert recommendations, or comparisons to other libraries. You do not need special software to do an evaluation, just some time and a clear definition of your goals. *Collection Evaluation in Academic Libraries: A Practical Guide for Librarians* will take you through the steps of gathering data and analyzing it, so that you can be comfortable even if you have never done a quantitative study before.

The intended audience of this book is mainly academic libraries, though the evaluation methods will in many cases be applicable to other types of libraries as well. Because evaluation can influence so many aspects of collection management, people in several different roles within academic libraries could potentially use the strategies described in the chapters that follow. If you are new to collection development, an evaluation can be a great way to learn about your existing collection as well as about the subject areas it covers. More experienced selectors will find practical and concrete ideas of how to use data to identify important authors, books, or journals, or create guidelines for weeding. Directors or heads of collection development can use the evaluation results when making budget requests or talking to other administrators about the library.

All of the techniques presented here can be done without using specialized software or any math more complicated than calculating percentages. Although this book introduces you to the latest software products for collection evaluation, WorldCat Collection Evaluation and Intota Assessment, it does not assume that everyone has access to these tools. You'll be able to pull data from software you already use, such as your library catalog and WorldCat. Instructions are provided for collecting holdings information from WorldCat Discovery, which will supersede FirstSearch at the end of 2015. The only software that is required for storing data and making calculations is Excel. You do not have to be an experienced Excel user to manipulate your data, however. Any function that is more advanced than typing numbers is described step-by-step.

What is distinctive about *Collection Evaluation in Academic Libraries* is that it not only explains how to collect data but also how to use your findings to improve your collection. The literature on collection development is often vague, referring to familiarity with the curriculum, major authors, and knowledge of your existing collection. It rarely says exactly how you would acquire this familiarity. An evaluation is one way to do so. Because collection evaluation can tell you so much about your patrons' needs, the disciplines you support, and the strengths and weaknesses of your current collection, it can be useful for anyone doing collection development. This book makes explicit connections between the data and your purchasing or weeding decisions, so that you can get as much as possible out of the evaluation.

Organization of This Book

Collection Evaluation in Academic Libraries: A Practical Guide for Librarians begins with an overview in chapter 1 of some of the reasons librarians do collection evaluation, as well as principles to keep in mind to ensure that your data is meaningful. Chapter 2 summarizes four different approaches to collection evaluation so that you can start thinking about which combination of approaches is the best fit for your goals and resources. You'll solidify your decision about which collection evaluation methods to use as you read chapter 3, which teaches you how to plan your project in a way that balances time, quality, and cost and also takes into account different colleagues' needs. Once you've finished the planning process, chapters 4–11 show you how to implement the collection evaluation.

Which approach you choose depends partly on what question about collection strength you want to answer. Do you have enough materials? Do you have the best materials? Do you have what your patrons want to use? The different approaches presented in this book each answer a different one of these questions. There are two methods that answer the question about what patrons want. The first evaluation method, presented in chapters 4 and 5, is benchmarking—comparing your library to other libraries or comparing different sections within the library using basic counts of items or titles. This method asks if the library has enough materials overall or on specific topics. Chapters 6 and 7 present the second method, list-checking, which involves comparing your collection to lists of expert recommendations to see whether you have high-quality materials. The third method, usage statistics, presented in chapters 8 and 9, assumes your goal is to provide materials your patrons will use. This method uses traditional measures of use such as circulation or downloads. Chapters 10 and 11 discuss citation analysis as an alternate way of measuring use. Citation analysis relies on the bibliographies in faculty or student work to reveal what your patrons are citing.

Each of the four collection evaluation methods is described in a pair of chapters: the first with the subtitle "Collecting and Analyzing the Data" (chapters 4, 6, 8, and 10) and the second with the subtitle "Interpreting and Acting on the Data" (chapters 5, 7, 9, and 11). The "Collecting and Analyzing" chapters describe situations in which you would want to use this method, a brief history of the method, advantages and disadvantages of using this method, possible sources of data, how to store and organize the data, and any calculations you'll need to do in order to interpret the numbers. The "Interpreting and Acting" chapters begin with how to draw conclusions about what your data means. These chapters address how you will know if the number of books you have on a topic is enough, or what amount of circulation counts as high use. They also note specific actions you can take based on your data, such as adding subscriptions, marketing your collection, or changing your approval plan.

A final action step that is common to many collection evaluations is sharing the findings with others: administrators, prospective students, or library colleagues who were not involved in the project. The last chapter of this book, chapter 12, advises you on how to present information in a way that is clear and relevant to your audience and that balances transparency with determining what message you send. Because so many people in your institution have a stake in having a strong library, your findings will likely be of interest to people other than those whose initial questions or needs prompted you to pursue the evaluation. If someone outside the library is pushing you to do a collection evaluation, the good news is it will end up benefiting you as well, and if the evaluation is your own initiative, it will probably benefit others. Not only will you find collection evaluation useful, with this book as a guide it will also be doable.

Reference

Brown, Karen, and Kara J. Malenfant. 2012. "Connect, Collaborate, and Communicate: A Report from the Value of Academic Libraries Summits." Association of College and Research Libraries. http://www.ala.org/acrl/sites/ala.org.acrl/files/content/issues/value/val_summit.pdf.

Acknowledgments

My research for this book involved not only written sources of information but also human sources, without whose help I could not have completed my work. Thank you to everyone who shared information with me, tracked down answers to my questions, and showed me how to use your software products. Sara Randall from OCLC provided a demonstration of WorldCat Collection Evaluation as well as trial access and answered questions over email. Jen John and Diana Hall, also from OCLC, helped me get set up with WorldCat Discovery and provided guidance with searching. Christine Goetz was my point person from ProQuest, arranging for me to have a demonstration of Intota Assessment and helping me get permission to reproduce screenshots. Ella Garrison and Mark Tullos provided the demonstration and the screenshots. Jennifer Knievel at the University of Colorado kindly sent me her spreadsheet of call numbers mapped to OCLC's conspectus divisions. Pat Wagner of Pattern Research introduced me to the iron triangle of project management many years ago, and it has been helpful to me ever since. I'm glad she was able to remind me what it was called so I could properly reference the concept here.

My editor, Sandy Wood, has been a pleasure to work with: responsive, encouraging, and helpful. Thank you.

Several people not directly connected to libraries have also provided essential practical support. Dustin Kidd of the Department of Sociology at Temple University, a former professor of mine, had useful suggestions on how to manage the project, which calmed me down several times when I didn't know how to move forward. Thank you for being so committed to mentoring students through the writing and publication process. My excellent student worker, Alexandra Bacon, who helped compile the data for several of the examples in this book, has gone a step beyond with every task I assign her.

I appreciate the friends, family, and colleagues who have been excited for me and expressed interest in my process and progress. I am lucky to have a good friend who not only wanted to write together but organized and hosted a writing retreat, complete with food, lodging, and a hiking break. Now that I am done, I will miss writing at Lauri Hyers's beautiful home, surrounded by trees and good company.

CHAPTER 1

How Collection Evaluation Can Benefit Your Library

IN THIS CHAPTER

▷ Reasons for Doing an Evaluation

▷ History of Evaluations

▷ Principles of Evaluation

▷ Different Kinds of Quantitative Data

Reasons for Doing an Evaluation

EVEN IF YOU THINK YOU KNOW NOTHING about collection evaluation, it is likely that you are already doing it in some form. You just might not call it by that name. Evaluation basically means any systematic way of answering the question "How are we doing?" More formally, it is the process of using some kind of data to answer questions about the quality and adequacy of a product or service.

Motivations for Collection Evaluation

The most common form of collection evaluation that librarians do is respond to requirements from accrediting agencies. Specific programs at a university, as well as the university as a whole, must be accredited on a regular schedule. Accrediting bodies for many academic programs want to see information about library holdings, although what they ask for is usually very general: the number of books and journals, size of the budget, and some comment on how the scope of the collection matches the curriculum. Although this is a very surface-level way to describe a collection, it can be considered an evaluation because the data is being used by outsiders to judge the quality of your library compared to others.

Another common evaluation that libraries do is use usage reports to decide which journals to renew and which to cancel. This is usually done out of financial necessity or as a commitment to spending money carefully. Although libraries have long tried to count how often print journals have been used by tallying each time an issue or volume needs to be reshelved, much more data is available now that collections are online. Using usage statistics to make renewal decisions can be a narrowly focused form of evaluation if it ignores whether you are supporting some disciplines more than others and does not consider what other journals you don't have that might get used even more. It is, nevertheless, a good beginning for data-driven decision making, and you can build on this initial evaluation to create a broader one.

There are many situations beyond these two in which collection evaluation can be useful. The professional literature has examples of people who undertook an evaluation in response to the creation of a new academic program. In this case, the goal was to find out what the library already offered to support the program, find gaps in the collection, and learn what the major books and journals were in the field so that the library could use this information to create its initial core collection. Another situation that shows up in the literature is when a group of libraries decide to evaluate each library's collection in order to plan a collaborative collection development project. When libraries work together to divide up collection areas, it makes sense for each library to collect in areas where it already has a strong collection. An evaluation helps identify which areas these are. Another recent use of collection evaluation has been evaluating new purchase models, usually patron-driven acquisitions, to see how a model is affecting the scope and usefulness of the collection. Libraries wishing to gauge the success of their patron-driven acquisitions programs can compare the breadth and usage of books acquired through the traditional librarian-selected model to books purchased at the point of need.

Evaluation as a Collection Development Tool

As the above examples begin to illustrate, collection evaluation can help with many aspects of collection management. From the basic task of selecting books to the more complex project of planning for a new purchase model, all collection management functions require some information about the existing collection and about patron needs, and there are certain questions you need to be able to answer in order to do the job well. Table 1.1 lists questions you might ask when doing different tasks. These questions are an expansion of the basic question, "How are we doing?" They ask in more detail what you ought to have that you don't, what you have that is not needed, and whether your holdings match patrons' needs. All of the questions in the table are ones whose answers can be found with one or more of the evaluation methods in this book. Even if your current informal or intuitive means of answering these questions have been helpful to you, it is likely that a formal evaluation will teach you something new about your collection that you can use to make informed decisions.

The literature about collection development tends to have very general suggestions of how to figure out what to add or remove from your collection. Textbooks will mention reading book reviews, checking for publications of major professional organizations, and becoming familiar with the university's curriculum and the library's existing collection.

Table 1.1. Information Needed to Manage a Library Collection

TASK	QUESTIONS TO ASK
Book and journal selection	What are patrons requesting on interlibrary loan? What are the most important titles in the field? What authors and topics are important to your patrons? What are patrons citing in their writing? In what subject areas do you have less than your peers? What do other libraries have that you don't? What formats do your patrons prefer? How do disciplines intersect or overlap?
Weeding or moving to storage	What is not getting used? Where does your collection overlap with consortial partners? How old are the books you have on this subject? Which sections have large numbers of unused books? Do your patrons use older materials? How old?
Renewing or canceling subscriptions	What is getting used? What are the most important titles in the field? How does the cost compare to the usefulness of the resource?
Training new selectors	In which subjects are patrons finding most of what they need within the library, and for which subjects do they have to look elsewhere? In which subjects is the collection larger or smaller than that of other libraries? What authors and topics are important to your patrons? What are the most important titles in the field, and do you have them? What are patrons citing in their writing? What do other libraries have that you don't? What sections need to be weeded?
Budget requests	What do aspirational institutions have that you don't? Are your patrons finding most of what they need within the library, or are they relying heavily on interlibrary loan or other sources?
Marketing	How many books and periodicals do you have? What are the unique strengths of your library? How does the size of your library compare to libraries at similar institutions?
Accreditation	What are the most important titles or databases in the field, and do you have them? How does the size of your collection in this area compare to libraries at similar institutions?
Evaluating new purchase models, e.g., patron-driven acquisitions	Do books purchased under this model get used more or less than books purchased under your previous models? Is this purchase model resulting in books on a variety of subjects, or is it skewed toward a few?
Planning collaborative collection development	In what subject areas do you have more than your partner institutions? Do you have any books or journals that none of your partner institutions have?

They often give the impression that collection development depends on knowledge that is accumulated over time and integrated in the selector's head. Johnson's classic book *Fundamentals of Collection Development and Management* is fairly typical in saying, "An experienced collections librarian is hard-pressed to explain exactly how he or she decides what to add and what to exclude" (Johnson, 2009: 103). An evaluation provides specifics so that you have an objective way of knowing in which areas your collection is larger than others or which sections are more heavily used. You can use your evaluation to generate a ranked list of the most used authors or journals. With data, you can learn about the needs of people you are unable to talk with directly: both what you are providing that they find useful and what they are using that you don't have.

Using Collection Evaluation for Relationship Building

Besides providing you with specific information that can help with decision making, collection evaluation can help in intangible ways by influencing relationships with people outside the library. In academic libraries, data can be a tool for outreach to faculty if you share your findings with them and solicit their feedback. Faculty sometimes think of themselves—subject experts and the ones planning the curriculum—as most qualified to say what belongs in the collection. Bringing your data to the faculty can demonstrate that you as a librarian have unique knowledge about the collection and user needs to complement the faculty's knowledge. Data can help reveal collection development as its own area of expertise, at the same time that it can provoke conversations with faculty in which they share expert knowledge about their curriculum and fields of specialization.

Using data to initiate a conversation can help, especially when there is a conflict between what faculty believe the library should have and what librarians believe. At many institutions, some faculty have questioned whether the library ought to be buying books at all, particularly in disciplines that rely primarily on journals for the latest research. If circulation reports show that books are being used to some extent, reviewing the reports with faculty can teach both you and them about patrons' needs. Including faculty in the process of interpreting the data can set you up to work together rather than arguing over conflicting impressions.

Evaluative data can affect librarians' relationship with administrators as well. With the increased focus on assessment and data-driven decision making in higher education today, having your own carefully considered strategies for collecting and using data demonstrates that you are keeping up with this trend. Wical and Kishel say that "the more librarians can speak the language of assessment in terms that administrators understand, the better their libraries will do in uncertain financial times" (2013: 186). When administrators see that the library is collecting its own assessment data, they not only know that the library is on board with the institution's culture of assessment, they are more confident in the library's ability to manage its resources.

History of Evaluations

Over the last decade, university administrators have been trying to build cultures of assessment at their institutions. One impetus for this effort was a report from the U.S. Department of Education's Commission on the Future of Higher Education, released in 2006, that called for greater accountability from universities in the form of publicly available data about cost and student learning. The commission recommended that the data be presented in a format that allowed students to easily compare different schools and make informed decisions about where to attend. This recommendation reflects a shift toward seeing students as consumers, which is a change that education policy makers say is a result of the high cost of higher education and the recent appearance of online alternatives to a traditional college education (Basken, 2012).

In addition to asking for universities to make information available to prospective students, the commission also requested changes in what information accrediting agencies will use in their review processes. The report says, "Accreditation agencies should make performance outcomes . . . the core of their assessment as a priority over inputs or processes" (U.S. Department of Education, 2006: 25). The agencies that accredit U.S. institutions of higher education have since altered their guidelines for measuring student learning (Brown and Malenfant, 2012), and the National Research Council recently undertook a three-year investigation of ways to measure the quality of a university (Basken, 2012). In addition, as national conversations have continued to emphasize accountability and assessment, universities have looked for their own ways to evaluate their quality and value beyond what is required.

The trend of increased assessment in education is happening not only in classrooms or among school administrators but in academic libraries as well. The addition of two new assessment-related professional development events and increasing attendance at these events attest to librarians' interest in the concept. The Association of Research Libraries began offering its Library Assessment Conference in 2006, and by 2012 attendance at the event had more than doubled from 215 to 560 (MacAyeal, 2014). In 2012, the American Library Association launched its institute, Assessment in Action: Academic Libraries and Student Success, which plans to accept a growing number of participants each year. Yet this new focus on assessment by professional associations does not mean it is a new concept. Although evaluation has just begun to be treated as its own area of specialization, libraries have been developing evaluation methods for more than a century.

The first library collection evaluation in America was conducted by Charles C. Jewett in 1850 as a report for the Smithsonian. It was not an evaluation of the Smithsonian itself but aimed to determine the capacity of all U.S. libraries collectively to support scholars (Johnson, 2009). Most of the specific methods described in this book were developed later, though still long before assessment became a buzzword. A project at the University of Chicago in 1933 used the list-checking method detailed in chapter 6 to compare its library's holdings to four hundred lists of recommended works (Lundin, 1989). Whereas list-checking requires finding lists devoted to particular subjects, the Clapp-Jordan formula, introduced in 1965, aimed to create a universal tool for evaluating all academic library collections. This formula calculated target collection sizes for academic libraries based on the number of faculty and students at the institution (Hiller and Self, 2004). It proposed a minimum size that constituted a core collection for any academic library, and then added to this baseline according to the size of the institution (Johnson, 2009).

Despite this long and varied history of collection evaluation methods, none of these methods has been widely used until recently. More commonly, although libraries have collected a lot of numbers, the numbers have not been meaningful. One set of numbers that libraries typically collect has been the kind requested in yearly surveys for the Association of College and Research Libraries (ACRL), the Association of Research Libraries (ARL), and the National Center for Education Statistics (NCES). The surveys ask questions about numbers of volumes owned, journals subscriptions, online database subscriptions, and expenditures. Because these numbers describe the entire collection without breaking it down by subject or year of publication or considering the quality of the resources, they do very little to help librarians determine the quality or usefulness of their collections. Several people have criticized these and similar organizations for perhaps inadvertently conveying to libraries that simply collecting numbers counts as meaningful evaluation (Hiller and Self, 2004; Brooks-Kieffer, 2009).

The shift from compiling numbers for surveys to attending institutes on assessment has come about due to several factors. One factor is the multitude of data that became available once libraries automated their catalogs. Another is the increasing variety of methods that have been developed since the Smithsonian evaluation in 1850. Gross and Gross (1927) conducted the first citation analysis in 1927, and the aforementioned University of Chicago list-checking project came soon after in 1933. The conspectus method, which significantly influenced the benchmarking techniques of chapter 4, was introduced in 1980. Around the same time the conspectus method was introduced, changes in organizational thinking prompted libraries to return to some of the methods developed in the first half of the century and use them more regularly. Hiller and Self (2004) say that strategic planning became widespread in the 1980s, which forced libraries to define goals and objectives and find ways to measure whether they had achieved these goals. During the same time period, libraries began to focus more on how they were used rather than simply on how much they contained. The 1990s saw the first use of LibQUAL+, a survey of library users' impressions of library services. By the end of the twentieth century, automated systems, a developed toolkit of evaluation methods, strategic thinking, and a focus on users came together to position libraries to begin evaluating their collections in ways tailored to their unique goals and user populations and designed to influence future collection development.

Principles of Evaluation

Nowadays, the literature advocates an evaluation process that differs significantly from the survey data libraries have traditionally collected. There are several guiding principles for a good evaluation. It should be geared toward the library's users, as a good library is no longer judged strictly by size but more by how well it meets users' needs. An educational institution might use multiple approaches to measure this, as students' needs are a combination of what they seek out themselves and what faculty want them to be using. For this reason, the evaluation should take into account faculty expertise and goals for their students. It should be granular, broken down by subject to create small enough subsections of the collection that you can tell what you should get more of and where you have more than you need. Most importantly, the data needs to tell you something about the library's performance, and there needs to be a way to act on what you've learned. Data that is not going to lead to some sort of action is not worth collecting.

While the methods described in this book all produce numbers, another guiding principle for a collection evaluation is that it should include reflection on aspects of the library that cannot be measured numerically. Many librarians will gather quotes about the importance of the library or its impact on patrons to help make a case about the library's value. In a dissertation by Linn, the university librarians he interviewed mention "weav[ing] the student story into [their budget requests] to make it a little more human" and creating "emotional ties . . . with examples of use by faculty or students" (2008: 123).

Incorporating stories along with the numbers is more than simply a tactic to manipulate those who decide your budget, however. Statistical measures cannot reveal what the library means to the people affected by it, whereas stories can. Bourg (2013), assistant university librarian for public services for Stanford University Libraries, reminds us that "the impact of our collections, our services, and our people . . . is very real and is also very, very, very hard to measure." Although this book focuses on what is measurable, you are encouraged to supplement the numbers with comments or reflections from your users.

Different Kinds of Quantitative Data

This book provides four different ways to measure the quality and usefulness of your library collection. Although the literature on collection evaluation often labels methods as quantitative or qualitative depending on whether they focus on the quantity or quality of the items in the collection, all four of the methods described here are quantitative according to the more common definitions of the terms. Quantitative data, as the term is usually used, involves numbers and measurements, whereas qualitative data consists of descriptive language reflecting individuals' experiences. However, though the methods are all quantitative, they do examine the quality of the collection as well as its size. Quality can be defined in at least three ways. It could mean having enough materials, the best materials, or the materials most desired by your patrons. Each method presented in this book addresses a particular one of these definitions of quality, with two methods addressing patron needs. Though the four methods follow different definitions of what makes a good library collection, in practice many libraries are balancing several goals for their collection, and most evaluations will combine two or more approaches.

Most of these methods should more properly be called assessment rather than evaluation. In the field of education, assessment is meant to imply a process that provides useful feedback, usually on student achievement or the effectiveness of instruction, that will benefit the person or institution being assessed. Evaluation implies more of a judgment applied to a final product and may also focus more on external standards. According to these distinctions, the word *assessment* seems more appropriate for most library projects. Although some of the evaluation methods in this book, such as those done for an accrediting agency, use external standards and produce a judgment, most do not. The library literature, however, more often uses the term *evaluation*, and this book will follow suit. When *assessment* is used here, it is usually in cases where the information being gathered is formative rather than a judgment, but *evaluation* can mean this too.

Librarians often struggle with trying to make sure their data is accurate enough to be used as a basis for decisions. Although the eloquent title of Bucknell's (2012) article on usage statistics for online resources, "Garbage In, Gospel Out," implies that librarians are too trusting of the available data, the opposite can also be true. Some people feel their data is so inaccurate as to be useless. Some well-known issues are that usage statistics vary depending on the interface patrons use and that circulation counts fail to account for in-house use. This book does not dispute the fact that data about library collections can be inaccurate and does not always tell us what we want it to. In fact, it acknowledges the shortcomings of each method along with the strengths. It is a basic premise of this book, however, that imperfect data can still be useful, and the quest for perfect data should not hold you back from making decisions based on what you found. Using even one of the methods in this book should equip you to make better decisions about your collection and to promote your library to others. In fact, it is likely that once you have collected data, you'll realize you can use it for even more purposes than the goal that originally motivated the evaluation. This book aims to show you how to make as much use of your findings as possible.

Whatever your level of technical knowledge, experience with collection development, or goals for your evaluation, the how-to chapters will help you get data and the interpretation chapters will help you use the data to improve your collection.

Key Points

With motivation and knowledge of some basic principles, you are ready to start planning your evaluation. As you begin, remember:

- An evaluation can tell you about whether your library collection is of sufficient size, quality, or usefulness.
- The data from an evaluation can help with all aspects of collection management.
- Unless it is required of you, do not collect numbers that are not going to help you make any decisions. A good evaluation will lead to some kind of action.
- Your evaluation should divide the collection into subsections so you will know in some degree of detail what you need to acquire or discard.
- An evaluation at an educational institution should take faculty perspectives into consideration.
- Your patrons' stories and impressions can complement the numerical data by demonstrating the impact of the library on individuals.

Your next step is to consider what questions you are trying to answer and which method or methods will help answer those questions.

References

Basken, Paul. 2012. "Quest for College Accountability Produces Demand for Yet More Student Data." *Chronicle of Higher Education*, May 17. http://chronicle.com/article/Quest-for-College/131910.

Bourg, Chris. 2013. "Beyond Measure: Valuing Libraries." *Feral Librarian*, May 19. http://chrisbourg.wordpress.com/2013/05/19/beyond-measure-valuing-libraries/.

Brooks-Kieffer, Jamene. 2009. "Yielding to Persuasion: Library Data's Hazardous Surfaces." In *Library Data: Empowering Practice and Persuasion*, edited by Darby Orcutt, 3–16. Santa Barbara, CA: ABC-Clio.

Brown, Karen, and Kara J. Malenfant. 2012. "Connect, Collaborate, and Communicate: A Report from the Value of Academic Libraries Summits." Association of College and Research Libraries. http://www.ala.org/acrl/sites/ala.org.acrl/files/content/issues/value/val_summit.pdf.

Bucknell, Terry. 2012. "Garbage In, Gospel Out: Twelve Reasons Why Librarians Should Not Accept Cost-Per-Download Figures at Face Value." *Serials Librarian* 64, no. 2 (August): 192–212.

Gross, P. L. K., and E. M. Gross. 1927. "College Libraries and Chemical Education." *Science* 66, no. 1713 (October): 385–89.

Hiller, Steve, and James Self. 2004. "From Measurement to Management: Using Data Wisely for Planning and Decision-Making." *Library Trends* 53, no. 1 (Summer): 129–55.

Johnson, Peggy. 2009. *Fundamentals of Collection Development and Management*. 2nd ed. Chicago: American Library Association.

Linn, Mott. 2008. "The Budget Planning Process in Higher Education: Evaluating Administrators' Strategies and Tactics." PhD dissertation, Graduate School of Library and Information Science, Simmons College. ProQuest 3467790.

Lundin, Anne H. 1989. "List-Checking in Collection Development: An Imprecise Art." *Collection Management* 11, no. 3/4 (October): 103–12.

MacAyeal, Greg. 2014. "A Culture of Assessment: Five Mindsets." *C&RL News* 75, no. 6 (June): 311–12.

U.S. Department of Education. 2006. *A Test of Leadership: Charting the Future of U.S. Higher Education*. Washington, DC. http://www2.ed.gov/about/bdscomm/list/hiedfuture/reports/final-report.pdf.

Wical, Stephanie H., and Hans F. Kishel. 2013. "Strategic Collection Management through Statistical Analysis." *Serials Librarian* 64, nos. 1–4 (April): 37–41.

Approaches to Evaluating Your Collection

Ways of Categorizing Approaches to Collection Evaluation

THERE ARE MANY APPROACHES TO EVALUATING a library collection, and these approaches differ in philosophy, focus, and purpose. In other books or articles about collection evaluation, the authors often classify evaluation methods into categories. This book does not use any of the various classifications but instead just describes each evaluation method separately. The categories that other authors have created can still provide a useful introduction to collection evaluation though, because they explain how different evaluation methods view the collection from different angles.

A common way to describe collection evaluation methods is to say that they are either collection-centered or user-centered. A collection-centered evaluation assumes that the collection can be inherently adequate or inadequate for the population it serves, regardless of how it is used. These evaluations compare the library collection to an external standard that specifies the desired size of the collection or which books or journals it should contain. A user-centered evaluation, on the other hand, assumes that what matters is not whether you have the same number of books as other libraries or the books someone else recommends but whether you have what your own patrons want. These evaluations measure how well the library is meeting patrons' needs by looking at their behaviors or asking them directly.

Another way to describe collection evaluations is by looking at whether they measure inputs or outputs. This is similar to the distinction between collection-centered and user-centered but can include even more ways of measuring a collection's strength. The collection itself is considered an input and usage an output. Other possible inputs could be the budget or books per student enrolled. Outputs have to do with what patrons gain from the library, so besides circulation, other outputs could be searches of the library catalog or the number of library materials placed on reserve.

A third way of classifying evaluation methods is by whether they are quantitative or qualitative. This division only applies to collection-centered evaluations. When collection development librarians use the terms *quantitative* and *qualitative*, a quantitative analysis means one that is concerned with the quantity of items the library owns, whereas a qualitative study looks at whether the materials are of high quality. Both quantitative and qualitative evaluations usually produce findings that are some kind of number, whether the number reflects the collection size, the collection strength, or how many of the top journals the library has.

Although the above divisions are the main ways of classifying collection evaluation methods, there are other ways you could potentially categorize them. Some methods work better for presenting results to people outside the library, while others work better for educating librarians about their own collection. Some methods make it easy to review the whole collection at once, while others are more useful for focusing on a particular field. The latter kind usually work better for evaluating interdisciplinary fields, whose resources fall within several different call number ranges. Another distinction between evaluation methods is that, while every approach can give ideas of new materials to purchase, only some of them can help with weeding.

Collection Evaluation for Academic Libraries leads you through four methods of doing a collection evaluation. Because each has its own distinct advantages and serves a unique purpose, the methods presented here are not arranged into categories. Each approach answers different questions, and each has a situation in which it would be the best option. Table 2.1 summarizes the four methods and provides highlights of what each can help with as well as what it cannot accomplish.

Four Methods of Collection Evaluation

Benchmarking

The first evaluation method this book covers is quantitative benchmarking. The primary question benchmarking answers is, does the library have enough materials? You'll usually answer this by comparing the numbers of books or journals you have to the amount owned by peer institutions. You can break down the collection by subject or format so that the data tells you which sections in particular need to grow. Dividing the collection by subject allows you to compare different sections of your own collection to each other or to see how holdings on a topic compare to enrollment in its corresponding department. Because benchmarking looks at the size of the collection, it is usually considered quanti-

Table 2.1. Comparison of Four Methods of Collection Evaluation

NAME	PROCESS	QUESTIONS ANSWERED	BEST METHOD FOR	SHORTCOMINGS
Quantitative Benchmarking	Comparing counts of book and journal holdings, either between your library and peers or between different sections of your library. Can also refer to comparing the size of the holdings on a subject to enrollment in the corresponding department or budget for that department.	Do you have enough books on this topic? Do you have as many books as your peers? How big a collection should you aim to have? How does your collection compare to enrollment in certain areas or spending in those areas? Which parts of the collection might need to be weeded?	Providing fast facts and comparisons to administrators or prospective students.	Tells you nothing about the quality of the books or their usefulness. You won't learn about the breadth of the collection within a broad subject category. Not useful for evaluating how your collection serves interdisciplinary areas.
List-Checking	Checking to see whether your library has access to titles on a list of expert-recommended books or journals.	Do you have the best or most important books on a topic?	Evaluating an interdisciplinary field. Building a retrospective collection on a topic.	Becomes cumbersome if you try to find enough lists to evaluate the entire collection. Existing lists might not quite match the focus at your institution. You can't use the same list in repeated evaluations. Does not help with weeding.

(continued)

Table 2.1. (Continued)

NAME	PROCESS	QUESTIONS ANSWERED	BEST METHOD FOR	SHORTCOMINGS
Usage Statistics	Using circulation reports or vendor-provided usage reports to see which of your resources get the most use. Reviewing interlibrary loan reports to see what items your patrons are using that you don't have and how often patrons are resorting to ILL versus using local resources. Comparing the costs of subscriptions to their usage.	Which sections of the library are heavily used and which are not? What percentage of patrons' needs are being met in-house versus from other libraries? What are the most requested items that you don't have? Does patron-driven acquisitions lead to buying books that won't get used again? Which parts of the collection might need to be weeded? Which journal subscriptions are heavily used and which are not? Are your subscriptions cost-efficient? Which subscriptions might you want to cancel?	Advocating for continued or increased funding for book purchases and journal subscriptions. Making renewal decisions. Evaluating a new purchasing model.	You can't compare print book use to e-book use, or print journals to e-journals. You can't compare cost per use for e-books that are available via subscriptions to those that were purchased with perpetual access. You will not learn which kinds of patrons used which materials.
Citation Analysis	Reviewing bibliographies from faculty or student work to see which books, journals, or authors are popular and how many of the cited resources are available through your library.	What journals and authors are important to the people whose work you are analyzing? Are journals more important in this field than books or vice versa? Do you have most of what your patrons are citing? Are your users citing books that you have electronically more or less often than books you have in print? Which databases have the largest numbers of articles your users are citing?	Learning about an interdisciplinary field. Learning what is important to a small program whose resources get used less than those for larger programs.	Does not capture usage for purposes other than publication. Cannot tell you which of your abstracts-only databases get used. Does not help with weeding.

tative and collection based. It is also a method that lends itself to providing information to outsiders, finding sections to weed, and evaluating the whole collection at once.

Libraries often do quantitative benchmarking in response to requests from people outside the library. Many people who are interested in the library but do not have it as their primary responsibility want to be able to get a quick sense of what the library is like but do not have the time to read an in-depth review of complicated tables. These people include prospective students, grant funders, and university administrators. A particularly important audience for benchmarking data is whoever allocates budgets at an institution, as comparisons between the institution and its peers can make a compelling case for funding the library's growth. National associations such as the National Center for Education Statistics and the Association of College and Research Libraries solicit various numbers from libraries describing their collections and services, which the associations compile into tools for comparison between institutions. These national surveys have been a major impetus for many libraries to gather basic quantitative data about their collections.

What makes benchmarking useful for communicating with people outside the library, however, is the same trait that makes the data less useful for librarians trying to do collection development: it is very simple. While the numbers allow outsiders to make a judgment at a glance, measures of size say very little about the content of a collection or what it means to those who use it. After completing a quantitative benchmarking, you won't know whether your books are in good condition, whether the journals you have are significant ones, or whether your books are appropriate for your users. In addition, because benchmarking usually involves dividing up the collection by call number ranges, you may not be able to tell how well you are serving interdisciplinary programs since these don't fit neatly within a range. You may be able to identify areas to weed if you can see that your collection in these areas is larger than your peers', but you will still want to find out if books are being used or if they are classics before you remove them.

List-Checking

The second method, list-checking, can fill in some of the gaps left by a benchmarking study. List-checking is also focused on the collection, but instead of being concerned with size, it asks whether your library has the best books, journals, or other materials on a given topic. For this method, you'll need a list of what materials are considered the best. The list can be produced by subject experts outside the library or derived from reports that show which journals are cited most frequently. A list-checking evaluation involves checking your library's holdings against the list to see how many of the titles on it you own or have access to.

Because list-checking requires finding a list of recommended items on a topic, it is most often used when librarians want to evaluate their resources supporting one particular program. It would be burdensome if not impossible to find enough lists to evaluate every topic that your library collects. If you are seeking to increase your budget in support of a specific program, it can help to make the case that you are missing certain titles from a list of important journals in that field, and you need funding to start these subscriptions. List-checking tends to be a desirable method for projects focused on interdisciplinary fields since focusing on one topic at a time and checking the list manually means there is no need to break the collection down into discrete subject classifications. For example, if you have a list of recommended books on Middle Eastern studies, you can check the list against your catalog without worrying about whether a particular book is history, sociology, or political science. It is also useful for starting a collection in a new area since the list will give you important older titles that an approval plan might not catch.

Lists can be very useful for selectors who are new to the fields for which they are responsible. A list of significant works on a given topic can teach librarians what is important in that field, and it can also provide direction on how to improve the collection. Once you've checked the list to see what you do and don't have, it is easy to turn the items you don't have into a purchase list. The problem is that after you've purchased the items you don't already own, you can't use the list again as an evaluation tool. List-checking works best as a one-time project. Another way in which list-checking evaluations are limited is that they cannot tell you what to weed. Because the lists are selective, no one expects that your collection will consist of *only* what is on the list, so not being on the list does not inherently mean the item should be weeded.

Usage Statistics

The next method, usage statistics, shifts from evaluating the collection by external standards to evaluating it based on how it is used. Like benchmarking, usage statistics can also be effective for communicating with administrators because usage is often seen as an indicator of value. If you are able to demonstrate that your patrons use a particular database, you can make the case that the resource is important to your users. If the library overall is getting a lot of use, you have a case that the library is important.

Although an evaluation based on usage has a different philosophy than one based on the size of the collection, analyzing usage statistics sometimes looks similar to analyzing benchmarks, at least when you are looking at books. Both methods involve dividing the collection into segments by call number and running reports to count what is in each part of the collection. With usage statistics, however, the number of items in each section is only a preliminary step that allows you to calculate how many checkouts per book occurred in that section. You'll use this ratio to identify which parts of the collection are heavily used and which are not. Another step can then be breaking down your interlibrary borrowing requests into the same call number ranges so that you can compare what your patrons are requesting from other libraries to what they use from yours.

While usage statistics are just one of several ways to evaluate a book collection, decisions about journal or database subscriptions almost always rely on usage. When you are paying for a subscription annually, it is reasonable to want to know whether the resource is being used before agreeing to pay for it again. Since 2003, Project COUNTER has provided a standard for how usage of online resources is tracked and reported. Most journal and e-book vendors provide reports that follow the COUNTER standards, and electronic resource providers that do not follow the standards will still offer some kind of usage reports. Libraries commonly use vendor reports to evaluate both journals and e-books purchased using a subscription model. Usage information is usually considered alongside the price in the form of a yearly cost-per-use figure that is calculated for each subscription. Items with a cost per use that is too high are usually discontinued.

Unlike the other evaluation techniques, usage statistics require you to look at different formats separately, as usage is measured differently for books than for journals. For books you're likely to be comparing one subject or call number range to another rather than looking at specific titles, whereas with journals you're making decisions at the subscription level, which could mean individual periodicals or large packages. In addition, the frequently used cost-per-use metric is only appropriate for materials you pay for by subscription. With one-time purchases, the cost has already been paid, and it would be cumbersome or even irrelevant to find the original purchase price for each book. The difference in usage metrics for one-time purchases versus subscriptions makes evaluation of e-books particularly complicated. Because e-books can be sold as either perpetual-access firm orders, subscriptions, or patron-driven acquisitions, you'll need to evaluate different parts of your e-book collection separately. As a result, usage statistics produce a very fragmented picture of the collection.

Although usage statistics can be helpful in deciding which sections of the library could use more books, which sections to weed, and which subscriptions to renew, data on patrons' usage of the collection does not perfectly measure what they need. Most users have a bias toward using what is readily available to them. The fact that your patrons are using a journal you subscribe to might not mean that it is important in their field; it means it was easy enough for them to access that they found it worth the effort. If your users are not experts in the subject they are researching, they might actually be using something inappropriate. Because your choice to purchase something increases your patrons' chances of using it, some deliberate collection of items from expert-generated lists can help steer patrons toward quality materials.

Citation Analysis

The last collection evaluation method, citation analysis, is another way of measuring usage. Bibliographies from faculty publications, dissertations and theses, or even undergraduate work can tell you what material types, authors, or specific items are important to your users. You can check your catalog for the items your users are citing and calculate how many of them are available through your library. Whereas traditional usage statistics are an anonymous and aggregate measure of what was used, citation analysis provides more specifics on who is using what. Although in some cases you won't know exactly who the creator of the bibliography was, you will know their area of focus and role within the institution. The information on what your users are citing and the availability of these resources allows you to learn about specific departments' use of the library as well as needs each department may have that you are not meeting.

Because citation analysis starts by targeting users and then figuring out what they are using, it usually works better than traditional usage statistics for revealing the needs of patrons in interdisciplinary fields. Whereas circulation statistics won't tell you if books on plants were used by biology students or environmental science researchers, collecting bibliographies from environmental science faculty will tell you for sure whether they use biology books, as well as what other disciplines they use. Citation data also allows you to compare departments or user groups. Bibliographies can reveal which departments or programs rely more heavily on books and which use journals almost exclusively. If you collect bibliographies that represent varying levels of research, you can learn which journals are more useful to beginning students and which are valued by experts. The picture you will get of your collection from citation analysis is more user-centered than any of the other methods because it is the only method that collects information from the users themselves.

Citation analysis comes with some of the same caveats as traditional usage statistics, as well as having its own unique shortcomings. As said before, all patrons are biased toward using what is available locally. This bias is less of a problem with citation analysis than with usage statistics because you can tell what kind of researcher was using each source. Inexperienced researchers, such as first-year students, may be using resources that are inappropriate, but faculty know more about what is acceptable to cite and what is important within their areas of interest. Given the choice between two scholarly and relevant books or articles, though, faculty may choose the one that is available through the library of their home institution, so citation data will still be somewhat skewed toward resources you already have.

One shortcoming of citation analysis that is not a problem with traditional measures of usage is that bibliographies do not capture all usage of library materials. They only tell you what was cited in a written work, and even then only in the ones you collected. Patrons could be using your resources for something other than writing papers. If a physical therapy student on a clinical rotation used an article, citation analysis would not tell you this. Citation analysis also cannot tell you whether your patrons find abstracts-only databases valuable for discovering articles to read. Because of the gaps in what it measures, citation analysis is not useful for weeding, though it can tell you what to keep and what new materials to acquire.

The Choice of Which Methods to Use

The decision of which method or methods to use for your collection evaluation will depend on what you are trying to accomplish. In some cases the method will be prescribed for you—for example, if you are participating in the accreditation review for one of your institution's programs and the accrediting agency requires a report showing how many books you own that support the program. Even if you are doing a collection evaluation for internal purposes, sometimes one particular evaluation tool stands out as the most appropriate for the situation. For example, libraries that are beginning to collect in an area where they previously had few materials usually look for a list of core materials on the subject and use it to check what they have. As stated earlier, reviewing the library's journal and database subscriptions almost always involves using usage statistics and calculating the cost per use for each subscription.

Sometimes a particular method is the most practical because it allows you to respond quickly to a time-sensitive request. If you've been asked to weed on short notice to free up space for other uses of the building, running reports on usage is an efficient way to make sure that decisions can be made with some justification. Although it would be preferable to also find or create lists of important works in the areas you're weeding, you might not be able to find an appropriate list or have the time to create your own. Usage reports let you cover more ground in less time. Likewise, if you find out journal prices have increased more than you can afford and you need to decide right away which subscriptions to cancel, checking to see which have not been used is a good way to make a fast decision. It would be preferable, however, to find out which journals are important in the field (using list-checking), seek faculty input, and possibly check whether your journal collection is much larger on certain subjects than others (benchmarking). If you are able to plan ahead and do an evaluation before there is an immediate need for action, you'll have more options when it comes to choosing which methods to use.

Because every evaluation method has its own strengths and weaknesses, ideally you should combine two or more of them to get the fullest picture of your collection and make the most informed decisions. Often it makes sense to combine a method that uses external standards (benchmarking or list-checking) with one that focuses on your users (usage statistics or citation analysis). For example, if you are planning to weed books that are unused (using usage statistics), you may want to check expert lists to see if they are considered important in the field (using list-checking). You can also combine a method that looks at the collection as a whole (benchmarking or usage statistics) with citation analysis, which hones in on particular users who might get overlooked in a larger-scale analysis. If your traditional usage statistics show that one of your databases has very low use, but you know that it serves a small program, you could get bibliographies from works by faculty in this program to figure out whether the journals in this little-used database are actually the most important to this small group of faculty. In this case, both methods would be necessary for making a decision: the low usage compared to other databases is not helpful information unless you know what the database means to the particular users it is meant for, but if you were to find that faculty or students from one program were not relying on a given database, you would not want to unsubscribe without knowing if it had low usage overall.

Another reason you might combine evaluation methods is if the primary evaluation method you are using reveals certain areas in which you need more materials but does not provide enough specifics on what to add. In this case, you can use another method to fill out the list of suggestions. If quantitative benchmarking reveals that you need more books on astronomy, for example, you can use the "Core List of Astronomy Books" (available at http://ads.harvard.edu/books/clab/) for ideas of specific books to buy. Alternately, or in addition, you could use reports of interlibrary loan requests, which are described in the chapter on usage statistics, to figure out what your users want that you don't have, and you could buy these. Similarly, if your usage reports show that you could benefit from more books on education reform, but your interlibrary loan reports provide only a few ideas of titles to buy, you could look at faculty publications to see what authors or specific books they cite.

You can also use several evaluation methods to balance competing philosophies of collection development. Some people adamantly believe that it is librarians' jobs as educators to guide students toward the best materials rather than purchasing in response to patron demand, while others believe that usage is the only true measure of value and therefore that purchasing should be driven by what patrons want to use. If your philosophy is a combination of both, you'll want to use both list-checking and usage statistics to evaluate your library collection and help you decide what to buy.

Nonmeasurable Aspects of the Collection

It is always a good idea not only to triangulate between different formal methods of collection evaluation but also to supplement numerical data with information on what is not measurable. There is a lot that matters about your collection that you won't be able to find out from any of the above methods. None of these techniques can tell you whether your collection represents diverse opinions on controversial topics or includes international perspectives. They do not tell you whether your books are in disrepair or whether they are too basic or too complex for the patrons they are meant to serve. The materials your library owns could be for the wrong audience, such as child development books that are targeted at parents even though your patrons are pre-service teachers or school counselors. A lot of these questions can only be answered by going to the shelves or looking at your online resources title by title. Although shelf-reading provides an impressionistic rather than systematic evaluation of the collection, it also allows you to look more closely at certain sections than a formal evaluation does.

Another important, hard-to-measure quality of an academic library collection is that it should meet the institution's pedagogical goals. Talking to faculty is sometimes the only way to find out if your collection is sufficient in this way. If a faculty member believes that students will learn best by reading examples of research that they can use as models for their own, then the library ought to focus on finding exemplary research studies to purchase rather than looking for guides to research methods. To some extent you can deduce what faculty are asking students to read by looking at what kinds of books get checked out, but understanding faculty's teaching strategies can give you additional insight into the difference between the books that get used and those that don't. The data you generate from any of the methods described here can be a great prompt for conversations with faculty, who will then provide perspectives that the numbers can't.

Not only is it hard to tell from numerical data whether or not your resources meet the institution's teaching objectives, none of the evaluation methods here can tell you what your resources have meant to your users. A particular book may have served as the backbone of someone's paper, or it could be something they cited once to pad their bibliography. The same book could be personally inspiring for one person and simply required reading for another. It could be checked out once by someone who found it essential or many times by someone who only glanced at it each time. The only way to figure out the impact of your resources is to gather testimonials from users, through surveys, focus groups, or a feedback form. You won't be able to compare how many testimonials you get for particular titles or subjects, but stories from users can help demonstrate the overall importance of the library and the value of keeping low-use materials in some situations, and quotes can be an accessible way to communicate with administrators or prospective students. Testimonials, as well as conversations with faculty and impressions from shelf-reading, can be combined with any of the techniques described in this guide to create a more complete picture of your library's collection.

Examples of Two Libraries and the Methods They Used

The professional literature has several examples of collection evaluations that other libraries have done. In these examples, you'll see how circumstances can influence what method you choose and how combining multiple methods can create a strong, multifaceted analysis. You can also see how an evaluation sometimes has additional benefits beyond accomplishing its original goal.

Example 1: Colorado State University Libraries (Culbertson and Wilde, 2009)

Motivation. The library wanted to request a budget increase to better support twelve doctoral programs. A new strategic plan provided an opportunity to justify the request based on how the money would support the strategic plan.

Evaluation Methods.

- Quantitative benchmarking of book collection compared to peer institutions
- List-checking with core lists created from faculty input and information on what was most cited in each field
- Analysis of citations by researchers at Colorado State; interlibrary loan reports

Nonmeasurable Elements. Faculty provided feedback on the numerical findings.

How the Data Was Used. The librarians calculated an amount of money they wanted to request based on the prices of specific core journals and the estimated cost of buying enough books to have at least 75 percent of the amount their peers had. The libraries reported their findings to the vice provost for graduate education.

Outcome. The libraries were able to get money to purchase electronic backfiles. The funding request was "bolstered . . . by both the data and the testimony of faculty that emerged as a result of this process" (Culbertson and Wilde, 2009: 13). The data has also been useful for accreditation reviews of the doctoral programs.

Example 2: University of Colorado at Boulder, Engineering Library (Wiersma, 2010)

Motivation. The university had added programs in bioengineering and biotechnology, areas in which the library had not previously collected heavily. The engineering library wanted to see how well it was supporting those programs and find weaknesses in the collection so it could improve.

Evaluation Methods.

- List-checking for journal holdings using several lists of recommended titles and a list created by combining the holdings of a peer group
- List-checking for books against *Choice* magazine's recommended titles
- Quantitative benchmarking of book collection against four peer libraries

How the Data Was Used. Librarians created a list of books that peer libraries owned that they did not and reviewed it for its fit with their own curriculum. The library purchased some of these titles and also changed its approval plan profiles to include more bioengineering and biomedical books.

Outcome. Librarians become more familiar with the existing collection. The collection grew significantly under the new approval plan, especially in biotechnology.

Key Points

Now that you have an overview of the main approaches to evaluating a library collection and some examples of how libraries have combined different methods, it is almost time for you to select which method or methods you want to use and start planning your evaluation. As you think about which methods to use, remember:

- Think about what questions you are trying to answer and choose the method that will provide the right kind of information for your purposes.

- Consider benchmarking or usage statistics if you want to weed or if you need to communicate about the library to people outside it.
- Consider list-checking and citation analysis when evaluating how well the collection supports an interdisciplinary program.
- Compensate for the shortcomings of one method by combining it with another.
- Make sure to supplement your data with a review of nonmeasurable aspects of the collection such as its physical condition or how well it supports faculty teaching objectives.

Chapter 3 will talk you through some questions to ask before you settle on a method and will help you plan for whichever method you choose.

References

Culbertson, Michael, and Michelle Wilde. 2009. "Collection Analysis to Enhance Funding for Research Materials." *Collection Building* 28, no. 1 (January): 9–17.

Wiersma, Gabrielle. 2010. "Collection Assessment in Response to Changing Curricula: An Analysis of the Biotechnology Resources at the University of Colorado at Boulder." *Issues in Science & Technology Librarianship* 61 (Spring). http://www.istl.org/10-spring/refereed1.html.

Before You Start

THERE ARE MANY REASONS TO CAREFULLY PLAN before you begin a collection evaluation project. Thinking about which parts of your collection you want to evaluate and what data you need can help you avoid collecting data that isn't useful, embarking on a never-ending project, or having to repeat steps as you figure out your procedures. Deciding what your co-workers' roles will be allows you to support them throughout the project. This chapter presents the planning process that should happen before you begin a collection evaluation project, from broad questions of goals and scope to smaller details such as how you'll organize your data.

As you think through the goals and details of your collection evaluation, it is helpful to remember that any project involves a three-way balance of depth, time, and cost, sometimes called the iron triangle of project management. Focusing heavily on any one of these factors will mean sacrifices to the other two, and the balance you strike will depend on your circumstances. An elaborately planned, in-depth evaluation may take so long that it never gets finished. At the other extreme, you might be in such a hurry to do an evaluation that you sacrifice depth and simply collect whatever data is easiest to obtain and analyze. If you are short on funds but have the time, you can do an analysis cheaply by deciding not to purchase any of the collection evaluation tools on the market, but it will take you longer to collect all the data manually. Whatever balance of depth, time, and cost you find, it's best if you arrive at this balance deliberately, with an awareness of your priorities and limitations. Your evaluation should have enough detail to make it useful and yet be simple enough that it can be completed in the time you have, using the financial resources available to you. To make this happen, you'll want to ask yourself several questions, shown in textbox 3.1.

Goals

The first step in planning a collection evaluation is to define your goals. Although your initial interest in doing a collection evaluation probably arose because there was something you wanted to find out about your library, your questions at this point may still be vague. You will be able to plan out the specifics of your evaluation better if you start with an explicit goal or several goals. Although this book describes the process of data collection before suggesting what you can do with the data, deciding what actions you want to take actually comes first. You should set goals and plan the evaluation, then collect your data, then follow the action steps that will improve your collection in the ways you'd intended to do from the beginning.

A goal is slightly different than the motivation for undertaking an evaluation. A motivation is what prompts you to do the evaluation: you need to make space for more

TEXTBOX 3.1.

QUESTIONS TO ANSWER BEFORE BEGINNING A COLLECTION EVALUATION

- What are your goals?
- What kinds of data do you need in order to meet these goals?
- Do your goals require you to look at every subject on which you collect and every material type? If not, which parts of the collection do you need to look at?
- How much time do you have to devote to this project?
- How often do you plan to repeat the evaluation?
- What data can you get from your catalog, internal records, WorldCat Discovery, or collection evaluation software?
- Will you be able to get the same kinds of data for every department or subject area you are evaluating?
- Given your time frame, budget situation, and the data you want to use, does it make sense for you to subscribe to a software tool designed to help with collection evaluation?
- What tasks will be the responsibilities of which of your co-workers?
- Are there likely to be fears or objections on the part of your colleagues? What will they need from you in order to successfully participate in the project?

study areas by removing something from the stacks; your art department is undergoing accreditation and has asked you for an analysis of library materials in support of its programs; you think patron-driven acquisitions will be a cost-effective way to grow your collection, but you aren't sure if the books you buy via this model will get used after they're purchased. A goal is more specific and includes what you want to do with your findings, including not only action steps but what kind of collection these actions should help you build. Some example goals are listed in textbox 3.2.

A goal should take into account your library's mission, so that it is targeted toward building the type of collection that your mission indicates. Does your library aim to serve faculty's research needs or only classroom needs? If your goal is to build a core collection, you should specify whether it is a research core or one for undergraduates. If your primary patrons are students, does your mission include meeting demand for any kind of materials, or do you specifically exclude certain materials such as textbooks, DVDs of popular television series, or leisure reading? Your mission will affect not only your action steps but also what method of evaluation you choose. Usage analysis supports a mission of meeting patron demand, while list-checking assumes the library's role is at least in part to direct students toward the best materials in their fields.

In some cases, the goals of your collection evaluation will be shaped by the needs of people outside the library. A major external criterion to take into account is the mission statement of the larger institution. Although the mission of the library should align with that of the larger institution anyway, telling administrators exactly how the library is supporting the institution's mission or strategic plan will benefit your library's reputation and strengthen your case when asking for any additional resources. If your institution's strategic plan involves finding cost-effective ways to support increased enrollment, for example, you might use usage statistics to eliminate subscriptions with a high cost per use, and you might also benchmark your collection against those of institutions whose

TEXTBOX 3.2.

EXAMPLES OF POSSIBLE GOALS
FOR A COLLECTION EVALUATION

- To gather information that allows you to cut your journals spending by 15 percent while maintaining a collection that combines heavily used journals and those having the highest impact in the field
- To determine whether you can make a case for increasing the budget in support of your institution's international studies program
- To weed enough books to create room for a collaborative work space, without removing anything that is regularly used or a classic
- To build a book and journal collection that will provide 80 percent of what patrons want to read
- To retroactively build a core collection in sports psychology, an area in which you have not been collecting
- To allow subject selectors to create informed collection development plans that take into account the overall significance of works in their areas of responsibility, faculty teaching strategies, and student usage habits

enrollment is close to your target. The data that you'd get from these two kinds of evaluation would show that the library is serving the interests of the larger institution and directly supporting its strategic plan. If the benchmarking reveals that institutions with your target enrollment figures usually have more library resources, your library can then use the evaluation to bolster a request for money. Referring to the strategic plan, the library can make a case that the money would support a goal that the institution has already identified as being important.

In addition to responding to the broadly defined needs of your institution, there are ways a collection evaluation can serve specific offices on campus. Your admissions office, for example, probably tells prospective students about the library and has an idea of what kind of information appeals to their audience. Asking them about their needs while your evaluation is in the planning stages ensures that you collect data that is relevant and helpful to them. Besides making you a good colleague, providing helpful data to other offices is in your own interest as well, as the other offices can use your data to promote the library.

While responding to the needs and mission of the rest of your institution, however, you should make sure your goals mesh with your own beliefs and expertise in collection development. Sometimes requests that come from outside the library conflict with what the librarians believe is best or are simply influenced by the requestor's unfamiliarity with contemporary libraries. There is often a way to respond to these requests according to your own views. If someone asks you to remove books in the art section to make room for a new office, you might respond that in fact these books get used much more than the physics books, and you would prefer to weed physics books and then shift. You can probably argue for a redefined goal of weeding the least used books to make room for the new office rather than weeding specifically art books. If an accrediting body wants to know what percentage of your budget is allocated toward English journals, you may want to explain that because journals in this field are inexpensive you are able to provide a large collection using a relatively small percentage of the budget, and you can provide a count of journals in addition to budget information. You should answer the question asked but can also explain that your own goal is to provide a number of journal titles that is proportionate to the enrollment in the program, or to provide the journals that account for 80 percent of student citations, and then offer data that shows you are doing so. Keeping your own collection goals in mind lets you respond to external requests in ways that meet the requestors' needs while still building your collection according to how you think best.

Scope

The next step after defining your goal is to start thinking about what information you'll need in order to pursue it. Understanding what information you need allows you to articulate the scope of your collection evaluation project, which in turn enables you to estimate how long the project will take you and to recognize when you are finished. Being finished doesn't mean you'll stop thinking about evaluation and move on to something else. It means there is a point in the process where you stop collecting data, look at the data you've collected, and take some actions. You can choose to repeat the process on a regular schedule if you would like assessment to be an ongoing part of your library's operations, but the evaluation won't be useful unless you go through the full cycle of collecting data, analyzing, and acting each time, and you can't move through the cycle unless the data collection step has an end point. To make sure your data collection process is bounded, you'll need to decide what questions you want to answer and for which segments of your collection.

Deciding which parts of the collection to analyze will probably be your first step in setting the scope. An evaluation could focus on resources that support a particular program or topic, no matter what their format, or it could focus on only a particular format, such as physical books or e-books, across all subjects. It is rare for anyone to evaluate all material types on all subjects in one go. Not only would this be a cumbersome project, but very few of the common goals or motivations for doing a collection evaluation require it. Many of the example goals above explicitly or implicitly reference specific parts of the collection: print and electronic journals on all subjects, all material types relevant to international studies, print books on all subjects or in the particular section where you need to free up space. Only the last goal in the bulleted list above, creating informed collection development plans, would ultimately involve looking at all material types and subjects, and even this goal can be pursued one subject at a time.

Evaluating all formats in one subject area is most appropriate when the impetus for the collection evaluation comes from a particular program, either a new program that needs an initial core collection or a program undergoing an accreditation review. An advantage to focusing on one program at a time is that you can look more holistically at how users from that program might experience the collection. Limiting your collection evaluation by subject can give you the time and brain space to compare multiple evaluation methods and material types and to integrate your numerical findings with faculty feedback and librarians' impressions of the collection.

Evaluations that deal with only one material type also have their uses. Sometimes you need to make a decision that only affects one material type. For instance, many libraries review all of their journals subscriptions at once when it is time to make renewal decisions. Looking at only one material type can also facilitate comparisons across the collection. If you want to know, for example, whether the art books in your print collection are "highly used," the only way to quantify this otherwise subjective label is to compare these books' circulation rates to those of the other books you own. Making comparisons across the collection does not always require looking at every subject area. You can make comparisons by looking at just a few call number ranges, or by comparing one section to the collection as a whole. If the Education Department at your institution is questioning whether you should be purchasing books for them, and you want to respond with data showing whether or not education books get used more or less than other books, you don't necessarily need to see circulation data for every discipline. You can keep the scope of your evaluation narrow, and get it done quickly, by comparing one discipline to the average for the entire collection, or by picking just a few other disciplines to compare it to. When you have more time, you might decide to expand the evaluation to include print circulation data related to all your programs.

The other piece of defining the scope of your collection evaluation, besides which formats and subjects you are evaluating, is what questions about the collection you want to answer. This will help you pick an evaluation method, as different evaluation methods answer different questions. Refer to table 2.1 in the previous chapter for a summary of which questions each evaluation method can answer. It's likely you'll want to use more than one method, but you do not need to use all four methods together. As you think about which methods would give you the information you want, you can tentatively decide which ones to pursue. You might tweak your plans later on as you think through how much time you have and how you are going to collect your data.

Time

Another important aspect of your collection evaluation project that you should consider before starting is how much time it will take. Ideally, you would set the scope of your project first and then create a timetable. There will certainly be cases, though, where time limitations are so clear from the outset that you set the scope by asking what you can get done in the time you have. If you are free to set your own deadline, however, you can identify what information you want and then estimate how long it will take to gather the information. Even when there isn't an external constraint, it is still a good idea to plan out how long you expect your project to take. Coming up with a schedule helps ensure that you'll complete the project.

Once you have an estimate of how long your collection evaluation will take, you can also plan how often you'll be able to repeat the process. The schedule for repeating the evaluation will depend not only on how long the project takes but on the method you are using. For some methods, you need to review multiple years of data in order to see patterns, so it wouldn't make sense for you to repeat the study every year. One such method is analysis of print circulation data. When looking at circulation data, having two to four years of data helps correct for the fact that some courses are not offered every year and materials for these courses may only get used when the course is running. If you decide to use four years of data for your usage analysis, then you can wait to repeat the evaluation until four years later, when you'll have new usage data to analyze. The one kind of evaluation many libraries do yearly is reviewing usage reports for electronic resource subscriptions, as renewal decisions are usually made yearly. A comparison to authoritative lists, on the other hand, is something you're unlikely to repeat at all. Once you've compared your collection to the list, you'll try to buy as much as you can afford that is appropriate to your collection, so a future analysis would only recap for you what you'd purchased since the last run-through.

You may need to alter your schedule as the evaluation progresses. If you'd planned to do something every year, and it took you a full year to collect the data, you might switch your schedule to every three years so you have time to change your selection strategies before you evaluate again, or simply to give yourself some time for other projects. Having a timeline in mind is still a good idea, though, as it will keep the project moving forward.

An additional time-related consideration is deciding the best time of year to do the evaluation. It's frustrating to decide in March that you want to cut something and then realize you just renewed it in January. Your administration probably solicits budget proposals at a specific time, and you don't want to begin an evaluation just after you've missed the window for using it to strengthen your budget request. The time of year will not always matter, but it's good to think about whether it might be an issue.

Data Needs

The scope and timetable of your collection evaluation provide some broad boundaries for the project. Your next step is to fill in some details on how you'll do it. The first detail to figure out is where you will get the data. Table 3.1 spells out what data you will need in order to do each type of evaluation and suggests possible places for you to get that data. In some cases there is more than one option. You might, for instance, get information about your own collection from your catalog or from WorldCat Discovery, if your holdings are

Table 3.1. Data Required for Each Evaluation Method

NAME	DATA NEEDED	POSSIBLE SOURCES OF DATA
Quantitative Benchmarking	Count of materials in your own collection, with the ability to sort or filter by format, subject, and possibly age	Local catalog WorldCat Discovery or WorldCat Collection Evaluation
	Count of materials in other libraries' collections, with the ability to sort or filter by format and subject	Other libraries' catalogs WorldCat Discovery or WorldCat Collection Evaluation
	A defined group of peer libraries or aspirational libraries	Library Statistics Program from NCES U.S. News rankings
	May compare holdings counts to enrollment or budget	Local records
List-Checking	Lists of recommended journals or books related to the subject under consideration	Lists can be found online or created in-house
	Whether or not you own or subscribe to the recommended titles	Local catalog
	Whether or not your peer libraries or aspirational libraries own or subscribe to the recommended titles	Other libraries' catalogs
Usage Statistics	Tallies of circulation of print materials in your collection, sorted or filtered by material type, subject, and date. You'll need to know the date last borrowed and preferably also the total number of checkouts within a given period. You can look at either the total number of checkouts within a subject or the total number of unique items checked out, preferably both.	Circulation reports from local catalog

(continued)

Table 3.1. *(Continued)*

NAME	DATA NEEDED	POSSIBLE SOURCES OF DATA
	Size of your collection on each subject and material type	Local catalog
	Counts of interlibrary borrowing requests placed within a given time period Report should include call numbers to allow sorting by subject	Reports from interlibrary loan software
	Estimated counts of usage of print journals, by title, within a given time period	Locally maintained tallies of how often each journal is reshelved
	Number of full-text downloads of each journal (for single-title subscriptions), database (for package subscriptions), or e-book collection (if subscription-based) within a given time period	COUNTER reports or other vendor-provided usage reports
	Cost per use of any subscriptions	Calculated from usage and prices. Pricing information should be in your own records of past spending.
	Subject distribution of e-books purchased via patron-driven acquisitions	Vendor-provided purchase reports (COUNTER reports do not include this information)
	Counts of postpurchase uses of e-books purchased via patron-driven acquisitions	Vendor-provided purchase reports (COUNTER reports do not include this information)
	Chart of how your budget is allocated by subject, if applicable	Local records
Citation Analysis	Bibliographies from faculty publications, dissertations and theses, or other student works	Databases that track citation, such as Web of Knowledge Institutional repository Institutional records of faculty publication Student work requested from departments

included there. In many cases you can still do the evaluation without every piece of data that is listed; you just won't be able to answer certain questions. For example, you can still benchmark your collection without having budget information; you just won't be able to answer questions about your budget. If you only have access to bibliographies from graduate students and not faculty, then do an evaluation using only graduate students. Most likely, any library will have the ability to do any of the four methods presented in this book, as the instructions take into account some variety in what data you'll be able to access. Your specific procedures, however, will depend on what data you have.

Making decisions at the very beginning about what data you want helps you to be consistent as you go through the process. If you intend your analysis to cover the entire collection, you'll want to use data that you can get for every department. This is harder to do for some methods than for others, but not impossible. If you are focusing on authoritative lists, you probably won't find one corresponding to every program your institution offers, so plan on using the techniques in chapter 6 to create some of your own lists. Citation analysis is particularly hard to keep consistent by department. If you are analyzing student work, do students in every department produce a dissertation, or do some departments offer no graduate programs? You might decide to only use faculty papers to get around the disparity of some departments having graduate students and others not, or you might decide that your goal is simply to see how well you support doctoral programs and look only at ones for which you can get dissertations.

Planning for data collection involves thinking about many small details. Since these details are specific to each evaluation method, considerations for each method are included in the appropriate chapters on collecting data. An example would be, when looking at print book circulation, needing to decide what material types you are including. If you have a collection of dissertations that are kept separate from books, are you interested in their circulation or not? In some cases, you won't be able to get the exact data you want—for example, if you don't want to include dissertations in your count of print books but can't easily identify them to remove them. Don't be discouraged if your data is imperfect as it will still be informative. Data always has flaws, but this does not make it meaningless. The purpose of thinking through your needs at the beginning of the project is to get as close as possible to the data you'd ideally want, even if you can't get everything just right.

There are only a few cases in which missing or flawed data would significantly limit your ability to do a collection evaluation. If your library does not have access to WorldCat Discovery or WorldCat Collection Evaluation, you will have difficulty doing benchmarking, as you'd be reliant on the quirks of several different libraries' catalogs. If your catalog's circulation reports are not in a format that can be exported into Excel, you will have difficulty using your usage statistics. This book tries to offer a variety of options for how to get data so that it should be very rare for any library to conclude they couldn't use a certain evaluation method at all.

Software Tools

One factor that will greatly affect where you get your data and the time it takes to collect it is whether or not you have access to a software tool for collection evaluation. At the time of this writing in 2014, there were two such products on the market. One is WorldCat Collection Evaluation, produced by OCLC, and the other is Intota Assessment, from ProQuest. Although this book is written so that you can do any method of evaluation without special software, evaluation software can speed up some of the processes of data collection, particularly when comparing your holdings to other libraries. Another benefit of using either of these two products is that they allow you to combine circulation data with other deselection criteria, provided you've been able to export the data from your catalog to be loaded into the evaluation software. Being able to look simultaneously at both a book's circulation and whether your peers own it, or circulation and whether it appears on a core list, can help you do well-informed weeding relatively quickly. The downside to using either of these products is that the data is less customizable than it would be if you collected it yourself. Although both products allow you to view your collection in subject-specific chunks and allow you to drill down to narrow subjects representing small sections of the collection, neither allows you to create reports for custom call number ranges that match the units at your institution. It should be noted that both products were relatively new at the time of this writing and may add more features in the near future.

WorldCat Collection Evaluation (WCE) provides reports that help with several of the evaluation methods described in later chapters. All the reports are set up as comparisons. You can compare your library's holdings to those of other institutions, including some preselected groups that come with the software. Examples of the preselected comparison groups are Top 10 Law Schools or Top 10 Liberal Arts Colleges. You can create your own custom comparison group or compare your holdings to the entirety of what is in the World-Cat database. Comparisons to other institutions facilitate the benchmarking techniques described in chapter 4. The report comparing your collection to what is in HathiTrust can help you identify titles to discard based on the knowledge that they have been preserved digitally and made available online. The software also provides comparisons to authoritative lists, facilitating the list-checking strategy described in chapter 6. It includes *Choice* magazine's Outstanding Academic Titles, Doody's Core Titles in the Health Sciences, and lists from *Booklist*, *Library Journal*, *School Library Journal*, and *Publisher's Weekly*.

All of these reports, whether they compare your collection to another library's or to an authoritative list, include a graph illustrating the percentage overlap between your holdings and those of the comparison group. You can also see how many of the libraries in your comparison group own each title. There is an option to export a title list, which you can use to identify either your unique holdings or titles that your aspirational institutions own that you might want to add. If you've uploaded circulation data into WCE (for libraries that use WorldShare Circulation it will be there already), this is included in the title list, so you can make weeding or purchasing decisions that combine aspects of benchmarking and usage analysis.

The other software product, Intota Assessment, also allows you to compare your holdings to other libraries (benchmarking) or to recommended lists (list-checking). Intota Assessment's tool for comparing your own library to others, called Peer Analysis, is designed more for making decisions at the title level than for benchmarking, so it requires some manipulation. This tool lets you run a report comparing sections of your collection title by title to your peers or to aspirational institutions. The report lists titles unique to you, shared titles, and those that your peers own that you don't. To use this information for benchmarking, you could export the table to Excel and total the number of titles you own uniquely, titles your peers own, and titles that overlap. The list-checking feature, which is found in the menu under Recommendations, only includes lists from Resources for College Libraries and Ulrich's core journals list. There is a tool called Deselection that combines list-checking and usage statistics to help you identify titles to weed but does not provide a comparison with other libraries' holdings. Intota includes a few features that WCE does not: manipulation of COUNTER-compliant usage reports for online resources and automatically generated answers to some questions about collections that appear on ACRL's annual survey and that of the British Society of College, National and University Libraries (SCONUL).

Although the two products provide similar information, there is a slight difference in the processes they support and the information they provide. Both products are designed to facilitate weeding, but for now only WorldCat Collection Evaluation is geared toward benchmarking and only Intota Assessment allows you to analyze COUNTER reports. Intota Assessment leverages its relationship with Resources for College Libraries and Books in Print, which are owned by the same company. Access to Books in Print is included with a subscription to Intota Assessment. Depending on what evaluation methods you are planning to do and how much money you have, you can decide if one of these two products will be more useful or affordable. Both products are adding new features regularly, and you should seek out updated and more detailed information than what is in this book if you are thinking of starting a subscription.

Human Resources

For a collection evaluation, as for any project, a major resource and possible challenge is the people who will be involved. If your library has multiple selectors assigned to different subject areas, you may want each person to review the data for their own area and use the findings in future collection development decisions. As librarians are often not trained to work with quantitative data, it is very possible that some of the people who could potentially use information revealed by collection evaluation will not really understand the findings. For someone without experience in quantitative research methods or statistics, it is easy to make an incorrect interpretation of a table—say, focusing on the low number of downloads from a certain database without taking into account that this can be explained by the small number of journals in the database. Others might not feel confident even trying to read the table. In some cases, librarians' discomfort in interpreting data is not due to inexperience so much as a difference in philosophy. Many social scientists do not believe numbers are a meaningful way to measure quality. If you have colleagues who feel this way, you don't want them to feel steamrolled by having to participate in a project they don't believe in, but you probably don't want to let them opt out of it either. Your collection evaluation will go more smoothly if you can listen to and support your colleagues so that they feel included rather than pressured.

If you are nervous about your own ability to train your colleagues in reading tables, or to interpret the data yourself, remember that this book is meant to guide you. The "Interpreting and Acting on the Data" chapter for each evaluation method tells you how you'll know what amount of usage can be considered high, what cost per use is too much, or when it's probably okay to weed items versus when you don't have enough information to make that decision. By reading this book and applying its instructions to your own collection, you will become familiar enough with interpreting numbers that you can explain the process to your colleagues.

In order to be able to support your colleagues, you need to decide who is going to be involved in the evaluation and what each person's role will be. Liaison librarians might be in charge of finding authoritative lists for their subject areas, for example, or collecting citations from their faculty's publications. Alternately, these people might have no involvement in the data collection but might be asked to use the findings to make decisions about purchasing or weeding. The division of labor will be different for each library, depending on the size of your workforce, the skills you each have, and who has the time. Deciding who is doing what will also help you estimate how long it will take to do the project.

Once you've identified who will be involved, let the relevant people know early on what you expect their role to be and also that you will be available to answer questions and orient them to the data. You don't want them to write off the project as something that you're handling alone that doesn't involve them or to worry that they are being forced to do something that they'll feel incompetent at doing. Telling them what kinds of numbers you will be collecting can ease apprehension about the analysis, as then the librarians are not in suspense about what they are going to have to work with. You can even ask them what kinds of data they'd find useful or what they want to know about their areas of the collection. They may be able to suggest changes that will make the project easier for them to complete. They will also be more interested in looking at data if it was gathered in response to a question they posed, and this increased interest might help balance out some discomfort.

In addition to fear or lack of skills, another challenge you might face is some co-workers' unwillingness to work with quantitative data. If someone whom you need to be involved in this project does not believe numbers can reveal anything meaningful, an approach that could help is to remind them that you are not discounting nonnumerical ways of evaluating the collection. Your evaluation can include asking faculty for their opinions, browsing the shelves, or checking the numbers against librarians' intuitive knowledge of the collection. The last of these, incorporating librarians' existing knowledge into your interpretation of the data, can help with another major reason for unwillingness to work with quantitative data: the belief that assessment implies distrust of your colleagues' professional skills. The literature on building a culture of assessment could also help you respond to this attitude if it is prevalent at your institution.

The common element to all the potential challenges just described is that your response should involve listening to your colleagues and incorporating their questions and existing knowledge into the evaluation. This may seem contradictory to the point made above about consistency in data collection, since accommodating everyone's preferences may result in different librarians using slightly different data. Some exceptions to the intention of consistency are okay, though, as long as you've established a minimum amount of data to collect for each department or segment of the collection. Henle and Cochenour (2007) provide a nice example of responding to selectors with varying appetites for data. When these authors were compiling usage data for their electronic resources, one of their library's selectors asked for a report broken down by hour, a level of detail that is beyond what would've been reasonable to make everyone review. They provided this information for the selector who wanted it without changing their expectations for the other selectors, thus combining a baseline consistency with some flexibility. Allowing someone to collect or review extra data, or offering some leeway in how the data is used, does not necessarily violate the goal of consistency and can give the relevant people some ownership of the evaluation project. Just be careful with those who want to go beyond the baseline that they do not let their task expand so much that they can't finish it on time.

Preparatory Steps

Once you've articulated your goals, set the scope of your project, decided on a timeframe, found your data sources, and begun a conversation with your colleagues, you are ready to move from the planning stage to the preparation stage. Part of preparation could entail creating some tools for your library to use. One of these tools is a system for dividing up your collection by subject, and the other is a list of peer libraries or aspirational institutions.

Dividing the Collection by Subject

As explained in chapter 2, two of the four collection evaluation methods in this book—benchmarking and usage statistics—require you to divide up your collection according to call number ranges. If you are using a software tool, you will have to use the divisions that are built into the software. For WCE these are the conspectus divisions, categories, and subjects, explained below. Intota Assessment provides classifications based on the sixty-one subjects included in Resources for College Libraries. In Intota Assessment, books or journals are assigned to a classification according to their subject headings, not call numbers. Libraries that are not using one of these two products, or those supplementing the software with other data, have several choices for how to divide the collection by subject.

The simplest way to divide your collection is by using the divisions that already exist within the call number system that you use. For example, if you use the Dewey Decimal System, you might treat the 100s as a unit and the 200s as a unit, and so on. For the Library of Congress, you could evaluate the As, the Bs, and so on. These are probably not the most meaningful ways to divide your collection, however. Four different letters in LC deal with history (C, D, E, F), while the letter B includes three different disciplines: philosophy, psychology, and religion. The divisions within the Dewey Decimal System are more consistent, but with only ten divisions, you'd end up with broad ranges of materials in each section. Other ways of subdividing your collection will make the analysis more meaningful but also more time-consuming.

One common way that libraries analyze their collections is by using the conspectus divisions and categories, a series of call number ranges created as part of an initiative of the Research Libraries Group in the early 1980s to standardize how libraries described their collections. This system created a series of twenty-five divisions representing general fields such as physical sciences or art and architecture. Within these twenty-five divisions are five hundred categories representing narrower topics such as sculpture or photography, which are further divided into four thousand subjects. Although OCLC no longer posts the entire series of call number ranges on its website, it can be found via the Internet Archive (at http://web.archive.org/web/20070416113618/http://www.oclc.org/collectionanalysis/support/conspectus.xls). Call numbers for both the Library of Congress and the Dewey Decimal System are assigned at the category level (i.e., the middle level). Divisions are made up of several categories, so the call number range for a division is simply the combination of all the ranges for its component categories.

Another option besides using the conspectus call number ranges is to create custom call number ranges that correspond with the departments or programs at your institution. Dividing your collection in this way is a little more time-consuming than using the conspectus categories because you will need to create the scheme yourself, but the result will be data that feels more meaningful to your institution. You can borrow from the schemes of other libraries, some of which have posted their call number maps online. Because the purpose of mapping call numbers to departments is to create units of analysis that are specific to your institution, though, you will probably need to adapt what you get from other institutions rather than simply using their maps. An advantage of institution-specific maps over the OCLC conspectus is that they can better treat interdisciplinary programs. For example, for disability studies the University of Michigan lists ninety-six different call numbers, covering psychology, physical recreation, law, education, and medicine. Creating institution-specific call number maps also probably results in data that will feel more relevant to stakeholders and might tie more closely with action steps. Textbox 3.3 summarizes the three options for dividing a collection into sections according to call numbers.

Identifying Peer or Aspirational Institutions

Benchmarking almost always involves comparing your collection to that of peer institutions, and comparison to peers could be useful for list-checking as well. If you are part of

---

TEXTBOX 3.3.

WAYS OF DIVIDING YOUR COLLECTION BY SUBJECT

Classes That Exist as Part of Your Classification System (i.e., A, B, C for Library of Congress; 100, 200, 300 for Dewey)

- Time Required: No time is required to create a map of call numbers to subject divisions. Involves running the fewest reports.
- Usefulness: Reports are the least meaningful.
- Tools: Outline of Library of Congress Classification (http://www.loc.gov/catdir/cpso/lcco/) and outline of Dewey Decimal System (http://www.oclc.org/dewey/resources/summaries.en.html)

Conspectus Divisions and Categories

- Time Required: Takes longer to do your analysis than the system above, as each division is the composite of many call number ranges representing different categories and you will have to run a report for each range.
- Usefulness: Reports are more meaningful, as they correspond with disciplines, though maybe not with the programs at your institution.
- Tool: OCLC's map of call numbers to conspectus categories (http://web.archive.org/web/20070416113618/http://www.oclc.org/collectionanalysis/support/conspectus.xls)

Custom Call Number Ranges

- Time Required: Time-consuming to create and use, as you will need to map your own programs to call number ranges and then evaluate the collection according to these ranges.
- Usefulness: The data will be meaningful to library liaisons, faculty, and administrators who are used to thinking about your institution in terms of its programs.
- Tool: Example from University of Michigan (http://www.lib.umich.edu/browse/categories/)

a consortium of libraries that serve similar student bodies to your own, you may have a group of peers that you routinely use for comparison purposes. If this is not the case, or if you want to compare yourself to libraries you aim to emulate rather than ones that are already similar, there are a few ways you can pick a group that you'll use for comparison.

To identify peer or aspirational institutions, a useful tool is the Library Statistics Program of the National Center for Education Statistics (NCES) (http://nces.ed.gov/ surveys/libraries/compare/). This tool lets you compare one library (presumably your own) to a group that you select. The tool is more useful for helping you find a comparison group than it is for actually doing the comparison, as the tool only contains very general information about each institution, such as counts of materials in various formats. To find a comparison group, you can select libraries based on several different variables. If you are looking for peers rather than aspirational institutions, you want to look at libraries that are already similar to you in the populations they serve (e.g., enrollment or degrees offered). Because the outcome of your own collection evaluation will be some knowledge of how your collection differs from your peers', you don't want to start out by limiting your comparison group to those with a similar-size collection to yours. You may not want to use budget as a criterion either, especially if you are hoping to use your collection evaluation to argue for greater funding. If you want to argue that other schools with the same amount of students and same degree levels have better-funded libraries and therefore larger collections, you can't do this by comparing yourself only to libraries with budgets similar to yours.

Since the NCES tool does not include a variable for the academic caliber of the school, you may want to generate a list of peers based on the above variables, look for additional information on these schools, and select from among them either schools that are ranked similarly to yours or those that are more highly ranked. The primary place to look for university rankings is *U.S. News*. If your institution has a national reputation, see http://colleges.usnews.rankingsandreviews.com/best-colleges/rankings/national-universities for universities or http://colleges.usnews.rankingsandreviews.com/best-colleges/ rankings/national-liberal-arts-colleges for liberal arts colleges. If your school is considered a regional institution, you may want to use the rankings of regional universities, available at http://colleges.usnews.rankingsandreviews.com/best-colleges/rankings/regional-universities.

If you are looking for aspirational institutions rather than peers, you'll want to look at the rankings first and may not use the NCES site at all. You can use the top-ranked institutions as your comparison group, or you can find ones whose collections you expect to be just slightly better than yours: the next tier up in rankings perhaps, or universities with similar rank as you but larger budgets (if you are not trying to make an argument about the size of your budget). If you are looking at how well the collection supports a specific discipline or program, rather than evaluating your entire library collection, your aspirational institutions will be ones with especially strong programs in your area of focus. *U.S. News* produces rankings of graduate programs in many different fields (http:// grad-schools.usnews.rankingsandreviews.com/best-graduate-schools), and professional associations also often create rankings as well. Search for a list of best graduate schools for your topic of interest, and select a list that was created by a professional association. Even if your collection only supports undergraduates, you'll probably use the graduate school rankings to find your aspirational institutions. Such lists will be more likely to exist than lists of undergraduate programs, and schools with graduate programs should be collecting in more depth, giving you more to aspire to.

Organization of Data

With these tools in place, the only remaining preparatory step is setting up a structure for organizing your data. Most likely you'll be storing the data in Excel, as this is a readily available tool. Wical and Kishel's (2013) survey of sixty-two academic libraries in Wisconsin found that 66 percent of respondents were using Excel spreadsheets to collect usage statistics for electronic resources. You could of course use Google spreadsheets instead. If you're not using Google, the spreadsheets can be stored either on your institution's intranet in file folders or on password-protected web pages. Make sure everyone who needs to use the spreadsheets has access to them and knows where they are.

It is recommended that, before you begin collecting any data, you create a blank spreadsheet with the rows and columns labeled. This is your template, and using it will make it easy for you to stay consistent as you tabulate data for multiple parts of the collection or as different subject librarians collect similar data. Since you've already established what amount of standardization is reasonable, all librarians who are collecting data can use the template as a concrete way to see what is required of them and can see how much leeway they have to adjust the collection evaluation to their personal preferences.

Before you begin filling in the spreadsheet, write down exactly what data you plan to collect. Be very specific. If you are going to collect usage from July 1 to June 30, write that down, so if you go back to collecting more data next week you can use the same dates. Note what formats and locations you included—did you include reference books in your count of books, or are those going to be separate? If you started counting holdings on December 5, all areas of the collection should count what you had as of December 5. If there is more than one report that gives the same data, write down which one you will use. When you've written your detailed plans, you are ready to start collecting data.

Key Points

This chapter has taken you through a thorough planning process that involves clarifying aspects of your project from its overarching goals to the details of data collection. In brief, the steps in this process are:

- State your goals at the outset, as they will influence the scope of the project and what evaluation methods you use.
- Decide what subject areas and material types you will be evaluating. You do not need to do everything at once. The scope of the project will affect how long it takes you to complete.
- Set a target for when you expect to finish and how often you intend to repeat the evaluation. If you have an externally imposed deadline, modify the scope if necessary so you can meet the deadline.
- Figure out where you will be getting your data, whether it is from WorldCat, your own catalog, local reports, or faculty publications. You will need different data for different evaluation methods.
- Identify which of your colleagues are going to be involved in the project and make sure to include them in the process from the beginning.

- Prepare for your data collection by making some decisions about the details: what system will you use for dividing your collection by subject, who is your comparison group, and where will you store your data?

You should now be more than ready to begin your collection evaluation. If your project includes benchmarking, you can go directly to chapter 4. Otherwise, you can skip to the chapters that introduce the methods you plan to use.

References

Henle, Alea, and Donnice Cochenour. 2007. "Practical Considerations in the Standardization and Dissemination of Usage Statistics." In *Usage Statistics of E-Serials*, edited by David C. Fowler, 5–23. Binghamton, NY: Haworth Press.

Wical, Stephanie H., and Hans F. Kishel. 2013. "Strategic Collection Management through Statistical Analysis." *Serials Librarian* 64, nos. 1–4 (April): 37–41.

CHAPTER 4

Benchmarking— Collecting and Analyzing the Data

PROBABLY THE OLDEST, MOST TRADITIONAL WAY OF EVALUATING a library collection is simply quantifying its size. Almost every library has at one point produced a list of numbers representing how many monographic volumes it holds and how many active serials subscriptions it has. These are the kinds of numbers that campus offices involved in promoting the institution tend to want, but they can frustrate librarians who are not always sure these numbers convey anything meaningful. Are these enough books? Is three hundred journal subscriptions impressive? Some point of comparison would make the numbers more useful. Try comparing your library's size to the library at a peer institution, and right away the numbers will seem more meaningful. Or compare how many history books you own with how many art books, or how many printed biology books with how many biology e-books. These numbers can provide information that can send a message about your library's strengths, make a case for better funding, or influence future collection development decisions.

Evaluating a collection through comparing quantities of items is usually called benchmarking. This chapter on benchmarking uses the term to refer to all kinds of evaluation that focus on numbers of books or other materials rather than what particular titles are owned or used. Although this may sound like a superficial form of analysis, this kind of data allows for simple communication with administrators as well as a bird's-eye view for librarians. Benchmarking data is often collected to share with people outside the library, though it can be useful for librarians as well.

Ways to Use Benchmarking

Which items you choose to count and whose collection you compare yourself to will depend on your audience and goals. If your audience is the National Association of Schools of Art and Design, which has asked about library resources as part of the accreditation process for university art departments, you'd only count art materials but would include all formats. Your admissions office, on the other hand, would want information on the entire collection. If you want to show parents of prospective students how you measure up against other institutions, you'd probably compare yourself to peers, while a plan for expanding the library would be better done by finding aspirational institutions. Libraries planning for collaborative collection development sometimes calculate the size of their holdings in different subject areas to help assign collection responsibilities. As with all evaluation methods discussed in this book, you will probably use the data in some way to drive future purchasing and weeding. You will decide what data to collect based on what message you want to send to whom, what decisions you might make based on the data, and what is available to you in terms of data, time, and staff.

Table 4.1 lists some goals that can be met using various kinds of numerical data. Although all the data is comparative, there are several possible kinds of comparisons: between institutions or between different parts of one library's collection. The second-to-last item in the table, deciding what to buy, is not strictly a form of quantitative comparison. When the process of quantitative comparison also provides an easy way to generate a list of titles to purchase, however, many libraries will want to use this list. The rest of this chapter uses different scenarios to illustrate the steps for gathering data using three different tools. There may not be an example here that uses the same data you want to use and the same tools that you have, but remember that as table 4.1 notes, in most cases benchmarking can be done to some degree with whatever tools you have.

The strength of quantitative data is its clarity in communicating with people outside the library. Big-picture, dashboard-type data is useful for those who want to assess the library at a glance. For example, an administrator in the communications office at Arcadia University has said that she likes "digestible information" and "fast facts" to use in promotional materials. If you uncover unique strengths of your library, translating these strengths into numerical "fast facts" can help you market this uniqueness to prospective students and their parents. Internal stakeholders such as the provost also often appreciate concise information that they can review quickly, though campus leaders may follow up by asking for more detail later. According to Ferguson (1992), administrators think in terms of competition with other institutions, for both students and faculty, and therefore comparative data will be the most meaningful for them.

Table 4.1. Ways to Use Benchmarking

GOAL	AUDIENCE	DATA NEEDED	POSSIBLE TOOLS
To advertise	Offices promoting the university, e.g., marketing or admissions	Fast facts Collection size in relation to competitors	Local catalog Library Statistics Program from NCES WorldCat Discovery or Collection Evaluation
To plan collaborative collection development	Consortial partners	Relative sizes of different segments of each library's collection	Shared catalog WorldCat Discovery or Collection Evaluation
To justify budget requests	Provost or financial officer	Size of collection in relation to libraries of peer institutions	Local catalog Library Statistics Program from NCES WorldCat Discovery or Collection Evaluation
To allocate existing budget	Librarians	Size of segments of the collection in relation to enrollment or to usage, or compared to universe of published material	Local catalog Local enrollment and usage data WorldCat Discovery or Collection Evaluation
To know what to buy	Librarians	Size of segments of collection compared to aspirational institutions, plus a title list	WorldCat Discovery or Collection Evaluation
To weed	Librarians	Size of collection, measured in segments of subject and year	Local catalog WorldCat Discovery or Collection Evaluation

In addition to communicating with administrators and the public, benchmarking data has historically been used to plan for collaborative collection development efforts. When the analysis is broken down by subject area, libraries in a consortium can identify areas in which their collection is stronger than the other partner libraries and can focus on building those subject collections to support the entire consortium. Conversely, consortia can identify areas of overlap between their collections and choose sections to weed, though this kind of data may be less useful for weeding if the data collection tool does not provide a title-by-title list of overlapping holdings. Chapter 5 includes some best practices on how to incorporate holdings information into planning for collaboration.

Benchmarking has its shortcomings as an evaluation method as well. Because comparisons between libraries, based solely on volumes held, describe the collection in such broad strokes, benchmarking data often needs to be supplemented with a lot more information before you can feel comfortable using it to drive any decisions. One reason the numbers don't tell you much on their own is that they don't indicate whether the particular books and journals the library provides are actually useful. Nowadays libraries often purchase large packages of electronic journals, which are padded with titles the library does not need and which inflate the size of the collection without necessarily improving it. It is possible the collection could be padded with inappropriate books as well, particularly if you haven't weeded in a while. Looking at the library's holdings for a given range of publication years can help tease out whether the library owns older or newer books, but this method still does not really measure the usefulness of the books. Despite these limitations, however, benchmarking analyses are valuable for how they can help you communicate about the library to outsiders, and in the correct circumstances they can help with decision making within the library as well.

History of the Conspectus Method

Since the early 1980s, a standard protocol has existed for describing a library in terms of the size of its holdings. This is the conspectus method, developed by the Research Libraries Group (RLG). Although this method of describing holdings quantitatively is no longer in use, it was prevalent for twenty years, and elements of it are commonly incorporated into quantitative measures of library holdings today. Created by nine research libraries in the late 1970s and early 1980s, the conspectus was intended to "become the cornerstone of a . . . national cooperative effort . . . among all the principal research libraries of the nation, for the eventual benefit of generations of scholars" (Gwinn and Mosher, 1983: 129). The goal was to create a standard way for libraries to describe their collection strengths and communicate these strengths to each other. RLG member libraries could collaborate to assign collection responsibilities to those who already had large collections in a certain area, or could "dispose of locally unneeded materials with the knowledge and assurance that materials [would] be available elsewhere" (Gwinn and Mosher, 1983: 130–31). The means of communication that RLG developed was a five-level scale that allowed libraries to rate their collections from minimal (level 1) to comprehensive (level 5) (Gwinn and Mosher, 1983; White, 2008). RLG also created a standardized way of dividing up collections into subject-based sections so that collections could be evaluated at a more granular level. The RLG conspectus contained twenty-five divisions, which were assigned Library of Congress classification ranges. These divisions were subdivided into five hundred categories of four thousand subjects (Bushing, 2001). A second conspectus was developed later by the Western Library Network (the WLN conspectus). It included divisions by Dewey Decimal Classification and expanded RLG's five-level scale into ten levels. Comprehensive collections were still considered level 5, but levels 1–3 were divided into 1a, 1b, and so forth. These new levels allowed smaller libraries to use the conspectus tool, as there was now more gradation at the bottom of the scale (Bushing, 2001; Lange and Wood, 2000).

The major shortcoming of the RLG and WLN conspectuses was a lack of consistent, objective means for assigning collection levels. Lange and Wood (2000) explain that the library literature in the 1980s provided a multitude of suggestions of how to assign a number indicating collection depth. The guidelines recommended "a variety of tools" such as "title counts, age of materials, expenditures . . . comparison of library holdings against standard lists and bibliographies, and citation studies" (Lange and Wood, 2000: 70–71) as well as usage data and user surveys. Instructions for translating the results of such comparisons into collection levels attempted to standardize this process but fell short. Webster gives the example that a library holding "15–20% of the titles in the major bibliographies" was considered to provide basic instructional support (2001: 155). Since libraries were in charge of selecting appropriate bibliographies themselves, though, this measurement was not uniform. In the end, picking a collection level indicator was a matter of judgment. White calls the conspectus scales "pseudo-evaluation," albeit well intentioned (2008: 171).

Legacy of the Conspectus Method

Neither the RLG nor WLN conspectuses are currently in use, though their legacies continue. RLG discontinued its conspectus tool in 1997 (Lange and Wood, 2000). After WLN became part of OCLC in 1999, the latter built on the WLN conspectus to create an automated tool for collection analysis (Bushing, 2001). OCLC's product, launched in 2005, was called WorldCat Collection Analysis. In September 2013, this product was superseded by WorldCat Collection Evaluation, discussed later in this chapter. Both WorldCat Collection Analysis and WorldCat Collection Evaluation built on the contributions of the conspectus method by using conspectus divisions and categories as units of analysis and providing the means to measure library holdings in these subject areas as well as to compare one's holdings to standardized lists. Although the conspectus method is no longer in use, some recent quantitative studies still use its divisions as units of analysis (Knievel, Wicht, and Connaway, 2006; White, 2008).

Although the original conspectus method was designed for research libraries, and WorldCat Collection Evaluation is only available to libraries who subscribe, any library can benefit from the models these tools provide for evaluating a collection. In developing these tools, RLG, WLN, and OCLC have created techniques for evaluation that you can use even if you do not have access to a product specifically designed for collection evaluation. Much of the data that WorldCat Collection Evaluation provides can be gathered manually by using the Discovery interface to search WorldCat, and if you do not subscribe to WorldCat, your own online catalog can provide some of the data. The different strategies for benchmarking illustrate well the iron triangle of project management mentioned in chapter 3, in which all projects rely on a balance of depth, time, and cost. Approaches that cost less money will generally require more time for data collection, whereas paying for an analysis tool will allow for a quick and easy project. The two major software tools are described in more detail below. This chapter describes three strategies for collecting benchmarking data, in order from the least to most expensive and most to least time-intensive, so that you can pick the one that fits your needs and resources.

Preparing for Benchmarking

The questions to address before benchmarking are the same as the general preparation steps spelled out in chapter 3: what are your goals, what information are you looking for, what formats or segments of the collection will you be including in the analysis, and what tools do you have available for collecting data? As always, the goal will determine whom you pick as your comparison group and what data you use. When choosing a comparison group, using the instructions in chapter 3, remember that if you are trying to make the case for greater funding, you shouldn't select peer institutions based on the size of their budget. You will want to find evidence that other schools with the same amount of students and same degree levels have better-funded libraries and therefore larger collections.

Another choice you will have to make is what subjects you'll be evaluating. If you are using collection evaluation software, you will need to subdivide your collection according to the categories the software program uses. If you are collecting data manually, using either WorldCat Discovery or your local catalog, you can either use the conspectus categories or your own customized call number ranges. If you are focusing on a specific academic program, which may not fit well within the conspectus categories, you might prefer to create your own units based on call number ranges that you choose.

Benchmarking Using Freely Available Tools

Comparison to Other Institutions

Once you have articulated a goal and made decisions about the details of your project, there are a few different ways you can gather data. The cheapest method, and one that is accessible to any library that can find the staff time, involves data that is freely available online or relies entirely on internal data. Lyons (2009) suggests simply searching your own catalog and then running the same searches in the catalogs of peer institutions. You can do several searches to get counts for different call number ranges. If you want to run separate searches by format, check each institution's catalog for all item types that might represent the same format. For example, Arcadia University's library catalog includes the item types of book, reference, and oversize, all of which should be included in a count of books. There might be certain items you want to exclude from your count, but you shouldn't do so unless you can exclude them for all the libraries you are benchmarking against. As an example, the children's book collection at Arcadia has its own item types, so it is easy to avoid counting a science book for second graders in the total count of science books, but this might not be the case for all libraries. If you can't exclude something for all libraries, it's better to include it across the board for the sake of consistency.

A larger problem when attempting to do a comparison using the method Lyons suggests is that few catalogs allow a search by a call number range. Most catalogs allow users to search by a specific call number, but even then results can be inaccurate. Glance at the results to see if a search for HV24 also returns HV245, for instance. This method would work best if you search by LC subclassifications, which are just the first two letters of the call number, but it would be difficult to do searches based on call number maps such as the ones described in chapter 3. Another caution when running separate searches by format is that many libraries do not assign call numbers to periodicals, so it might not be possible to do a comparison of the relative sizes of libraries' periodical holdings. Also, some catalogs truncate search results at fifty and therefore cannot provide useful data. Although a comparison using peer libraries' public catalogs has the advantage of being free, it is also prone to distortions in the data due to inconsistency between catalogs.

Internal Comparison

If you are doing an internal comparison, that is, comparing some sections of your collection to other sections, you will likely be able to do this using only your own catalog and internal data. Such an analysis will not, of course, show how you compare to competitor schools or help you plan for collaborative collection development, but it can inform budget allocations and communications with the faculty about support for their departments. The section on WorldCat Discovery later in this chapter includes an example of how benchmarking within your own collection can show you your library's purchasing history in different subject areas. You could gather this data from your own catalog as well, as long as your catalog allows you to limit a search by publication date, item type, and call number range.

Internal comparisons can also compare holdings to enrollment or budget data to provide context. You might want to look at how many books per student you have in different subject areas, or see how the number of subscriptions for each department compares to the amount spent on these subscriptions. Table 4.2 shows a brief analysis that uses enrollment data. The table shows serials subscriptions at Arcadia University broken down by department or program. Note that some departments are equivalent to disciplines and others are structured around a particular profession. Despite this apparent inconsistency, these categories match the administrative units at the institution and will make more sense to both faculty and the librarian liaisons to these departments than any other categories would. To

Table 4.2. Serials Spending Compared to Enrollment at Arcadia University

DEPARTMENT	NUMBER OF TITLES	% OF TITLES	CREDIT HOURS	% OF TOTAL CREDIT HOURS
Anthropology	3	0.96%	116	0.98%
Art and Design	11	3.51%	5,516	4.85%
Biology	12	3.83%	5,825	6.26%
Business	9	2.88%	5,338	5.74%
Chemistry	21	6.71%	2,557	2.75%
Education	34	10.86%	8,244	8.86%
English	62	19.81%	10,691	11.49%
Forensic Science	3	0.96%	1,153	1.24%
Genetic Counseling	25	7.99%	832	0.89%
Leisure	14	4.47%	n/a	
Library (for staff use)	20	6.39%	n/a	
Math	12	3.83%	3,875	4.16%
Modern Languages	3	0.96%	3,013	3.24%
Peace and Conflict Resolution	7	2.24%	1,121	1.20%
Physical Therapy Program	46	14.70%	6,002	6.45%
Physician Assistant Program	22	7.03%	9,237	9.92%
Political Science	8	2.56%	1,520	1.63%
Psychology	28	8.95%	4,839	5.20%
Public Health	25	7.99%	1,295	1.39%
Religion/Philosophy	2	0.64%	994	1.07%
Sociology	13	4.15%	3,745	4.02%
Total	313*		93,077	

* some titles are counted multiple times

perform a similar comparison at your own institution, you would want to use the departmental units at your school. If you use a subscription agent, they will be able to provide a list of journals subscriptions. Your registrar's office or provost will have enrollment data.

Because journals in some fields are much more expensive than in other fields, it is useful to see not only what percentage of subscriptions support each department but also what percentage of the budget is spent on each department. Comparing this information to the percentage of credit hours in this department can then reveal which departments are underserved and which ones to prioritize if there is money to add subscriptions in the future.

WorldCat Discovery: Some Expense, Some Labor

Comparison to Other Institutions

The procedures above rely on data that can be obtained for free, either from in-house sources or on the Internet. Many academic libraries have access to an additional tool that can also be very useful for comparison: the WorldCat database, provided by OCLC. Libraries that subscribe to and include their holdings information in WorldCat can use the WorldCat Discovery interface to search the database and compile data at no extra cost other than staff time. Discovery was released in beta in 2014 and made available to all libraries that subscribed to FirstSearch. To use it, you will need to register with OCLC and receive a URL for Discovery. This step will be required when Discovery supersedes the FirstSearch interface at the end of 2015.

Since most academic libraries already pay for a subscription to WorldCat, using its public interface for data collection will often be a good option. You can gather data using a straightforward method that McClure (2009) designed for using the FirstSearch interface to compare her holdings to those of other libraries. Although Discovery is still under development, the documentation (http://www.oclc.org/support/help/Searching-WorldCatIndexes/default.htm) shows that fielded searching is intended to work similarly enough to FirstSearch that McClure's techniques should also work in Discovery. McClure's goal was to use a tool to which she already had access to "mimic some of the features of OCLC's WorldCat Collection Analysis, a subscription product" to which her library did not have access (2009: 79). The advantages of McClure's technique over using local library catalogs are that her method involves searching the holdings of the peer or comparison group through a uniform interface, one that allows searches by call number range. Furthermore, since OCLC records usually include both an LC and a Dewey call number, you can make comparisons with libraries that use either system. Even serials records will have call numbers, so they can be included in the comparison. The disadvantage is that OCLC usually includes multiple bibliographic records for the same book or journal, whereas the library's holdings symbol would only be attached to one record. This will skew the results to make the library look like it has a smaller percentage of potential materials in a given field than it actually has. In other words, if there are four records for one book, and one of those records indicates that the book is held by your library, the numerical count will show that you have 25 percent of the books in the list, when you really have all of them. This would mainly be an issue when comparing your own holdings to all potential purchases. If you are comparing your library's holdings to another library's, their holdings symbol will also only be attached to one record for each book as well, so the comparison will be more accurate.

McClure's method can be used to compare a library to the universe of all published materials, or to the holdings of a select group of peer or aspirational institutions. McClure used a method that fell in between the two, creating a composite of four libraries with strong collections in the subject area of interest to her and treating that composite as the "universe" of appropriate material. She explains that she did this because if she had only searched by call number, her results would've included a lot of nonacademic books that would not be appropriate for her library. The four libraries she and her colleagues selected were large university libraries with well-respected programs in the fields of interest to her study. She does not explain how they identified these libraries, but you can create your own aspirational comparison group using the instructions in chapter 3. Once you've created a comparison group, you will need to find the OCLC holdings codes for all the libraries in it, which you can do by using the Directory of OCLC Libraries (http://oclc.org/contacts/libraries.en.html). Look up each library and note its three-letter holdings code.

To do benchmarking using WorldCat Discovery, you'll need to configure the Knowledge Base so that WorldCat is one of the databases you can search using the Discovery interface, and you'll need a staff account for login. If your library is currently using Discovery, you'll have set up these required steps already. Go to your institution-specific Discovery URL and log in, then go to the Advanced Search screen, which will look like figure 4.1. Make sure you are only searching WorldCat by clicking on Add or Remove Databases in the upper right and seeing that only WorldCat (not WorldCat.org) is checked. Click Done to close the list of databases and return to the Advanced Search screen. Since the fields that you'll be searching (LC or Dewey Decimal Class Number and Holding Symbol) are not listed as options in the dropdown, leave the dropdown set to keyword and type in the field codes manually. You'll use lc: for a Library of Congress Class Number, dd: for Dewey, and li: for Holding Symbol.

Build your search string carefully using the tips in textbox 4.1. Add whatever limits you have chosen for your search—for example, books only or no juvenile materials. If desired, you can also limit your search by year or run several searches representing different decades.

As with the comparison method using free tools, run searches for each call number range and for each library in your comparison group. When you do your search in Discovery, you'll use the field code li: to limit your search to records that have a particular holdings symbol attached. To limit your search to only items held by Boston University, for example, you'd do a keyword search for li:BOS. You may choose to treat the comparison group as one unit, as McClure did, in order to compare your holdings to the universe of published materials. This will allow you to see the relative strengths and weaknesses of your own collection

Advanced Search

Figure 4.1. Discovery Advanced Search.

TEXTBOX 4.1.

HOW TO SEARCH FOR CALL NUMBER RANGES IN DISCOVERY

- Select keyword from the dropdown menu if it is not already selected.
- In the search box, type in the beginning of the call number, followed by wildcard symbols (#) to replace any digits that will vary across the range. *Example*: HD725# will return results for all 4-digit classification numbers starting with HD725—in other words, HD7250 through HD7259.
- It is important to use the wildcard symbol (#) rather than the truncation symbol (?). The truncation symbol means there could be any number of digits in place of the symbol, whereas each wildcard symbol specifies there should be exactly one digit in its place. *Example*: HD72? (truncation symbol) could return HD72, HD729, or HD7295. HD72# (wildcard symbol) will return only three-digit call numbers beginning with HD72.
- You can use multiple wildcard symbols in a row. *Example*: To search for HD1000–1999, use HD1###.
- For a small range, you can enumerate the possible call numbers and list them using the OR operator. *Example*: HD7255 OR HD7256.
- Narrower classifications should work in Discovery as well. *Example*: RZ275.S65.

Although somewhat clunky, this method does allow for very specific ranges. The following string searches the range RM695 to RM844, for physical therapy:

RM695 OR RM696 OR RM697 OR RM698 OR RM699 OR RM7## OR RM80# OR RM81# OR RM82# OR RM83# OR RM840 OR RM841 OR RM842 OR RM843 OR RM844

(for example, if you have a higher percentage of materials on rehabilitation therapy than on surgery) rather than comparing the size of your collection to that of another library. To search the comparison group's holdings altogether, combine the different libraries' codes using OR and put the field code li: in front of each symbol. Refer back to figure 4.1 to see an example search using the string li:PFM OR li:EMM OR li:FUJ OR li:BOS, to search for items held by University of Pittsburgh Health Science Library, Emory University Health Science Center Library, University of Florida Health Science Center, or Boston University.

Table 4.3 is an example of findings from using this method to compare Arcadia University's book holdings for physical therapy to those of the four libraries that were searched in figure 4.1. These institutions admit a similar number of students per year as Arcadia, but because their total library expenditures are much larger, the expectation is for them to have larger collections on almost every subject. The call number ranges are simplified from those offered by the University of Michigan on the website mentioned in the previous chapter.

The percentages in table 4.3 look low, but remember they are comparing the holdings of one library to four larger libraries put together. If the goal was to make the case that the library needed more books, or to tell prospective students how strong Arcadia's collection is, it would be better to compare Arcadia to other libraries one at a time. This

Table 4.3. Arcadia's Physical Therapy Book Holdings versus a Comparison Group

CALL NUMBER RANGE	SEARCH STRING	ARCADIA'S BOOK HOLDINGS	COMPARISON GROUP	ARCADIA'S HOLDINGS AS PERCENTAGE OF OTHERS
GV711	GV711	5	18	27.78%
HD7255–HD7256	HD7255 OR HD7256	1	46	2.20%
RA781	RA781	14	62	22.58%
RC1200–RC1245	RC120# OR RC121# OR RC122# OR RC123# OR RC1240 OR RC1241 OR RC1243 OR RC1245	25	269	9.29%
RD52P59	RD52.P59	1	1	100%
RD97	RD97	16	149	10.73%
RD736	RD736	0	0	n/a
RD756–RD757	RD756 OR RD757	3	37	8.10%
RD997	RD997	0	0	n/a
RE827	RE827	0	2	0%
RJ53	RJ53	0	2	0%
RL684P57	RL684.P57	0	0	n/a
RM695–RM844	RM695 OR RM696 OR RM697 OR RM698 OR RM699 OR RM7## OR RM80# OR RM81# OR RM82# OR RM83# OR RM840 OR RM841 OR RM842 OR RM843 OR RM844	5	40	12.50%

(continued)

Table 4.3. *(Continued)*

CALL NUMBER RANGE	SEARCH STRING	ARCADIA'S BOOK HOLDINGS	COMPARISON GROUP	ARCADIA'S HOLDINGS AS PERCENTAGE OF OTHERS
RM863–RM950	RM863 OR RM864 OR RM865 OR RM866 OR RM867 OR RM868 OR RM869 OR RM87# OR RM88# OR RM89# OR RM90# OR RM91# OR RM92# OR RM94# OR RM950	3	35	8.57%
RX395.S66	RX863.S66	0	0	n/a
RZ275.S65	RZ275.S65	0	2	0%
UB360–UB366	UB360 OR UB361 OR UB362 OR UB363 OR UB364 OR UB365 OR UB366	0	5	0%

kind of comparison would involve the same steps as described above, using only one library's holding code at a time. As McClure points out, a comparison to four peer libraries allows you to see the relative strengths of your own collection. Although Arcadia has only five books on coaching (GV711), for example, the chart shows that this is pretty good compared to what other libraries have. The other four libraries together have eighteen; therefore Arcadia has 27.78 percent of what the comparison group has. The numbers are similarly high on fitness (RA781, 22.58 percent). Remember that in this example one library is comparing itself to four other libraries, so having one quarter of what the comparison group has seems reasonable. More importantly, the 27.78 percent is higher than the percentages owned in other call number ranges, so this subject is not a gap in the library's collection. In these cases the percentage is high because none of the libraries included in this comparison have strong collections on these topics. This might be because coaching and fitness are only tangentially related to physical therapy. This example is a reminder to keep the curriculum in mind when interpreting data. A relatively strong collection on fitness is not something to tout if this is not part of the program's curriculum.

A possible data error that could come from using Discovery is that libraries will not always list their electronic holdings in OCLC, and certainly not the titles they make available to patrons through patron-driven acquisitions. These would be titles that the library does not own (yet) and has not paid for, but which are made available through records in the catalog so that the library can purchase them as they are accessed. For example, due to a large patron-driven acquisitions program, Arcadia's library makes considerably more available to patrons than is apparent from OCLC. Local catalogs might be the only option for comparing e-book holdings. For items other than books or journals, WorldCat might not work for benchmarking, as libraries are less likely to attach their holdings symbol to items other than books or journals with title-level subscriptions.

Internal Comparison

Another way to use WorldCat Discovery is to produce comparative data about your own collection, similar to what WorldCat Collection Evaluation can provide. In table 4.4, the print book collection at Arcadia University's Landman Library is broken down by department/program and decade of publication. The complete data is shown graphically in figure 4.2. This shows in what years peak purchasing occurred and gives a sense of the ages of the books in Arcadia's collection. Although e-book holdings would also be relevant, they cannot be included in this table if they are not included in WorldCat. This kind of comparison is not useful for serials because their "publication date" is usually when they were first published with the current title and does not reflect the actual currency of the serials collection.

The data in table 4.4 and figure 4.2 is organized by departments and programs for a couple of reasons. One is that, although the categories look irregular—some being disciplines and others professions, some overlapping with others—information organized this way will make more sense to the various people who will view the data. Faculty are affiliated with a particular department, as are liaison librarians, so this data refers to units they are used to thinking about and care about. It may also be easier to generate action steps when the data is broken down by department. Not only is it clear which faculty members to talk to about buying additional books, but the library's purchasing budget is broken down by these same categories and could be adjusted if the data prompts the library to make changes in the allocation. While all twenty-four of Arcadia's programs were analyzed, for clarity only six are included in the table or graph. By chance, the total number of programs that Arcadia offers is almost the same as the number of conspectus categories (twenty-five). An institution that served many more programs might find it simpler to analyze their collection by

Table 4.4. Print Book Holdings at Arcadia University by Department or Program and Year of Publication

	CALL NUMBERS	1950–1959	1960–1969	1970–1979	1980–1989	1990–1999	2000–2009	2010–2013	TOTAL
Education	L	47	273	331	600	1,694	1,696	331	5,036
English	P, PE, PN, PR, PS	1,546	3,878	2,500	2,516	3,394	3,929	717	21,939
Modern Languages	PA–PD, PF–PM, PQ, PT	744	1,731	661	369	560	462	50	6,065
Peace and Conflict Resolution	JZ4835–end of JZ, KZ	11	33	15	9	81	203	44	403
Political Science	J–JZ3875, K–KW	169	612	459	461	875	1,213	221	4,223
Sociology	HM–HV5840	97	323	436	665	1,019	844	250	3,721

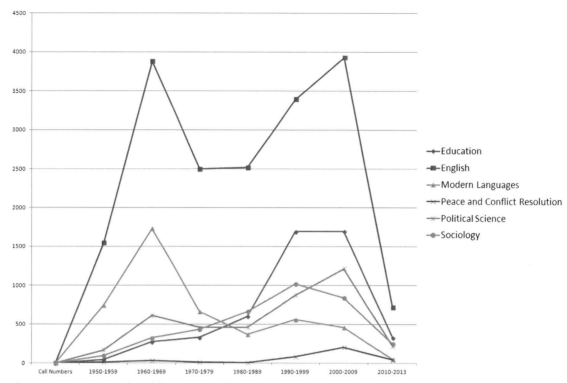

Figure 4.2. Print Book Holdings at Arcadia University by Department or Program and Year of Publication.

conspectus categories. Libraries using WorldCat Collection Evaluation to do this kind of analysis in a quicker and more automated way will have conspectus categories and their subdivisions as the only option.

To collect this kind of data using WorldCat Discovery, go back to the Advanced Search screen. Again, make sure that you are logged in with a staff account and that WorldCat is the only database selected. Limit the location to your institution using the dropdown menu at the bottom of the screen. In the dropdown menu for Format, select Book. For the year, type in a decade range. The system will accept 0000-1900 for the pre-1900 range, though the count will be inflated as this range also includes publications with no year. In the search box, leave the field selection as keyword and type the field code lc: (or dd:) into the box, followed by the call number you want to search for. Use the instructions in the sidebar to create your search strings.

When reading the graph in figure 4.2, there are a few points to be aware of. First, all the lines drop off on the right side because the last data point, 2010–2013, only covers four years, whereas the others all cover decades. Chapter 12 will explain why it is better to make sure each date range covers the same amount of years, but for now you can just be careful to note the different date ranges when reading the graph. Another note is that some of the categories overlap, so that a book might be counted for both peace and conflict resolution and political science, for instance. This is not necessarily a problem, as it simply means the same books could be useful to more than one department.

What this data tells us even without looking at the collection in more detail is something about the library's purchasing history. At a glance, it is clear that Landman Library purchased books heavily in the 1960s. Purchasing dropped off in the 1970s and 1980s and began to climb again around 1990. Patrons browsing the shelves are likely to find a lot of books from the 1960s in numbers that make newer books hard to find. To some extent any library that is buying fewer books in the current decade than in the past may be doing so because they have moved money toward e-book purchasing, or because print circulation is declining, or the institution's needs have changed. Again, more context will affect what conclusions you draw from the data.

WorldCat Collection Evaluation: Additional Expense, Less Labor

Making a table like the one just shown is very easy if you're able to use WorldCat Collection Evaluation (WCE). On the spectrum of analysis methods, WorldCat Collection Evaluation is the most expensive but least time-consuming. In order to use it, you need to already have a subscription to WorldCat and be regularly attaching your holdings symbol to records when you acquire new materials and removing it when you weed. An annual subscription to WorldCat Collection Evaluation is an additional expense on top of subscribing to WorldCat, but it has the benefit of allowing you to make the comparisons described in the previous section without typing out such long search strings or running three hundred separate searches. The disadvantage in terms of functionality is that you can't customize your call number ranges. WCE will only let you analyze your collection using the conspectus divisions and categories.

WorldCat Collection Evaluation is structured as a series of comparisons. It offers a comparison to a peer group that you've selected, a predefined comparison group such as top medical schools, or to the whole WorldCat database. For each kind of comparison, except the comparison to WorldCat, there are two different reports you can run: benchmarking or unique/shared. Both reports will tell you how many of the titles in your collection are unique to your library and how many titles are also owned by the comparison group. The primary difference between the two reports is that the benchmarking report shows what the comparison group owns that your library does not. The unique/shared report only shows your own library's holdings, but it tells how many of the titles in your collection are owned by one other library, two other libraries, and so on. The benchmarking report is more useful for comparing collection sizes, whereas the unique/shared report is more useful for comparing titles. Both reports output a graph showing the extent of overlap, and both can also provide a detailed list in Excel format of which titles are owned by your library and which by others. If you're doing a comparison to the WorldCat database as a whole, the benchmarking option is not available, as this report would need to list everything that is in WorldCat that your library does not own, and this would be a lengthy and not very useful report.

Comparison to Other Institutions

To benchmark your library against a peer or aspirational group, start by clicking Manage Comparisons on the left side of the screen. This will bring you to the screen shown in figure 4.3. Start by using the dropdown menu labeled Comparison Type. The options will be Peer, Pre-Defined, Authoritative, Hathi, or WorldCat. Select Peer if you want to create your own group of up to fifty peer institutions. Select Pre-Defined to use one of the comparison groups that comes with the software, such as top medical schools, top MBA programs, or ARL libraries. Once you select a type, the available comparison groups will appear in the box in the middle of the screen. In figure 4.3, because the comparison type Pre-Defined has been selected, the box is labeled Available Pre-Defined Groups. Click the plus sign next to a group to add it to your active comparisons. Then click the Create a Comparison button.

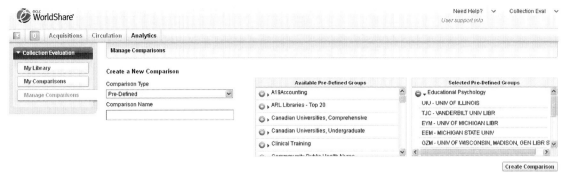

Figure 4.3. Create a New Comparison.

Next, click the middle link in the left menu, Active Comparisons, to see a list of all the groups you have used for comparison in the past, including the one you just selected. There will be three links next to each comparison group: Benchmarking, Unique/Shared Titles, and Comparison Title List. Click on Benchmarking. The resulting report will look like figure 4.4.

You can customize the benchmarking report in a few ways. One way is by limiting the report to only compare resources within a certain subject area. The list of Available Subjects near the top of the screen shows the conspectus divisions. You can expand a division to see the categories within it and then expand a category to see the subjects within that category. Select a division, category, or subject by clicking on it and then clicking the > arrow to add it to the list of Selected Subjects. Then click Refresh Chart to get a new chart showing only the subjects you've selected. The chart will combine all the selected subjects, so if you want separate numbers for each subject, you'll need to run the report again for

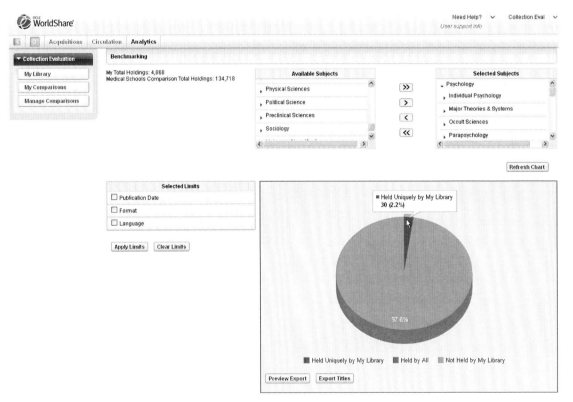

Figure 4.4. Sample Comparison Using Benchmarking Tool.

each. You can also limit the report by format, language, or publication date. If you select more than one format or language, the chart will include all the options you selected.

The pie chart in figure 4.4 shows the number of psychology materials in all formats owned by the library in question compared to the number owned by all the top medical schools combined. The percentages in the chart add up to 100, with the total number referring to the number of items owned by this library and the comparison libraries put together. To describe the size of your own holdings compared to the comparison group, you need to do some simple math. The number of items you own is the number Held Uniquely by My Library plus the number Held By All ("All" being your library plus the comparison group, not necessarily all libraries within the group). The number of items owned by the comparison group is the number Held By All plus the number Not Held By My Library. Although the pie chart only shows percentages, figure 4.4 shows that you can mouse over the wedges of the pie to see absolute numbers.

An advantage of using WorldCat Collection Evaluation is that not only can you compare the relative size of your collection to others, you can see exactly which titles you own that your comparison group does not and which titles your peers own that you don't. To see a title list, click Export Titles. You can retrieve the list via an FTP site. The title list will tell you how many of the libraries in the comparison group own each title.

Internal Comparison

WorldCat Collection Evaluation also offers a detailed report on your own library. This report, called My Library, is similar to the information provided by WCE's predecessor software, WorldCat Collection Analysis, which provided the chart Jennifer McClure was trying to mimic. Therefore, the chart shown in figure 4.5, from WCE, looks similar to the one in table 4.4, which was made using McClure's technique for searching WorldCat. Both tables list

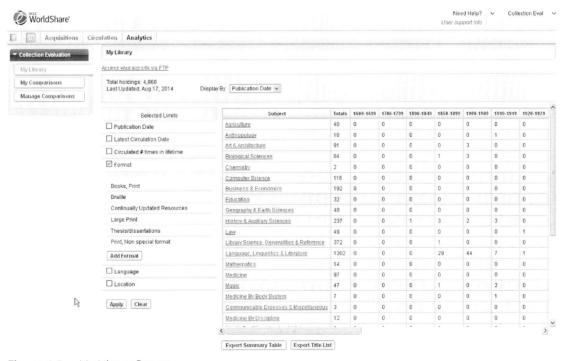

Figure 4.5. My Library Report.

subjects down the left side and date ranges across the top. In figure 4.5, the subjects on the left side represent conspectus divisions rather than the customized call number ranges you might use if you were collecting the data through another means. You can click on a division to see a chart that shows the categories within that division, and you can then click a category to see the subjects within the category. There are also options to limit the table so it only counts certain formats or certain years. The report does not display in graphical form, though you could export the table, save it in Excel, and then use Excel to create your own graph.

Overall, the advantages of using WorldCat Collection Evaluation for benchmarking over running searches in WorldCat Discovery are that the former lets you select conspectus divisions easily without typing in long strings of call numbers and offers preselected comparison groups. The detailed title lists can also be useful for deciding what to weed or what to add, as chapter 5 will explain. If you've sent OCLC your circulation data, they will load it into WCE for you so you can easily take into account both circulation and overlap with other libraries when evaluating specific titles for weeding. The disadvantage of automating the benchmarking process is that you lose some flexibility, since you can only divide your collection according to the conspectus divisions, categories, and subjects. You might also have to do a little bit of data manipulation on your own—for example, to compare the size of your collection to your peer group rather than looking at the overlap in holdings. Still, this product can save a lot of time.

Intota Assessment: Another Software Option

Another software tool you could consider using for collection evaluation is Intota Assessment, released by ProQuest in 2014. It offers seven different reports, of which the relevant one for benchmarking is Peer Analysis. Intota Assessment does not have a report comparable to WCE's My Library report. To compare your library to others, click on Choose Your Report in the top left corner of the screen to select Peer Analysis. Since the only libraries you can choose as peers are other Intota customers, for the time being there are fewer institutions you can compare yourself to than there would be if you were using WorldCat Collection Evaluation. The report is shown in figure 4.6.

As the figure shows, you have a choice of different schemes for subdividing your collection by subject, though as in WorldCat Collection Evaluation there is no way to create custom subdivisions that match your institution's programs. The schemes you can choose are Library of Congress, Dewey, RCL (the sixty-one subject areas used in Resources for College Libraries), or CR (subdivisions specific to career resources). The LC classifications are based on the Library of Congress subject headings, not call numbers. Intota also offers three levels of specificity for subject classification: within each subject heading, you can select a category and a subcategory.

The Peer Analysis report, shown in figure 4.6, produces a list of book titles rather than a summary of how many titles you and your peers own on the selected subject. The columns on the right list the peers you have selected, and the Xs in each column show you which books are owned by which libraries. In the screenshot, the library performing the comparison is Marlboro, and its holdings are listed in the second-to-last column on the right. You'd need to export the report to Excel and do your own math to calculate how many titles each peer library owned. The product was still relatively new at the time of this writing, and it may add features in the future that make it more conducive to benchmarking. At the moment, its most useful features are the report that is designed to

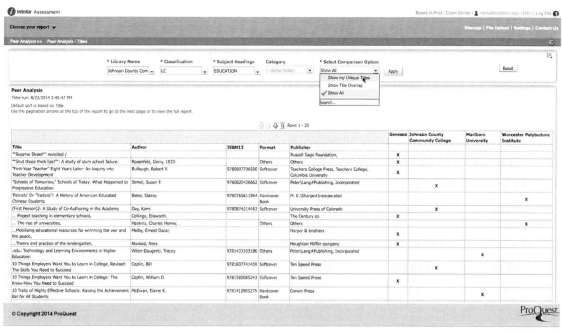

Figure 4.6. Intota Peer Analysis. Reproduced with permission from ProQuest LLC, © 2014 ProQuest. www. proquest.com.

help with deselection and its ability to pull together usage reports from various sources. Another benefit to Intota Assessment is that it is linked to Books in Print and provides much of the information from the latter within the Assessment interface. A subscription to Intota Assessment also includes access to the Books in Print website.

Key Points

Each tool described above has its own unique benefits, whether they be availability, efficiency, flexibility, or consistency of data. At the moment, WorldCat Discovery seems like the most desirable tool for the majority of libraries—it is something to which many academic libraries already have access, and it provides a uniform way to compare across collections. The local catalog likely has more complete information, however, and it is of course accessible to libraries that do not use WorldCat. WorldCat Collection Evaluation has the advantage of greatly speeding up data collection and providing title lists that translate into simple action steps for collection development. As you decide which tool to use and what data to collect, keep in mind the following:

- Benchmarking is useful for communicating with people outside the library—for example, when requesting a bigger budget, promoting your institution to prospective students, or doing collaborative collection development.
- Numbers relating to the library collection are only meaningful when compared to other numbers.
- Depending on your goals, you may choose to compare your library to peer institutions or aspirational institutions, or to compare some sections of your collection to other sections.
- Aim for consistency between how you count your own library's resources and how you count other libraries' resources.

- Benchmarking can be done using freely available tools, the commonly available Discovery interface to WorldCat, or WorldCat Collection Evaluation, a specialized tool that is available as a subscription. ProQuest's Intota Assessment also has a report that could be useful for benchmarking.
- Generally, the less a tool costs, the more time is involved in using it to collect data.

All of the types of data described in this chapter, whatever tool is used to collect it, can lead to multiple action steps, which the next chapter addresses.

References

Bushing, Mary C. 2001. "The Evolution of Conspectus Practice in Libraries: The Beginnings and the Present Applications." Paper presented at the Czech and Slovak Library Information Network, Czech Republic, May 29.

Ferguson, A. W. 1992. "The Conspectus and Cooperative Collection Development: What It Can and Cannot Do." *Acquisitions Librarian* 4, no. 7: 105–14.

Gwinn, Nancy E., and Paul H. Mosher. 1983. "Coordinating Collection Development: The RLG Conspectus." *College and Research Libraries* 44, no. 2 (March): 128–40.

Knievel, Jennifer E., Heather Wicht, and Lynn Silipigni Connaway. 2006. "Use of Circulation Statistics and Interlibrary Loan Data in Collection Management." *College and Research Libraries* 67, no. 1 (January): 35–49.

Lange, Janice, and Richard Wood. 2000. "The Conspectus: A Tool for Collection Assessment and Description." In *Encyclopedia of Library and Information Science*, vol. 66, supp. 29, edited by Allen Kent, 67–78. New York: Marcel Dekker.

Lyons, Lucy Eleanor. 2009. "Collection Evaluation: Selecting the Right Tools and Methods for Your Library." In *Library Data: Empowering Practice and Persuasion*, edited by Darby Orcutt, 37–51. Santa Barbara, CA: Libraries Unlimited.

McClure, Jennifer Z. 2009. "Collection Assessment through WorldCat." *Collection Management* 34, no. 2 (March): 79–93.

Webster, Janet. 2001. "Oregon State University Libraries' Collection Assessment Project." Paper presented at the IAMSLIC 2000: Tides of Technology 26th Annual Conference, Fort Pierce, FL, October 16.

White, Howard D. 2008. "Better Than Brief Tests: Coverage Power Tests of Collection Strength." *College and Research Libraries* 69, no. 2 (March): 155–74.

CHAPTER 5

Benchmarking—Interpreting and Acting on the Data

AFTER GATHERING QUANTITATIVE DATA, you will want to use the data for the goal you established at the beginning. Before making any changes to your collection, if doing this was a goal, you need to make sure you understand what the data is telling you. Sometimes the same numbers can tell two or more different stories. Do not be quick to conclude anything without questioning whether your numbers might mean something other than what you first assumed. You may want to supplement the quantitative data with your own or other people's impressions of the collection or with one of the other kinds of data described in this book, such as usage statistics, to help you make interpretations. This chapter presents ways to question the numbers in order to see if they mean what you think.

After figuring out, to the best of your ability, what story the numbers tell, you will move on to taking action based on the results of your evaluation. The actions might be very simple and exactly the ones you had in mind when you began—for example, providing some fast facts to your admissions office. They might also be more complicated, particularly if you are planning to modify your selection strategies or weed based on the data. If you followed the advice in chapter 3 on working with colleagues who are not numbers people, you'll probably already have some thoughts about how to combine the data with other forms of evaluation. Supplementing benchmarking data with other information is a good idea when doing anything with numbers beyond just reporting them to your institution, a national survey, or an accreditation agency. As you start trying to figure out what the numbers mean, it will become clearer what other information you need.

Interpretations of the Numbers

One of the first questions you will probably have when looking at benchmarking data is, "Is this enough books (or journals)?" There really is not a specific amount that is enough, though comparing yourself to peer institutions will give you a sense of whether your library is smaller than those at similar schools. Another way to define "enough" is by comparing some sections of the collection to others. This is what McClure (2009) did in the study described in the previous chapter. Although her data did compare her library's holdings to those of other institutions, in interpreting the results she made comparisons only within her own collection. Because her library held 72 percent of the top one hundred French titles and only 27 percent of the top one hundred Spanish titles, she concluded that she needed to rework her library's collection strategies to focus on building their Spanish collection. Following her example, you could also focus on the parts of your collection that fare especially poorly in comparison to other libraries. If your library has at most 5 perent of all academic publications in any subject area, or 80 percent of the amount your peers have, focus on the subsections of the collection in which you have only 2 percent of all published works or only 60 percent of what your peers have. Consider these the sections in which you don't have enough. You can still think big and try to request money to make the whole collection bigger, but in the near term it makes sense to improve the collection where there are gaps. Remember to focus on percentages instead of looking at which sections have fewer books in absolute terms. You may have fewer books on a subject just because there are fewer books published on that topic than others.

Even percentages don't tell the whole story, though. Your institution's needs are unique, and there may be a valid reason you have a smaller percentage of the universe of Russian books than you do Spanish books. Maybe the Russian program is much smaller or does not include as many literature classes as the Spanish program. You may know enough about your institution's programs to make this interpretation on the fly, but you can also supplement the numbers more formally using circulation or enrollment data to show why there is less demand for books on some topics than others. When using enrollment data, take into account the degree your institution grants in each program, as a master's-level program will probably need more books than an undergraduate program.

Besides figuring out if you have enough books to meet the demand at your institution, it's worth putting some thought into whether you have good books. One issue that is simple to check for is whether the collection is old. Having a lot of books on a certain subject looks good, but it might mean nobody has weeded that section in years. The instructions in the previous chapter for running several searches limited by year and comparing holdings across decades (results shown in table 4.4) can help reveal if your collection is skewed toward older materials.

There are some qualities of a collection that can only be assessed by either reviewing a title list or going to the stacks. One of these qualities is the target audience of the materials. You may have books that are not really aimed at students—for example, if they are for patients rather than medical professionals, or parents rather than teachers. This probably isn't the case unless there was a major problem with how collection development was done in the past, but it's something to think about. In addition, holdings could also be unevenly distributed within the range, such that your entire collection of books on folklore consists of stories from Norway, for example, and you don't actually have this subject well covered at all. Checking the shelf might help identify these issues.

Talking to faculty is another way to assess whether the materials owned are sufficient for their academic needs. Faculty can explain if there is a certain kind of book they use in class, or which assignments require students to do reading beyond what's in their textbooks and which don't. Their feedback can help clarify whether the sections with few holdings are areas in which you should collect more, or whether the size of these sections is actually okay. After reviewing the data and supplementing it in an appropriate way, you should feel ready to take some actions based on the data. Ways of supplementing benchmarking data are summarized in table 5.1.

Your Library's Strengths

As stated in chapter 4, basic numbers are often used to tell people outside the library about the collection. Your university's marketing or admissions staff, someone writing a grant application, or a department that is doing a program review might be satisfied with numbers that only show how many books you own or journals you subscribe to, as this is probably what they asked for. Remember from chapter 3, though, that it is sometimes okay to provide more information than you've been asked for. A great time to do this is if someone does not know to ask about newer formats. If you're asked how many DVDs you have, and you want to also provide a count of streaming video files, this extra information will probably be welcomed. Just make sure when providing extra information to keep it brief and relevant.

Another piece of information you might provide, besides the basic counts that were requested, is hidden collection strengths. For example, you may own some unique titles that would be of interest to your community. WorldCat Collection Evaluation and Intota Assessment will identify which books your library owns that the comparison group does not. If these are books you are proud to own, rather than books you should have weeded, make it a point to share this information. It may be relevant to an accrediting agency

Table 5.1. Ways to Supplement Benchmarking Data

WHAT BENCHMARKING DOESN'T TELL YOU	HOW TO FIND OUT
Are these enough books (or journals)?	Collect circulation data (see chapter 8) Compare holdings to enrollment
Is the collection too old?	Run reports that count your holdings by year
Are the books appropriate for your patrons?	Review a title list or check the shelves
Does your collection meet faculty's teaching and learning goals?	Ask them

or your admissions office (remember, they are too busy for irrelevant information!), but even if not, consider advertising your unique holdings in your own way, such as through a display or in a campus newsletter.

Unique or unusual holdings can also be good candidates for digitization. You'll want to check manually that your holdings are actually unique, as Orcutt and Powell (2006) found that 80 percent of the titles WorldCat Collection Analysis said they owned uniquely were actually owned by other libraries. Either the other libraries had different editions, or their holdings were simply tied to an alternate record in WorldCat. It is also of course important to make sure you have permission to digitize items and to verify that they have some value to potential users of the digitized collection.

Collaborative Collection Development

Another major goal of quantitative benchmarking—in fact, the intended purpose of the RLG conspectus—is to plan for collaborative collection development. These kinds of initiatives never quite took off the way the creators of the RLG conspectus hoped, however. Librarians have speculated on the possible reasons: competitive instincts between institutions, librarians' desire for control over their own collections, faculty preference for having materials on their own campus, and librarians' and administrators' frequent use of collection size as a stand-in for collection strength (Ferguson, 1992; Johnson, 2009; Seiden et al., 2002). Collaboration has been increasing in recent years, though, according to Mallery and Theus (2012), due to the economic recession that began in 2008. History is repeating itself, as several of the more successful collaborative collection efforts grew out of economic difficulties during the Depression.

Although quantitative data is essential for figuring out which libraries should collect what, infrastructure is even more important when starting out. A shared catalog is important so patrons can easily find out what is available to them from the consortium (Dominguez and Swindler, 1993). An efficient interlibrary loan (ILL) system is of course also key, so that borrowing from other institutions can be as simple a process as possible (Mallery and Theus, 2012; Shelton, 2003). In order for materials to move quickly through the ILL system, it is still necessary for the collaborating institutions to be near each other. If collaborative purchasing is going to involve any electronic resources, there will also need to be shared funding.

With the basic infrastructure in place, the next step is to decide how to divide up collecting responsibilities. This is where the benchmarking data becomes useful. Librarians from the Triangle Research Libraries Network say they have found that it makes the most sense to divide responsibilities for collecting research-level materials but let each library buy materials to support its own undergraduate curriculum (Dominguez and Swindler, 1993). Each library needs to feel that they are satisfying their patrons' basic needs before they will be willing to talk about collaboration. When deciding which research areas to assign to each library, the Triangle Research Libraries Network assigns areas of specialization based on faculty interests and existing collection strengths. Dominguez and Swindler also advise not assigning to any library the responsibility for specializing in something tangential to the academic programs it supports, as it will be hard to justify purchasing in this area when money is short. Their consortium provides guidelines to collaborating libraries only on what to collect rather than what not to collect so that nobody feels that participating

TEXTBOX 5.1.

BEST PRACTICES FOR COLLABORATIVE
COLLECTION DEVELOPMENT

Required Infrastructure

- Shared catalog
- Rapid processing of requests for books owned by consortial partners
- Geographic proximity
- Shared funding source if purchasing electronic materials, as the license will have to include all of the collaborating institutions

Collection Guidelines

- Each institution should aim to provide instructional materials for its own patrons. Divide collection responsibility for research-level materials only.
- Assign participating libraries responsibility for building research-level collections in areas where they already have a relatively strong collection and that support their own faculty.
- Do not assign an institution responsibility for collecting in an area that is tangential to its curriculum.
- Do not prohibit or discourage libraries from purchasing in each other's areas of specialization if their users want them to.

in the collaboration will force them to hold themselves back from purchasing things their patrons want. Most libraries that participate in collaborative collection development will sometimes purchase in areas that their collaboration plan has assigned to other libraries, particularly if they are responding to a faculty request.

Another type of collaboration that sometimes occurs is identifying "last copies" of works, that is, a copy that one library in the consortium promises to keep in perpetuity so that others can feel free to discard it. This requires a title-by-title comparison of holdings rather than just a comparison of how many books each library owns. If you don't have a shared catalog with the libraries you are collaborating with, or a subscription to WorldCat Collection Evaluation, you could use Discovery to look up which titles the other libraries own, though this would be laborious. A shared catalog could provide title-level information, as could WorldCat Collection Evaluation. If you are able to upload circulation data to WorldCat Collection Evaluation, you could combine this data with holdings information in order to identify titles to weed.

Budget Requests

When doing an evaluation for just your own library rather than as part of a consortium, there are also a variety of ways to use the data. For example, comparing your collections to peer institutions can be helpful in making the case to administrators for additional funding. For Linn's (2008) dissertation on the library budgeting process, he interviewed library directors and other academic administrators who make budgeting decisions. Several of them said they found it helpful to use comparative data when making a budget request, especially when the comparison group was well chosen to include similar schools or competitors. Use whatever numbers will help make your case, as long as you are honest and keep it simple. Besides collection size and budget, you might want to include an explanation of how you chose the comparison schools.

Another important element to include in the budget request is an explanation of what you would do with more money if you had it. For example, you might spell out that your collection is smaller than that at Competitor School X, due to a smaller budget, *and* if your budget were to grow you would use it to purchase a database that School X owns and that your faculty has requested as well. If faculty are willing, it can also be helpful to have them speak directly to the people who decide the budget so that it is clear that your requests are in response to an academic need. When talking about what you need, Linn says, make sure also to highlight what the library is doing well, as the administration or board will not be inspired to invest in a unit that talks only about how poorly it is performing. The trick is to present yourself as making good use of the funds you currently have while showing you could do even better with more money and being specific about what you will do.

Selection Tools and Processes

Quantitative benchmarking can help you make better decisions about using the money you already have. As mentioned earlier, comparing the numbers across different sections of your own collection can help you identify gaps. Filling these gaps should involve more than a big one-time purchase. If you use approval plans, think about modifying them so you'll get more books on the subjects where your numbers are low. Approval plans are an arrangement with a vendor, who will automatically deliver books matching a profile set by the library customer. The library not only can specify in its profile the subjects of interest but can identify publishers to include or exclude, a price cap, and a collection level (i.e., everything in this area or only key works). The library is able to return items it doesn't want, usually within thirty days, though the goal is to avoid this additional labor by customizing the profile so that most of what arrives is wanted. If faculty are amenable, you can do as McClure (2009) did and ask them to help review shipments and provide input on whether the approval plan is bringing in appropriate titles.

If you do not use approval plans, or supplement them with firm orders selected title by title, there are other ways to modify selection processes to help fill gaps in the collection. Try seeking out more sources of information on what is being published. Faculty can be a resource for recommending sources of reviews or names of authors or publishers they respect. There are also e-mail lists for librarians with a particular subject specialty, and you can ask the list for suggestions. To find an e-mail list, look at the divisions and roundtables of the American Library Association.

Benchmarking can also produce lists of books for one-time purchase. When using WorldCat Collection Evaluation to compare your library to the top libraries in a particular area, you can export a list of titles that many of the other libraries own. You will probably not want to automatically buy everything in the list but may winnow it down to fit within your budget, checking along the way that the titles are appropriate for your own collection. If you are using WorldCat Discovery, you can sort by most widely held and use the top results as a suggested purchase list for your own library. Obviously, the strategy of purchasing based on what other libraries own makes the most sense if you are not comparing yourself to libraries with whom you have a collaborative collection development arrangement.

A Starting Point for Weeding

In addition to purchasing, comparative data can also help with weeding. Reviewing data on your collection by year, as shown in figure 4.2, can reveal if the collection is skewed toward older books that might need to be weeded. Most libraries will have a larger number of books that are more than ten years old than books that are less than ten years old, as the former category covers a much larger span of time. However, having more books published between 1960 and 1969 than books published between 2000 and 2010 probably means weeding hasn't been done in a while. Keep in mind, though, that this is not the only possible interpretation of this type of data. As noted earlier, if you have purchased fewer print books in recent years, it might be because you're buying more e-books. Data from WorldCat Discovery might be missing e-book data since not all libraries include their e-book holdings in WorldCat. (If your e-book vendor sends you MARC records through WorldCat Cataloging Partners, your holdings will be in WorldCat. Otherwise, you need to have added them yourself.) If you have a lot of e-books that WorldCat doesn't know you have, consider repeating some of the searches using your local catalog. Either combine the results for print and e-book holdings, to show total book purchasing, or make separate counts to illustrate the shift in formats. If necessary, compare your e-book holdings to other libraries by searching their public catalogs.

In deciding what to weed, you should use more data than just the simple counts of how many books you own with a given publication year. Even libraries that do not have official collaborative agreements sometimes look at where their holdings overlap with other institutions, only weeding what they can see their consortial partners own. As already stated, you can figure this out using either a shared catalog, WorldCat Discovery, or WorldCat Collection Analysis. Start with a list of books that are more than a certain number of years old, and then look up which other schools own them. You will probably also want to find out if the books have been used in recent years and if they are classics. Future chapters discuss how to get this information. The CREW Manual (Larson, 2008) offers the acronym MUSTIE for weeding considerations. According to the CREW system, books should be considered candidates for weeding if they are misleading, ugly, superseded, trivial, irrelevant, or available elsewhere. Weeding involves combining many different kinds of information. In sum, consider:

- Overlap with other libraries' holdings
- Local usage (circulation)
- Age of the item
- Condition of the item
- Relevance to the collection
- Significance of the work

Key Points

Although quantitative benchmarking provides only a general overview of the collection, there is a lot you can do with the data.

- Look beyond the numbers to see if your data tell you what you think they do. Consider going to the shelves or meeting with teaching faculty.
- Although collaborative collection development is challenging, it can be done if certain essential elements are in place, such as a shared catalog and an efficient interlibrary loan system.
- For collaborative collection development, assign collection responsibilities based on each library's existing strengths and its institution's academic programs. Collection guidelines should define what libraries should purchase rather than what they should not purchase.
- When making budget requests using comparative data, be brief but do explain to the decision makers the ways your collection falls short, what you would do with more money, and ways you are managing your current budget well.
- Comparing different areas of your own collection can identify gaps so you can adjust purchasing to buy more in these areas.
- If the comparison group does not consist of libraries with which you are collaborating, you may want to make a list for purchase based on what the comparison libraries own.
- Quantitative data can also point out areas where a library needs to weed, though weeding should also take into account circulation statistics and other considerations.

When the outcome of an evaluation is more purchasing, libraries will of course want to think about what are the best books to own. Identifying if your library has the right books is the topic of the next chapter.

References

Dominguez, Patricia Buck, and Luke Swindler. 1993. "Cooperative Collection Development at the Research Triangle University Libraries: A Model for the Nation." *College and Research Libraries* 54, no. 6 (November): 470–96.

Ferguson, A. W. 1992. "The Conspectus and Cooperative Collection Development: What It Can and Cannot Do." *Acquisitions Librarian* 4, no. 7: 105–14.

Johnson, Peggy. 2009. *Fundamentals of Collection Development and Management.* 2nd edition. Chicago: American Library Association.

Larson, Jeanette. 2008. *CREW: A Weeding Manual for Modern Libraries.* Austin: Texas State Library and Archives Commission.

Linn, Mott. 2008. "The Budget Planning Process in Higher Education: Evaluating Administrators' Strategies and Tactics." PhD dissertation, Graduate School of Library and Information Science, Simmons College. ProQuest 3467790.

Mallery, Mary, and Pamela Theus. 2012. "New Frontiers in Collaborative Collection Management." *Technical Services Quarterly* 29, no. 3 (March): 101–12.

McClure, Jennifer Z. 2009. "Collection Assessment through WorldCat." *Collection Management* 34, no. 2 (March): 79–93.

Orcutt, Darby, and Tracy Powell. 2006. "Reflections on the OCLC WorldCat Collection Analysis Tool: We Still Need the Next Step." *Against the Grain* 18, no. 5 (November): 44–48.

Seiden, Peggy, Eric Pumroy, Norm Medeiros, Amy Morrison, and Judy Luther. 2002. "Should Three College Collections Add Up to One Research Collection? A Study of Collaborative Collection Development of Three Undergraduate Colleges." *Resource Sharing and Information Networks* 16, no. 2: 189–204.

Shelton, Cynthia. 2003. "Best Practices in Cooperative Collection Development: A Report Prepared by the Center for Research Libraries Working Group on Best Practices in Cooperative Collection Development." *Collection Management* 28, no. 3: 191–222.

CHAPTER 6

List-Checking— Collecting and Analyzing the Data

IN THIS CHAPTER

▷ Definition and History of List-Checking

▷ Advantages and Disadvantages of List-Checking

▷ Suggested Checklists

▷ List Selection

▷ Preparation for List-Checking

▷ The Data Gathering Process

▷ Software Tools

Definition and History of List-Checking

WHILE COMPILING NUMBERS ON THE SIZE OF YOUR COLLECTION, you may have questioned whether high numbers really indicate a good collection. With collection quality in mind, many librarians have approached evaluation by asking whether or not they had the best books on various topics. A common way of assessing quality is by comparing the collection to a list of books recommended by experts. This is called the checklist, or list-checking, method of evaluation. If the list being used is small and very selective, it is sometimes called a core list. Because list-checking is focused on evaluating the quality of a collection rather than its size or how well it meets user needs, it is often described as a "qualitative" approach. Despite evaluating the quality of a collection, list-checking is a quantitative assessment tool according to the more traditional use of the term in social sciences research, in that the assessment produces a numerical measure of how many of the items on the list a library owns.

The first known collection evaluation using list-checking was undertaken by Charles Coffin Jewett, assistant secretary at the Smithsonian Institute, in 1849. Jewett's project relied on citations from textbooks and checked the holdings of the Smithsonian against these citations (Meehan and Nisonger, 2005). Another notable evaluation project came from the University of Chicago in 1933. This project had a remarkable scope: it used four hundred different lists and involved two hundred faculty members (Lundin, 1989; Meehan and Nisonger, 2005). According to Bushing (2001), however, list-checking did not become widespread until the 1970s, when an increase in published material meant that a library could have a large collection without necessarily having high-quality or important works. Although the literature has fewer studies of list-checking than quantitative comparison or analysis of usage statistics, it is nevertheless a common evaluation method today. Anne Lundin sees lists as "such a basic form of communication among libraries and among scholars that their viability remains constant. . . . [The] appeal [of list-checking] is perennial" (1989: 111).

Advantages and Disadvantages of List-Checking

Advantages

List-checking is in some ways the simplest of the evaluation methods discussed in this book. It requires the smallest amount of numerical data, and it has the advantage of not requiring special software. Many assessment software products include list-checking capabilities, but it is easy to do an evaluation using only your catalog. Although the simplicity of list-checking makes it appealing, occasions when it makes sense to use this evaluation method are limited to a few specific situations. When your circumstances and goals are a fit for this method of assessment, though, you can gain a lot from the evaluation.

Lundin (1989) notes that list-checking is a strategy best suited to libraries with specialized goals. Maybe your library is large but you want to know how well it supports a certain narrower topic, or you might work in a small special collection and want to show that you support your area of focus as well as or better than larger, general collections do. Evaluating a medium-sized or large library's entire collection is obviously possible, as was done at the University of Chicago in 1933, but remember that evaluation used four hundred lists. More often list-checking evaluations have a narrower focus that is more manageable.

The list-checking method is often used to evaluate collections on interdisciplinary topics. Studies by Bolton (2009) and Bergen and Nemec (1999) illustrate why this is the case. In an article about her evaluation of a women's studies collection, Bolton explains that she used list-checking because women's studies is a field that does not fit within distinct call number ranges, and it is also not well described by Library of Congress subject headings. Using a bibliography of essential women's studies titles was the only way she could get an overall sense of an otherwise scattered collection. Bergen and Nemec had a very similar motivation in choosing list-checking to evaluate their collection on drug resistance. Although they felt that subject headings from the Library of Congress and the National Library of Medicine were a good way to identify books in this field, they had the same issue as Bolton regarding call numbers—books on drug resistance were not gathered within one or even a few common ranges. If you have done a quantitative study like those described in chapter 4, you probably used call numbers in some way to divide your collection by discipline. List-checking can help you focus on some topics that would not have gotten attention in your previous analysis because they were spread out across different disciplines.

Another occasion when list-checking is useful is when you are trying to build a retrospective collection on a particular topic. A core list will contain standard titles that have demonstrated lasting significance and can help you identify older titles that are still useful. This can be helpful if your library is trying to support a new program and you have begun collecting in an area that you haven't previously. A regularly updated list will also contain some newer books, but for the most part what it will do is create a foundation, and you will want to seek additional tools for keeping the collection strong going forward.

List-checking can also be helpful, and sometimes even required, when academic programs are seeking accreditation. The American Chemical Society lists as one of their criteria for bachelor's programs that the institution's library must subscribe to at least fourteen journals from their recommended list, and the titles should be distributed across subfields of chemistry. Although ACS is unusual in how specific they are in their requirements, criteria for other subjects suggest that other accrediting organizations might also like to see a list of key titles the library owns. The Accreditation Manual of the Master's in Psychology and Counseling Accreditation Council asks for a "description of [the] applicant institution's library, including . . . information specific to publications relevant to psychology" (MPCAC, 2014). Since you won't want to list every psychology publication you have, compiling the titles that you have from an authoritative list can be a good way to present information to the accrediting body.

Disadvantages

Even when list-checking is useful, there are some shortcomings to this method. It is possible that what an expert picked as the key resources in a field might not be what your library needs. The materials could be inappropriate for you or just might not get used. A study by Tonta and Al (2006) shows that what is important to the world at large doesn't necessarily match the needs of a particular institution. Their study looked at journal impact factors, which are often used to determine core journal lists, and found that higher-impact journals were not cited any more often by their students than lower-impact journals. Even if you use a list that was created for undergraduate students, and you are collecting for this same population, your students might not use what is on the list, as every school's curriculum is slightly different. Although most libraries will aim for a balance between buying what will get used and maintaining a classic core, some have a philosophy that emphasizes usage much more heavily, and these libraries will probably not give as much weight to authoritative lists.

List-checking is also not as useful for external audiences as some other methods of evaluation. Although lists can be helpful in an accreditation process, and faculty might be interested in seeing lists of which core journals or essential books you own, the subject-specific nature of lists means that they do not convey the big picture of the library. Furthermore, because list-checking involves looking closely at specific titles, it does not produce the kind of fast facts that an admissions or marketing office would want.

There are a few additional limits to what can be done with this technique. Unlike the method described in the previous chapters, list-checking does not help you identify unique holdings. You also can't repeat a list-checking evaluation for multiple years with the same list. Once the evaluation is completed, a library is likely to select new materials based on what was on the checklist, and once the list has been turned into a selection tool it can no longer be used to evaluate the collection. Despite its shortcomings, however, list-checking can be useful in the situations described earlier, particularly if the list is well chosen. Textbox 6.1 summarizes when and when not to use list-checking.

Suggested Checklists

Lists come in several different forms. Some will have tiers, where the titles in the top tier are the most important to own and others are recommended but not essential. Lists of journals are usually ranked, which helps make these lists adaptable to large or small libraries. A smaller library could focus on collecting titles in, say, the top quarter of the list, while a larger library could try to subscribe to the top half or more. Others might be annotated, allowing you to judge for yourself whether a given title is essential based on the annotation. There are many existing lists to choose from, or you can create your own. Textbox 6.2 names several lists and where to find them. Some additional core lists are included in journal articles about the process of creating them. To find a list on a subject that is not included in the textbox, do a literature search for the phrase "core list," "essential titles," or "recommended books or journals" and the subject.

Doody's Core Titles in the Health Sciences

A significant tool for collection development in the health sciences is Doody's Core Titles in the Health Sciences (DCT) (http://www.doody.com/dct/default.asp). DCT has been

TEXTBOX 6.1.

WHEN AND WHEN NOT TO USE LIST-CHECKING

When to Use

- When evaluating a specialized collection, particularly one on an interdisciplinary topic
- When building a retrospective collection
- When preparing for an accreditation review

When Not to Use

- When trying to create a heavily used collection
- When creating marketing materials
- When doing repeated evaluations

TEXTBOX 6.2.

A SELECTION OF CORE LISTS

Multisubject

- Doody's Core Titles in the Health Sciences, http://www.doody.com/dct/Content/DCTHistory.asp (subscription-based)
- Journal Citation Reports, http://thomsonreuters.com/journal-citation-reports/ (subscription-based)
- Magazines for Libraries, http://www.serialssolutions.com/en/magazines-for-libraries/ (subscription-based)
- Resources for College Libraries, http://www.rclweb.net (subscription-based)
- SCImago Journal Rankings, http://www.scimagojr.com
- YBP Core 1000, http://www.ybp.com/acad/core1000cover.htm

Specific Subjects

- Core List of African-American Studies Journals, from the African-American Librarians Section, Association of College and Research Libraries, http://afasacrl.wordpress.com/publications-and-resources/core-list-of-afas-journals/
- Core List of Astronomy Books, compiled by a committee from several universities, http://ads.harvard.edu/books/clab/
- Harzing's Journal Quality List (for Business), http://www.harzing.com/jql.htm
- CPT (Committee on Professional Training) Recommended Journal List, from the American Chemical Society, http://www.acs.org/content/dam/acsorg/about/governance/committees/training/acsapproved/cpt-journal-list.pdf
- Core List for an Environmental Reference Collection, from the Environmental Protection Agency, http://www2.epa.gov/libraries/core-list-environmental-reference-collection
- Basic Library List, from the Mathematical Association of America, http://www.maa.org/publications/maa-reviews/basic-library-list
- Essential Nursing Resources, from the Interagency Council on Information Resources in Nursing, http://www.icirn.org/Homepage/Essential-Nursing-Resources/Essential-Nursing-Resources-PDF.pdf
- Basic Resources for Pharmacy Education, from the American Association of Colleges of Pharmacy, http://www.aacp.org/governance/SECTIONS/libraryinformationscience/Pages/LibraryInformationScienceSpecialProjectsandInformation.aspx
- Core Psychology Journals, from the Psychology Committee, Education and Behavioral Sciences Section, Association of College and Research Libraries, http://www.corepsychologyjournals.org/main.aspx
- Core Public Health Journal Project, from the Public Health/Health Administration section of the Medical Library Association, http://www.phha.mlanet.org/blog/wp-content/uploads/2011/06/Health-Behavior-and-Education-PH-HA-Core-Journal-Project.pdf
- Core Books in Women and Gender Studies, from the Women and Gender Studies Section, Association of College and Research Libraries, http://libr.org/wgss/corebooks.html

endorsed by the Medical Library Association and has been called the "gold standard" of selection tools for medical libraries (Moyer, 2013: 47). This database was launched as an online subscription product in 2004 by Doody Enterprises, a publisher of book reviews, and was intended to fill the void left when the previous core list for medical sciences, the Brandon/Hill list, ceased publication. It includes reviews of print books, e-books, and software in 121 areas of medicine and associated health fields and is updated annually in May. Although designed for libraries to use as an ongoing selection tool, its inclusion of older classics makes it suitable for evaluation as well. The list is meant for both hospital libraries and academic health sciences libraries and includes a wide range of subspecialties, such as clinical medicine, nursing, dentistry, veterinary medicine, history of medicine, and medical ethics.

Doody's uses a unique selection process for its core lists, involving the work of two hundred specialists. Content specialists, who are academic faculty in the health sciences, propose books to be added to the list of core titles. A group of library selectors then rates each title from 0–3 on five criteria: authoritativeness of author and publisher, scope and coverage of subject matter, quality of content, usefulness and purpose, and value for the money. A title that receives zeroes across the board will not be included on the list. Books that score all threes are designated as essential core titles, resulting in a tiered list that allows smaller libraries to focus on the more important titles (Spasser, 2005).

Journal Citation Reports

Journal Citation Reports (http://wokinfo.com/products_tools/analytical/jcr/), an online product from Thomson Reuters, provides lists of journals in over 230 science and social science disciplines ranked by impact factor. The impact factor is a number created by Thomson Reuters in conjunction with their Web of Science database. It measures how often, on average, the articles published in a particular journal are cited in other journals. The number of published articles in the journal in a two-year period is compared against the number of times these articles were cited in the following year. The number of citations divided by the number of articles equals the impact factor. A journal with a higher impact factor is presumed to be more influential in its field than one with a lower impact factor.

Although Thomson Reuters (2014) describes Journal Citation Reports as the "recognized authority for evaluating journals," many scholars have criticized the impact factor as a measure of a journal's significance. Criticisms include the fact that the calculation of the impact factor only takes into account citations in journals that are indexed in Web of Science and only counts citations in journals rather than books, and that impact factors are not comparable across disciplines. Wagner (2009) points out that the top-cited journal in biochemistry has an impact factor of 31.190, while the top social work journal has only 2.352, yet this does not mean that biochemistry journals on the whole have more impact than social work journals. Biochemistry articles usually have longer reference sections than social work articles, so any useful biochemistry article will probably be cited more often than a social work article. Another shortcoming of impact factors is that having a high impact worldwide does not necessarily mean a journal will be highly used at a particular institution, as mentioned earlier.

Resources for College Libraries

One of the most prominent authoritative lists for books is Resources for College Libraries (http://www.bowker.com/en-US/products/rcl/rcl/index.html). This online database is the successor to *Books for College Libraries*, which was first published by ALA Editions as a multivolume set in 1967 with the goal of "describing an ideal undergraduate core collection for the library of a liberal arts college or small university" (Badics et al., 2007: 243). The editor of *Choice* magazine, which has been involved in the preparation of *Books for College Libraries* since the beginning, says the latter is a "recognized ... standard ... whose durability ... borders on the amazing" (Rockwood, 2004: 1020). *Books for College Libraries* was released in three print editions before being renamed Resources for College Libraries (RCL) and going online in 2007 as a subscription product. The name change reflected the addition of e-books and websites to the list; RCL still does not include journals. Titles are added and removed every year, though age does not automatically result in a title being removed from the list. As its "goal is to identify the best titles regardless of publication date" (Rockwood, 2011: 620), some older titles are retained in RCL if they are deemed to have continued value. Titles in RCL are selected by subject specialists, who are usually academic librarians or college professors. Editors may vary in their criteria for including books on their recommended lists. For example, Badics and colleagues (2007) explain that the gender studies specialist relied on syllabi for undergraduate courses as a measure of the importance of a work, whereas other editors did not necessarily take syllabi into consideration.

RCL lists books in sixty-one different subject areas. The subjects are intended to correspond with undergraduate majors and minors at universities and are not based on either standard call number schemes or the categories devised for the conspectus method. A significant improvement that was made at the time of the name change was the addition of more lists corresponding with interdisciplinary subjects, such as medieval studies, gender studies, and several area studies. Because of the search function of the online version, users can also generate on the fly a core list for a topic that is not one of RCL's sixty-one subjects. Keyword searching can cull titles from several different lists to form a core list on a specialized topic. RCL editors occasionally publish brief articles in the magazine *Against the Grain* surveying classic titles in a particular discipline. The article series is called "Collecting to the Core," and the articles are available on the RCL product website.

List Selection

Using an Existing List

When selecting a list to use in your evaluation, there are a few things you should look for. Think about whether the audience and goals of the list match your patron population and goals. A list that is intended to define a core collection for undergraduates might not be helpful for a research institution. There are also some ranked journal lists that were created to help faculty identify the most prestigious place to publish their work, or for tenure committees to evaluate candidates' publications. If you are not at a research or doctoral-level institution, the best journals for your students might not be the same as the ones in which your faculty publish. A community college might not have a mission to support faculty research and might want to select journals instead based on their accessibility for students. Aim to use a list that was created for a population similar to yours. If you can't find one, you can probably still use the list you have, but you'll want to adjust your expectations of how much of the material on it you should own, and you'll also need to be more selective later on when deciding which items from the list to buy.

Besides being created for different populations, authoritative lists are also created for different goals. You'll want to avoid lists of the top books of the past year, as these serve a different goal than retrospective lists. There is no reason to expect you would own a significant number of, say, the American Library Association's Notable Books of the Year before they were named as notable books, so comparing your collection to this list is not an evaluation. Annual lists can be helpful guides of what to purchase, and you may already use them for ongoing collection development. For an evaluation, however, it is better to use lists that include retrospective titles, both because these are titles you already had the opportunity to buy and because such lists allow you to evaluate the overall collection on a subject rather than just the previous year's purchases.

Another kind of list to avoid is one that you have already used. If you conducted an evaluation last year and then followed up on it by reviewing the titles you didn't own and acquiring the ones you felt fit the scope of your collection, then you will learn nothing new from doing another evaluation with the same list. Even if you haven't done a list-checking evaluation, you might have used some core lists already to get ideas for purchasing. You can't do an evaluation based on a list that you already used for purchasing, as you already know you'll have most of the titles that you would want. Because of problems with repeating an evaluation, you will probably do list-checking only once for any given subject.

Creating Your Own List

If there is no list available on the topic you would like to evaluate, there are several ways to create your own. The most common ways are by looking at other libraries' holdings or by looking at citations. McClure (2009) created a core list of titles in French, Italian, and Spanish literature by looking at the one hundred books in each area owned by the largest number of libraries. She concluded that the popularity of these books was a sign that they would be important to all libraries that collected literature from these three countries. Bergen and Nemec (1999) and Webster (2001) used a slightly different method, focusing on the collections of libraries they had identified as being strong in a certain subject. They searched libraries' catalogs by subject and kept track of which materials were owned by two or more of their comparison libraries. This method is labor-intensive, as it involves a lot of catalog searching. To create a core list using other libraries' catalogs, first identify libraries that you believe have strong collections. These might be ones with highly ranked graduate programs in your subject or special collections devoted to the subject, like the National Agricultural Library. Do keyword searches for your topic in one library's collection and make a list of all the titles you find. Then search for these titles in the second library's catalog. If you have a third comparison library, narrow your list to anything held by the first two and search for these in the catalog of the third library.

You can also use citation analysis to create core lists. Don't use citations from your own patrons' work, because citations by your own patrons are an indication of what they've used, and you'd really be doing a usage evaluation rather than identifying core works. Using citations as a form of usage analysis is the topic of chapters 10 and 11. Citation analyses that look more broadly at what gets cited in the published literature of the field are more appropriate for making an authoritative list, usually of journals. The list would be based on the same principle as the impact factors in Journal Citation Reports, namely, that a work that is cited more times is more important than works cited less. If you are using citation analysis to create your own core list of journals, it will differ somewhat from JCR because you'll be looking at how often the journals are cited within a particular field rather than how often they are cited by anyone.

To create a core journals list based on citations, you need to have at least one journal you already know is significant in the field. In the case of Kushkowski and Shrader (2013), who created a list of core journals on corporate governance, there was only one journal in existence dedicated solely to their topic, so this was their starting point. Other ways you would identify a journal to start with are asking subject experts or looking at a ranked list of journals in a broader field (say, business) and scanning down from the top until you find one devoted to your narrower subfield. You can assume this is the highest-impact journal in your subfield and can figure out what else is important in this subfield by looking at what journals are cited within this one. If you want to be even more thorough, you can repeat the citation analysis with the journals that come out as most cited in your first round. Black (2012) suggests starting with a journal known to be significant, looking at its citations, identifying the two journals that are cited the most in that journal and looking at what *they* cite.

Even if you have found one or more existing lists that are appropriate for you, you may choose to modify the lists to create tiers. Tiered lists add a layer to the evaluation by allowing you to compare whether you have more of the higher-tier, more important titles than the lower-tier titles. Tiers can also help you focus your collection and evaluation efforts on the most important titles on the list. There are a few ways to create a tiered list. If you're able to find more than one list on the same topic, you can follow the example of Dennison (2000). Comparing two lists, he considered a title top-tier if it was on both lists. If it was only on the more selective list (i.e., the shorter one), he considered it second-tier. Titles on only the less selective list made up the lowest tier. If you have a list that is ranked, you can create tiers by making a cutoff at a certain point in the rankings so that the first one hundred titles are the first tier, the next one hundred are the second tier, and so on. You could also take an unranked list and look up how many other libraries own the items on it. Items with over one thousand holdings in OCLC could be the top tier, items owned by 500 to 999 libraries could be the second tier. Chapter 7 describes a few ways you can use these tiers, although tiers are not necessary for a list-checking evaluation.

Preparation for List-Checking

Once you have found or created a core list on your topic of interest, there are a few questions to address regarding the data collection. One would be whether or not owning a different edition of a given title will count as a match. Another question is whether you will count titles the library makes available but does not own, such as titles that are in the catalog as part of a patron-driven acquisitions program and that will be purchased on demand. As it might be impossible to tell from another library's catalog whether or not all materials in the catalog are owned, and as patrons will care more about access than ownership, it makes sense to count nonowned materials that are included in the library catalog.

You won't know at the outset how much of the list you are aiming to have, so you'll probably want to pick some other libraries to compare yourself to. This does not mean comparing the size of your overall holdings, as described in chapter 4, but comparing what percentage of the list your peers own to what percentage you own. As in chapter 4, pick your comparison libraries to fit your goals. If you are trying to show that your small, specialized collection is so carefully selected that it is as useful for research on a particular topic as a larger and broader collection, you will want to use well-respected, large institutions as points of comparison. Bergen and Nemec (1999) compared their own library's holdings to those at the National Library of Medicine to show that they own almost as many titles on drug resistance as the NLM. If you are doing the evaluation as part of a review for accreditation, you might compare yourself to other accredited schools of a similar size.

You will probably want to calculate some additional numbers to help you interpret the data. Meehan and Nisonger (2005) provide context by noting how many total books they have in their collection that are on the same topic as their list. If you are comparing your library to others, you may want to do the same. You might also compare the total size of your library to the libraries you are using for comparison. Chapter 7 shows how you can use these numbers to help interpret the results of the list-checking.

The Data Gathering Process

Once you've found your list, decided on guidelines of what counts as a match, and picked comparison institutions, the list-checking process is very simple. Just look up all the titles on the list in your catalog and in the catalogs of the comparison libraries. Keep a list of the titles in Excel and note next to each one whether or not you have it. In separate columns, note whether each comparison library has the item. If you use a 1 to indicate you have the material and 0 to indicate you don't, you can sum each column at the bottom. Then use the total at the bottom to calculate the percentage of titles owned by each library. The example below shows what the data from a list-checking evaluation could look like.

What follows is a list-checking evaluation that compares Arcadia University to the three universities with the highest-ranked EdD programs in the United States. Since these universities are larger and have more extensive library collections than Arcadia, they are likely also to have more of the books on the checklist. Still, seeing the variation in how many of the recommended books each library owns can help set a goal for Arcadia's collection. The data illustrates the point made earlier that list-checking does not usually produce data that would help market the school, as Arcadia has fewer books than the comparison schools. The list-checking exercise can be internally useful, though, in showing whether the library's collection development practices are on-target.

The list used for this example is called "Bibliography of Research Methods Texts," and it was created by the ACRL Instruction Section in 2009. The introduction to the document says it "provides information on research methods relevant to library and information science," though in fact only a few pages of the bibliography list books that are geared specifically toward library and information science (ACRL Instruction Section Research and Scholarship Committee, 2009). The rest are about general social science research methods. The list includes a few books on quantitative methods but focuses mainly on qualitative methods (e.g., surveys and interviewing). Although it is a bibliography rather than a ranked list, all the annotations are positive, and therefore it can be considered a list of recommended books. Titles are selected by committee members for their quality rather than chosen based on how many libraries own the books.

The "Bibliography of Research Methods Texts" is appropriate for evaluating Arcadia's collection as this is an area in which the university actively collects materials. The library science section of the list was excluded from the comparison, as there is currently no library science program at Arcadia University. The main users of research methods texts at Arcadia are students in the EdD program, which is Arcadia's only doctoral program in the social sciences. The comparison group, therefore, is made up of the top three schools in *U.S. News and World Report*'s rankings of EdD programs: Vanderbilt, Johns Hopkins, and Harvard. The three comparison schools have a Carnegie Classification of doctoral/research, whereas Arcadia is ranked as a master's-level institution. These three schools all have PhD programs as well, which may or may not require more research than the EdD. The EdD degree is intended to be a degree for practitioners, whereas a PhD prepares people to be researchers. In practice, though, the programs at many schools are similar, though EdD programs usually have fewer requirements (Shulman et al., 2006). EdD programs usually do involve a dissertation, as Arcadia's does.

Excluding the books on library science, the "Bibliography of Research Methods Texts" contains sixty-six titles. As table 6.1 shows, Arcadia owns somewhat less than half of these. The three comparison institutions own more, with percentages that range from 65.15 to 81.82 percent. The chart adds context by including the total size of each library's book collection, where numbers are available. Although there is no formula for calculating how much of a given list your library should own, chapter 7 will show some ways you can use numbers like these to decide on a target that feels reasonable to you.

This example evaluation also demonstrates how to make and use a tiered list. Table 6.2 shows how many books are owned by all three comparison schools, two, one, or none. Since the bibliography was not based on popularity (i.e., whether or not a book was widely owned did not factor into whether or not it was included on the list), this calculation adds a measure of popularity to the evaluation. Looking at the list divided into tiers shows that Arcadia's purchasing is in line with what is generally popular among books on this topic. Arcadia is much more likely to own the more popular books than the less popular ones. Of the thirty-three books that are owned by all three comparison schools (i.e., the top tier), Arcadia owns 66.7 percent, whereas of the nine books owned by only one of the three top-ranked schools (i.e., the third tier), Arcadia only owns 11.1 percent. The higher percentage of titles owned for the top tier compared to the lower tiers shows that Arcadia is making similar decisions to the other schools about which titles are important to purchase.

Table 6.1. Research Methods Texts Owned by Arcadia and Three Comparison Libraries

	ARCADIA UNIVERSITY	VANDERBILT UNIVERSITY	JOHNS HOPKINS UNIVERSITY	HARVARD UNIVERSITY
Total Books and E-Books*	109,600	4,395,668	3,720,477	Not reported
Books from Bibliography (including e-books)	30	50	43	54
Percentage of Books from Bibliography Owned	45.45%	75.76%	65.15%	81.82%

* Total Books and E-books data from NCES Library Comparison http://nces.ed.gov/surveys/libraries/compare/

Table 6.2. How Many Schools Own Each Book

HOW MANY COMPARISON SCHOOLS OWN	HOW MANY BOOKS	HOW MANY ARCADIA OWNS	PERCENTAGE ARCADIA OWNS
3	33	22	66.7%
2	20	7	35.0%
1	9	1	11.1%
0	5	0	0.0%

Software Tools

There are several products that can speed the process of checking a library's holdings against a core list. This chapter briefly describes two: WorldCat Collection Evaluation and Intota Assessment, the same products shown in the chapters on benchmarking.

WorldCat Collection Evaluation

As shown in chapter 4, WorldCat Collection Evaluation is a tool for making comparisons between a library and a comparison group. The group is often a set of other libraries, but the software treats authoritative lists as if they are a comparison group and benchmarks the target library against the list. When creating a comparison, the software offers five options: Peer, Pre-Defined, Authoritative, Hathi, or WorldCat. Selecting Authoritative will give you the choice of a variety of lists, including ones from *Choice, Booklist,* Doody's, *Library Journal, Publisher's Weekly,* and *School Library Journal.* The lists are all multidisciplinary and include books but not journals. Many of these lists come from review sources that libraries use as selection tools, and they might not be appropriate for an evaluation if selection decisions have also been based on the same source. In addition, there is not a way to compare someone else's library to an authoritative list, only your own. Nevertheless, if these lists are appropriate for your library, WorldCat Collection Evaluation can be an efficient way to do list-checking.

Chapter 4 offers more detailed instructions on navigating the menus in WorldCat Collection Evaluation and running a comparison report. As in that chapter, the benchmarking report is more useful here than unique/shared, because it shows what titles are in the comparison group (i.e., the authoritative list) that your own library doesn't have. Figure 6.1 shows an example benchmarking report that compares a library's holdings to the Sociology and Anthropology sections of *Choice* magazine's Outstanding Academic Titles list. The arrow in the figure is pointing to where the screen identifies the comparison (as OAT). You can click on Export Titles under the pie chart to see a list that includes both your own holdings and the titles on the authoritative list.

Intota Assessment

In 2013, Serials Solutions released a product called Intota Assessment (http://www.serialssolutions.com/en/services/intota/assessment) that allows libraries to gather a multitude of collection information in one place. Assessment is one module of a multifaceted library management system that includes acquisitions, license management, and discovery features. The product information page describes Intota Assessment as providing a "total

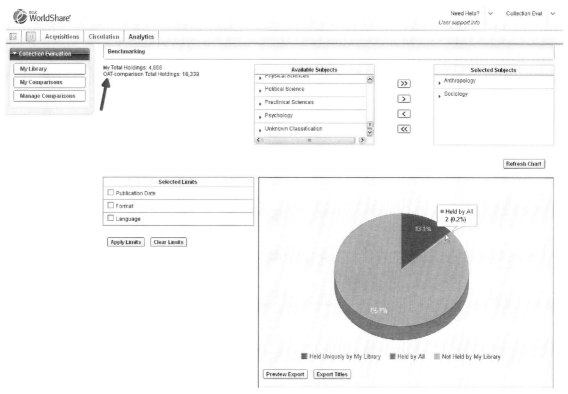

Figure 6.1. A Comparison to an Authoritative List Using WorldCat Collection Evaluation.

picture of holdings, usage and overlap for both monographs and serials, in both print and electronic formats" (Serials Solutions, 2014). This product supersedes the Bowker Book Analysis System, which was available from 2005 to 2014 and which allowed libraries to compare their holdings to Resources for College Libraries. Intota Assessment allows this same comparison and additional evaluation tools.

It includes reports in seven areas: cost per use, usage, accreditation, recommendations, deselection, overlap, and peer analysis. The peer analysis report was described in chapter 4. The report that you'd use for comparison to an authoritative list is the one called recommendations. Two authoritative lists are available as recommendations reports: Resources for College Libraries and Ulrich's Core. This is fewer lists than WorldCat Collection Evaluation offers, but by providing Ulrich's Core the software allows libraries to list-check their journal holdings, which WorldCat Collection Evaluation does not.

To compare your library collection to Resources for College Libraries, first click on Choose Your Report in the top left corner. Then click Recommendations, then Compare to RCL Chart. This will bring you to a table that lists subjects down the left side. These are the sixty-one subjects used in Resources for College Libraries. For each subject, the table provides a count of how many titles from RCL are Held by Library or Not Held by Library. It also tells you the total number of titles in RCL for that subject and the percentage of these titles held by your library. There is a link above the table for exporting to Excel. Intota Assessment makes it easy to export any of its reports to Excel, PDF, or PowerPoint files.

Click on one of the numbers in the table to see a full title list represented by the number—for example, titles on law held by your library. Figure 6.2 shows one of the title lists that the Compare to RCL Chart produces. Because Intota Assessment pulls information from Books in Print, the title list is fairly extensive in the details it provides.

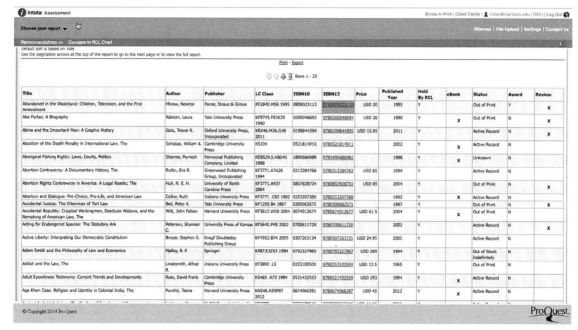

Figure 6.2. Comparison to RCL Using Intota Assessment. Reproduced with permission from ProQuest LLC, © 2014 ProQuest. www.proquest.com.

Besides bibliographic information, it also notes whether or not a title is in print, whether it has won an award, and whether a review of it is included in Books in Print. You can click through to Books in Print to find out what the award is or see the reviews. This could be helpful later if you plan to buy some of the books on the authoritative list.

Key Points

Although less versatile in its potential uses than the benchmarking method of evaluation, list-checking is a well-established process that can be useful in particular situations. It is a good option if your library is preparing to support a new program in an area where you have not previously collected and is helpful for specialized, interdisciplinary collections whose materials may not be gathered within a single call number range.

- List-checking is most appropriate for evaluating a collection on a particular topic and is especially useful for interdisciplinary fields.
- There are many lists available. Look for one that is retrospective and that is intended as a list of recommendations for libraries.
- Do not do an evaluation based on a list you previously used to guide your purchasing.
- Although some software automates the list-checking process, it can also be done very simply by looking up recommended titles in your library catalog.

The list-checking method does not lend itself to data that you can share with external stakeholders other than accrediting agencies, but it has the benefit of providing straightforward steps for improving the collection, which will be discussed in the next chapter.

References

ACRL Instruction Section Research and Scholarship Committee. 2009. "Bibliography of Research Methods Texts." http://acrl.ala.org/is-research/.

Badics, Joe, Robert Kelly, Paula Storm, Twyla Racz, and Walter Hogan. 2007. "Part 1: Resources for College Libraries and RCLweb." *Choice: Current Reviews for Academic Libraries* 45, no. 2 (October): 243–46.

Bergen, Phillip L., and Dolores Nemec. 1999. "An Assessment of Collections at the University of Wisconsin–Madison Health Sciences Libraries: Drug Resistance." *Bulletin of the Medical Library Association* 87, no. 1 (January): 37–42.

Black, Steve. 2012. "How Much Do Core Journals Change over a Decade?" *Library Resources & Technical Services* 56, no. 2 (April): 80–93.

Bolton, Brooke A. 2009. "Women's Studies Collections: A Checklist Evaluation." *Journal of Academic Librarianship* 35, no. 3 (May): 221–26.

Bushing, Mary C. 2001. "The Evolution of Conspectus Practice in Libraries: The Beginnings and the Present Applications." Paper presented at the Czech and Slovak Library Information Network, Czech Republic, May 29.

Dennison, Russell F. 2000. "Quality Assessment of Collection Development through Tiered Checklists: Can You Prove You Are a Good Collection Developer?" *Collection Building* 19, no. 1: 24–26.

Doody Enterprises. 2014. "Frequently Asked Questions." http://www.doody.com/DCT/Customer ServiceCenter.asp?SID={E430BE3A-9386-41A8-80E5-DB6D1EC5C146}.

Kushkowski, Jeffrey D., and Charles B. Shrader. 2013. "Developing a Core List of Journals in an Interdisciplinary Area." *Library Resources & Technical Services* 57, no. 1 (January): 51–65.

Lundin, Anne H. 1989. "List-Checking in Collection Development: An Imprecise Art." *Collection Management* 11, no. 3/4 (October): 103–12.

McClure, Jennifer Z. 2009. "Collection Assessment through WorldCat." *Collection Management* 34, no. 2 (March): 79–93.

Meehan, William F., III, and Thomas E. Nisonger. 2005. "The Rowing Collection in the Free Library of Philadelphia OPAC: A Checklist Evaluation." *Collection Management* 30, no. 4: 85–104.

Moyer, Jennifer E. 2013. "Doody's Core Titles 2012." *Charleston Advisor* 14, no. 4 (April): 47–49.

MPCAC (Master's in Psychology and Counseling Accreditation Council). 2014. *Accreditation Manual.* Norman, OK: MPCAC.

Rockwood, Irving E. 2004. "Books for College Libraries: The Sequel." *Choice: Current Reviews for Academic Libraries* 41, no. 6 (February): 1020.

———. 2011. "A Tale of Two Siblings: RCL and CHOICE." *Choice: Current Reviews for Academic Libraries* 49, no. 4 (December): 620.

Serials Solutions. 2014. "Intota: Book and Serials Analysis." http://www.serialssolutions.com/en/ services/intota/assessment.

Shulman, Lee S., Chris M. Golde, Andrea Conklin Bueschel, and Kristen J. Garabedian. 2006. "Reclaiming Education's Doctorates: A Critique and a Proposal." *Educational Researcher* 35, no. 3 (April): 25–32.

Spasser, Mark A. 2005. "Review of Doody's Core Titles in the Health Sciences 2004 (DCT 2004)." *Biomedical Digital Libraries* 2, no. 5 (June): 1–5.

Thomson Reuters. 2014. "Journal Citation Reports: Quick Reference Card." http://wokinfo.com/ media/pdf/qrc/jcrqrc.pdf.

Tonta, Ya Yar, and Umut Al. 2006. "Scatter and Obsolescence of Journals Cited in Theses and Dissertations of Librarianship." *Library and Information Science Research* 28, no. 2 (Summer): 281–96.

Wagner, A. Ben. 2009. "Percentile-Based Journal Impact Factors: A Neglected Collection Development Metric." *Issues in Science & Technology Librarianship* 5 (Spring). http://www.istl.org/09-spring/refereed1.html.

Webster, Janet G. 2001. "Oregon State University Libraries' Collection Assessment Project." In *IAMSLIC 2000: Tides of Technology—Proceedings of the 26th Annual Conference*, edited by James Wilbur Markham and Andrea Louise Duda, 152–56. Fort Pierce, FL: International Association of Aquatic and Marine Science Libraries and Information Centers.

CHAPTER 7

List-Checking— Interpreting and Acting on the Data

IN THIS CHAPTER

▷ Percentage of Titles Owned

▷ Interpretation of Tiered Lists

▷ Decisions about What to Buy

▷ Core Lists as an Educational Tool for Selectors

▷ Core Lists as a Supplement to Patron-Driven Acquisitions

OF THE EVALUATION METHODS PRESENTED IN THIS BOOK, list-checking has the most obvious action steps, since the list itself is a ready-made order request. List-checking can do much more than determine a one-time purchase, though. Although this evaluation method is only appropriate in a fairly narrow set of situations, list-checking can help in many ways within these situations. It can tell you whether or not your collection has a strong core and help you convey your strengths to accreditation agencies. You can use an authoritative list to evaluate your current selection process and familiarize new selectors with the collection. Core lists can also help libraries transition to patron-driven acquisitions. Building a core and finding strategies to grow this core as new materials are published can ensure that the library still plays some role in guiding patrons to the "best" materials even while letting users' self-stated needs drive most selection decisions. This chapter describes how you can interpret the results of list-checking both to evaluate your collection and then to improve it.

Percentage of Titles Owned

Now that you've gathered numbers showing how many items from the authoritative list your library owns, you may still be wondering if you have enough. As with quantitative comparison, there is not a definitive number of titles you should have. Even if you did this evaluation in response to an accreditation review, most associations do not require a specific number of library materials. Although defining a list as "core" implies that libraries should own the entire list, none of the studies mentioned in this or the previous chapter found a library that owned everything on its checklists. Whether or not your library owns enough titles from an authoritative list is a subjective judgment. The data you collected comparing your holdings to other libraries can help you make this judgment.

If the other libraries you chose for comparison are similar in size to yours, you will want to have a similar percentage of titles from your authoritative list. If the comparison schools are larger than yours, on the other hand, they will probably have more of the core titles. The data in table 6.1 comparing Arcadia University to three research-level institutions illustrates this. Arcadia has 45.45 percent of the books on the authoritative list, whereas the other libraries have amounts ranging from 65.15 percent (Johns Hopkins) to 81.82 percent (Harvard). The numbers on the overall size of each library can help put these percentages in context. Johns Hopkins's collection, for example, is thirty-four times the size of Arcadia's, with 3.7 million books. Since Arcadia's library collection is so much smaller than any of the comparison libraries, the target for Arcadia's core collection of research methods texts can also be smaller. If your comparison libraries are larger than your own, your goal can be to own a percentage of the list that is somewhat below what the comparison libraries own.

Looking at the range between the comparison libraries can help you figure out what range is acceptable for you. Using the example from chapter 6 again, there are 16.67 percentage points between the amount of the list Johns Hopkins owns (65.15 percent) and the amount Harvard owns (81.82 percent). If your comparison institutions are similar in size and caliber to yours, you'd want and expect your own results to fall between or very close to the results you found for the other institutions. If your library is smaller than the others, you might own less than the lowest amount owned by any comparison school. Arcadia owns 19.7 percentage points less than the lowest-scoring comparison school, with 45.45 percent of the books compared to Hopkins's 65.15 percent. Since the gap between Arcadia and the lowest-scoring comparison school is larger than the gap between the three comparison schools, Arcadia might want to increase its holdings of core research texts to bring it closer to the lowest-scoring comparison library. There is no absolute rule that says your holdings can only vary so much from other schools, or that a school half the size of another school should own half as many core titles, but looking at the range between the schools can help you set a goal that feels reasonable to you.

Since your comparison libraries will not be exactly the same as yours in terms of population served, you can also think about any possible differences in patrons when deciding if you need to have the same number of books from the list as they do. Although you probably selected comparison schools that had similar programs to yours, this is not always possible. For example, if your university offers a master's program in sociology and you used a ranked list of graduate programs to find comparison schools, they might offer PhDs as well. A study by Bolton (2009) found that the higher the degrees granted by a program, the more titles from the authoritative list its library tended to own. If your institution does not support PhDs in a field, you will probably not have as many books or journals from the checklists as schools that offer PhDs. You can still use these schools to help you set a target, but know that your aim will be somewhat lower than theirs.

Interpretation of Tiered Lists

If you used a tiered list for your evaluation, you'll have some additional numbers to look at. As chapter 6 mentions, tiered lists allow smaller libraries to focus their collecting efforts on the most crucial titles while larger libraries try to purchase as much as they can from the entire list. Large or medium-sized libraries can benefit from tiered lists as well by using the tiers to add a layer of analysis to an evaluation.

Dennison (2000) used a tiered list to test the effectiveness of his library's selection process. His analysis used a chi-square test, which is a statistical test used for data that fits into distinct categories. In this case, each journal belongs to a category (tier 1, 2, or 3), and which category it is in should ideally determine how likely it is that the journal will also fall into a second category (subscribed or unsubscribed). In Dennison's case, the outcome was different for journals in tier one (they are likely to fall into the "subscribed" category) than for journals in tier two or three (they are less likely to fall into the "subscribed" category). Dennison's test showed a significant relationship between what tier a journal was in and whether or not the library subscribed to it. His library was more likely to subscribe to journals that were on both lists than on only one. Dennison concluded that this meant his library was making valid collection development decisions and did not need to significantly modify their practices.

A simpler way to use tiers is just to calculate how much you own from each tier and eyeball the numbers. For the "Bibliography of Research Methods Texts," no chi-square test was done. If you look at table 6.2, you can see without a statistical test that Arcadia University is more likely to own books from the highest tier than the lower ones. The library owns 66.7 percent of the titles from the highest tier, 35 percent of the middle tier, and 11.1 percent of the lowest tier. If you can see from your own numbers that you own more titles from the highest tier, and progressively fewer from each lower tier, you can feel comfortable asserting that your selection practices are effective in terms of matching what the experts recommend. If the tabulated data were to show that the collection did not match the tiered authoritative list, obviously a change in selection processes would be in order. The section below describes how lists can inform future selection.

Decisions about What to Buy

Once you've seen which titles you don't have from your authoritative lists, you will probably want to go out and buy them, especially if you found that you have fewer books than the libraries you compared yourself to. An authoritative list should not be sent directly to the acquisitions unit without review, however. Before purchasing, consider whether the items you don't already own would be appropriate for your library. They may be in subfields that you are deliberately not collecting, in languages most of your patrons don't read, or outside your collection development policy for other reasons. You may want to ask faculty for their opinions of the items on the list that you don't own. It is possible that well-respected titles are still not the most relevant to your curriculum. Your usual collection development criteria are still in effect, with the exception of whatever guidelines you may have about restricting purchases to recently published works only.

One common criterion for collection development is that the library should purchase items that it expects patrons to use. Although the premise of list-checking is that expert recommendations take priority over user demand, in practice you may want to balance these two selection criteria by selecting the titles from the authoritative list that you think are most likely to get used. One way to predict use of items that you don't already have, especially journals, is by looking at interlibrary loan data. If your patrons have been requesting a certain journal on interlibrary loan (ILL), it is reasonable to assume they would continue using it once it became available at their own library. If the book or journal has never been requested on ILL, though, this does not necessarily mean that no one would use it if you owned it. Previous research has shown that patrons are more likely to use materials that their library owns (Beile, Boote, and Killingsworth, 2004). Purchasing core books or subscribing to core journals that have not been requested on ILL can be a way to guide students toward important works in their subject areas. If you find that there are many more appropriate titles on the list than you can afford, however, looking at past ILL requests can help you prioritize which to get.

There are several other ways to winnow down the list if it is impossible to buy all of the relevant and appropriate items. If you are using a tiered list, you can buy all the appropriate materials from the top tier and then proceed to the lower tiers if you have money. If your authoritative list is divided into subfields, another option is to do keyword searches of your catalog and see in which subfield your current collection is the smallest and then buy more books in this subfield than the others. A third way for academic libraries to select which core titles to purchase, mentioned above, is to ask faculty for input.

If you cannot afford to buy all the titles you want, know that you don't necessarily need the exact titles that are on the list. Although you may wish to get these titles for the sake of showing an accrediting body that you have them or for strengthening your collection in general, you can still have a relevant and useful collection without it matching the authoritative list exactly. It's possible you might already own a lot of similar titles that meet the same needs as the materials on the list. For example, the checklist used in the previous chapter, "Bibliography of Research Methods Texts," contains thirty-four books from Sage Publications, making up about half the bibliography. Landman Library at Arcadia University owns or has access to fifty-nine books on research methods from Sage, many of them by the same authors that are on the authoritative bibliography. As the document is "intended to be selective rather than exhaustive" (ACRL Instruction Section Research and Scholarship Committee, 2009), it seems possible the list makers did not themselves believe libraries needed to own the exact titles they had included in their bibliography. Kronenfeld and colleagues state this explicitly with regard to their list of core titles in public health; when it comes to textbooks, they say, "if a library already has other current texts in these areas, they will not necessarily need the ones listed here" (1985: 44). This does not negate the usefulness of the list, as the list-checking process has provided you with an evaluative measure, recommendations of what materials to buy, and information about key authors or publishers in the field. Try to figure out how your collection differs from the authoritative list by comparing publishers, authors, and the audience of the works. This will help you determine whether there is a real gap in your collection, and in the process you will have learned about both your collection and the topic you are evaluating. You may still choose to buy the materials you don't have, or you may conclude that you are doing fine.

If the evaluation you are conducting is in response to an accreditation, the ideal time to make the list to show your accrediting agency would be after you have decided what to purchase and sent the requests to your acquisitions department. Once the items are on order, you can add them to your list of what you own, making your collection look that much better than it did before.

Core Lists as an Educational Tool for Selectors

Once you have compared numbers and purchased selected titles from the list, the list-checking process can continue to affect your collection development by educating you about your own collection and the field you are evaluating. The time you spend looking up specific titles in the catalog will likely make you more aware of which resources your library already provides. Because the bulk of online journals are purchased as part of packages, even if you are a subject specialist you may not know exactly which titles your library has and may not have previously needed to identify the most important titles. List-checking can also improve your or your selectors' familiarity with the disciplines that you work with by teaching you what the major journals are in these fields or identifying classic books, major authors, and important publishers. Identifying classics also tells you what not to remove from the collection despite advanced age or low use. Use a nonpublic note field in the library catalog to note that something is a classic or core title so that you or future librarians will know not to weed it.

In addition to familiarizing you with your own collection, list-checking can help with future collection building. The lists are likely to include multiple works by the same major authors, and certain publishers will probably also show up repeatedly. You can add the authors or publishers to an approval plan, or if you do not use approval plans you can request the publishers' catalogs and set up alerts of future publications from these significant authors. Even if the classic authors are no longer publishing, there are probably new books that build on and refer to their work, and familiarity with their names can help you see how these new books fit into the scholarship of the field.

Core Lists as a Supplement to Patron-Driven Acquisitions

Background on Patron-Driven Acquisitions

After you have built a strong core and used the authoritative list to teach you how to identify future important works, you may feel comfortable turning some of the rest of the selection over to your patrons. Authoritative lists can supplement patron-driven acquisitions by ensuring that the collection retains a core of major works even when a significant part of the selection is user driven. Patron-driven acquisitions is a relatively new purchasing model that has been growing in the last fifteen to twenty years. Although libraries have always been open to patron requests, patron-driven acquisitions, or PDA, refers to programs that integrate the process of patron requests with other library functions, making the connection between requesting and purchasing nearly seamless so that the library can provide desired books to patrons at the moment of need. Such programs go by many different names, such as demand-driven, on-demand, or user-driven acquisitions. All of these terms highlight a contrast with the traditional model of "just-in-case" purchasing, in which librarians preselect materials based on educated guesses of what their users might need in the future.

A common way of soliciting patron requests is by merging interlibrary loan and acquisitions. Users submit a request form and librarians make a decision of whether to buy or borrow the requested item. This system is the most common for patron-driven acquisitions programs involving print books. Another form of PDA, more common for e-books, replaces the approval plan with records that are loaded into the catalog. Rather than shipping books to the library for approval, a vendor sends batches of MARC records that the library imports into the catalog. Users can then discover books in the catalog and click a link in the record to purchase the item. Libraries usually establish criteria on which requests to purchase or which records to load into the catalog so that purchases will fit the library's usual collection criteria.

Since the early 2000s, PDA has been growing in popularity due to technological advances as well as budget restrictions. The first known implementation of patron-driven acquisitions for print books was by Bucknell University in 1990, and it ran into problems because the acquisitions staff did not know at the time of order whether the books were actually available (Nixon, Freeman, and Ward, 2010). Now that online vendors show availability on their websites, it is much more feasible for libraries to make the decision to buy an item at the moment of need. The widespread use of electronic catalogs makes it feasible to preload large amounts of records for items not yet owned to make these available for request, and the emergence of e-books means it is possible to make a book immediately available when a user clicks on the catalog link. Drake University in Iowa imports records for print books that it does not yet own into its catalog and includes in each record a link to a request form (Koch, Welch, and McDonald, 2013). Software created by SUNY Geneseo facilitates the integration of PDA and ILL by automatically gathering information to help librarians make decisions. The software, called the Getting It System Toolkit (GIST), is an open-source add-on to the ILLiad interlibrary loan software that provides additional information to the staff interface, such as which consortial partners own the item, its price and availability on Amazon, and whether there is a free online version (see http://www.gistlibrary.org/illiad).

Tight budgets also make PDA an appealing option. It is an efficient use of library funds since every title purchased through this method gets used. Several studies have shown that not only do PDA purchases get a guaranteed initial checkout from the requestor, but they continue to be borrowed more often than titles purchased the traditional way (Pitcher et al., 2010; Walker, 2012). In times of tight budgets, replacing some of the library's approval plan or other just-in-case purchasing with demand-driven purchases can be a practical decision.

Using Authoritative Lists with Patron-Driven Acquisitions

There is some concern among academic librarians about turning over selection entirely to users, however. Walters points out that part of the mission of academic libraries is to teach, and part of a teacher's role is to identify the most important works for students to read. A librarians' role, he says, is to "guide patrons to the works that librarians and faculty, as experts, have found to be most useful" (2012: 204). Librarians who believe in the merits of both user-driven and just-in-case purchasing that helps guide users to important works can combine the two approaches. Limited purchasing from core lists can ensure that your library still owns important titles that you want to encourage students to use, even if the majority of purchasing is now driven by user requests.

The librarians at Drake University say they want to maintain a core print collection selected by librarians and faculty to supplement their PDA purchasing. To them, it makes the most sense to limit PDA to titles that they would have felt less certain about purchasing and to continue their traditional just-in-case purchasing for titles they can tell in advance will be significant (Koch, Welch, and McDonald, 2013). Core lists can therefore be a useful piece of the process of implementing patron-driven acquisitions.

To combine an authoritative list with patron-driven acquisitions, you'd want to begin with a retrospective evaluation using a list such as Resources for College Libraries. To make sure that the core is up-to-date, follow the suggestions above for using the list to educate yourself about significant authors and important publishers. You should also find an annual or continuously updated list that you can check regularly. RCL is updated continuously, and a new edition of Doody's Core Titles in the Health Sciences comes out each year. *Choice* magazine's Outstanding Academic Titles list is a well-respected annual core list, and the library vendor YBP publishes quarterly core lists on their website. If you reach a point where patron-driven acquisitions represents the majority of your purchasing, you will be spending less time on selection than before but will be reviewing the lists as they come out to maintain your core.

Key Points

List-checking can serve several purposes related not only to evaluation but also to future collection development. To get the most out of your list-checking activity, here are some points to remember:

- There is no firm rule of how much of the list you should have. Decide if you have enough by comparing your library's holdings to other libraries, taking into account the differences between your library and the others.
- When deciding what to purchase from the list, use your usual collection development criteria and also consider what you already own.
- Use the list to educate yourself. Look for repeated authors and publishers so you can buy more from them in the future.
- To keep your core collection up-to-date, you can use an annual list and buy the new titles each year.

As the discussion of patron-driven acquisitions above shows, building a strong core is not necessarily at odds with building a collection based on user needs. Using usage data to evaluate and shape your collection is the subject of the next chapter.

References

ACRL Instruction Section Research and Scholarship Committee. 2009. "Bibliography of Research Methods Texts." http://acrl.ala.org/is-research/.

Beile, Penny M., David N. Boote, and Elizabeth K. Killingsworth. 2004. "A Microscope or a Mirror? A Question of Study Validity regarding the Use of Dissertation Citation Analysis for Evaluating Research Collections." *Journal of Academic Librarianship* 30, no. 5 (September): 347–53.

Bolton, Brooke A. 2009. "Women's Studies Collections: A Checklist Evaluation." *Journal of Academic Librarianship* 35, no. 3 (May): 221–26.

Dennison, Russell F. 2000. "Quality Assessment of Collection Development through Tiered Checklists: Can You Prove You Are a Good Collection Developer?" *Collection Building* 19, no. 1: 24–26.

Koch, Teri, Andrew Welch, and Lisa McDonald. 2013. "Adding PDA for Print? Consider Your Options for Implementation." Paper presented at Charleston Conference: Issues in Book and Serials Acquisitions, Charleston, SC.

Kronenfeld, Michael R., Janet E. Watson, Caroline A. Macera, and Jennie J. Kronenfeld. 1985. "A Recommended Core Book List for Public Health Libraries." *Medical Reference Services Quarterly* 4, no. 2: 39–52.

Nixon, Judith M., Robert S. Freeman, and Suzanne M. Ward. 2010. "Patron-Driven Acquisitions: An Introduction and Literature Review." *Collection Management* 35, nos. 3–4 (June): 119–24.

Pitcher, Kate, Tim Bowersox, Cyril Oberlander, and Mark Sullivan. 2010. "Point-of-Need Collection Development: The Getting It System Toolkit (GIST) and a New System for Acquisitions and Interlibrary Loan Integrated Workflow and Collection Development." *Collection Management* 35, nos. 3–4 (June): 222–36.

Walker, Kizer. 2012. "Patron-Driven Acquisition in U.S. Academic Research Libraries: At the Tipping Point in 2011?" *Bibliothek Forschung und Praxis* 36, no. 1 (March): 125–29.

Walters, William H. 2012. "Patron-Driven Acquisition and the Educational Mission of the Academic Library." *Library Resources & Technical Services* 56, no. 3 (July): 199–213.

CHAPTER 8

Usage Statistics—Collecting and Analyzing the Data

Applications and Complications of Usage Statistics

WHILE MOST LIBRARIES TRY TO COLLECT WORKS with lasting significance, the main mission of many libraries is to provide the materials their patrons want to use. When materials are heavily used, the library is both satisfying user needs and spending money well. Libraries' missions vary, of course, with some stringently removing unused books from the shelves and others keeping nearly everything for the sake of maintaining a historical record. Whether or not your primary goal is to have a heavily used collection, however, usage statistics will almost definitely be helpful to you in some way. You can use usage data at a very fine-tuned level—for example, to serve a particular course by seeing which books on its topic are the most used—or at a very broad level, such as determining to what extent print circulation is declining as your e-book collection grows. If your collection development philosophy includes both providing a classic core and satisfying patron demand, a combination that is not uncommon, you can use usage data in conjunction with other methods of evaluation like the checklist method described in the previous chapters.

Evaluating your collection using usage data is somewhat more complicated than the previous methods. It provides a finer-tuned view of the collection than benchmarking and therefore relies on more numerical calculations. Because there is a wide range of questions that usage data can help answer, you may want to analyze the data in multiple ways. Another complication is that you will need to do a separate analysis for each format—books, e-books, print journals, and electronic journals—as usage of each type is measured so differently. In some ways analysis of usage data can be easier than benchmarking, however. You should be able to do it using only data from your own institution, as it is not relevant that items might get used more or less by other institutions. There is no special software required besides your integrated library system, and you won't need to search for outside resources like you would with the checklist method. While you will need to think carefully in the beginning about your goals and what data will help you meet them, any library should be able to do some amount of usage analysis.

Usage of books is measured differently than usage of journals, and electronic materials are measured differently than print materials. Book usage has traditionally been measured by checkouts, while print journals that don't circulate commonly have their use measured by counting the times staff has needed to reshelve the volumes. These measures are not comparable, since the first is a count of borrowing and the second counts in-house use. Books and journals that are available electronically are measured in yet another way, through vendor-provided reports on how often patrons have accessed them. Unlike usage statistics for print materials, which have no way of measuring how many pages of a book or articles from a journal your patrons have read, statistics for electronic resources usually count usage by section, either a book chapter or journal article. Usage of online materials tends to be much higher than print, both because electronic resources are easier for patrons to access and because measures of online usage are more sensitive than measures of print. Just glancing at the full text of an article, for example, would count as usage. Because the means of measuring are so different, you cannot compare usage of one format to usage of another. This chapter will therefore describe how to evaluate each format separately.

Even though usage data is very fragmented, it can serve many purposes and is frequently used by libraries. You can use usage data to:

- Adjust the budget according to which materials have declining use (probably print materials) and which have increasing use (probably online resources)
- Identify sections of your print collection to weed
- Identify heavily used areas so you can continue to purchase in these areas
- Dialogue with faculty about their needs, particularly faculty who say they don't need books
- Make renewal decisions for subscriptions to journals and e-book collections
- Justify continued funding for subscriptions
- Evaluate patron-driven acquisitions to see how this purchasing model affects your collection
- Show stakeholders that the library is being used, even if fewer people are using the physical building

Circulation of Print Books

Usage of print books has traditionally been measured using circulation records. You can use the same data for audiovisual items that circulate, though for clarity's sake this section is written as if it is only about books. Circulation data is obviously only available for materials that can be checked out (i.e., not reference books), but it is a very useful measure in cases where it is available. Data on checkouts can show whether books are used more heavily in some subjects than others and whether usage of print books is going down over time as the library acquires more e-books. When collecting circulation data, you should pair it with measures of your holdings. If you are going to say "twenty books were checked out last week," you need to know whether that was twenty out of the one thousand on the shelf, or whether you only have thirty and the twenty that got borrowed represent two-thirds of the books on a specific topic. Because you'll be starting with numbers showing the size of different sections of your collection, the process of evaluating circulation data begins similarly to quantitative benchmarking, described in chapter 4. There are a few additional questions to ask when you are beginning a usage analysis, though, in order to make sure your holdings numbers and circulation numbers refer to the same segments of your collection.

What Materials to Include

In order to be consistent as you collect numbers related to holdings and circulation, it is important to think carefully about what kinds of materials you want to include in your analysis. Later on you may also be comparing usage of books that you own to requests for books through interlibrary loan, so it's worth giving some thought ahead of time to what the ILL data will look like as well. If you won't be able to exclude a certain type of material from your ILL data, for example, you should probably not exclude it from the holdings data either. Think about how you will be collecting each kind of data and what information will be available to you. You should be able to get holdings and circulation counts from reports in your integrated library system (ILS). Spend some time in the beginning of the evaluation process looking at how the reports are structured and what kind of information they can provide and deciding which ones will be best for you to use. As you figure out your criteria for what to include in the analysis, write down what you come up with so that you'll remember to use the same criteria each time you gather data.

Materials you should definitely exclude from the holdings and circulation data are reference material, archival materials, and anything else that does not circulate (see textbox 8.1). It is important also to exclude items that are on order from both holdings and circulation reports, as these are not yet held and have not had a chance to circulate. Knievel, Wicht, and Connaway (2006) mention excluding government documents, as these are acquired based on the depository status of the library rather than selected item by item. If you are a depository library, it will not be useful for you to analyze whether specific government documents get used more than others. This will also be true of dissertations and theses if you routinely collect all of your own students' work and allow it to circulate. You should also either remove reserves from the holdings and circulation data or analyze them separately from the rest of the circulating collection. Both usage and selection are very different for reserve items than for other materials, as they are purchased with a guarantee that they will be used by many students, and the library usually receives explicit instructions from faculty on what to purchase. An analysis of reserves usage will serve different goals from other usage analysis, probably goals related to evaluating your services rather than the collection.

Since circulation counts will be based on items rather than bibliographic records (i.e., if a two-volume set is checked out it will count as two circulations, although the volumes are part of the same bibliographic record), the holdings count should also be based on items. When running reports for holdings or circulation, limit your reports by item type so that you're starting out with only books. Filtering by location could also be a way to sort out the materials you want to exclude. If reference books have the same item type as circulating books, location could be the only way to differentiate these materials. If you are not able to filter your reports in a way that's useful to you, put as much information as possible in the report so you can sort it manually. Exporting reports to Excel and sorting by item type, location, or call number can make it easier to find the items you want to delete. For example, you might delete anything with no call number if in your library this means it is on order.

After spending some time thinking about what you want to include and what you can exclude, you may realize that you can't sort all the data in the ways you want. Just do the best you can. If you can't remove dissertations from your circulation data, it won't invalidate everything you'll learn from the analysis.

Dividing the Collection by Subject

Although you won't be comparing your library to other libraries, you will be comparing some sections of your collection to others. Chapter 4 discusses several ways of dividing the collection into subject-based sections. One method is to use the conspectus divisions. These twenty-five groupings describe broad disciplines and are mapped to call numbers. The mapping is quite complicated, however, as each discipline is spread throughout multiple call number ranges. Each division is made up of multiple categories, which are defined by a specific call number range. Computer science, for example, is one of the smaller divisions, made up of only three categories. These categories map to the call numbers HF5548, Q300–385, and QA75–76. Since these call number ranges are not adjacent to each other, you'd need to run a separate report for each category and then add the numbers to get circulation and holdings data on the computer science division. You may decide to keep your numbers separate and do your analysis at the category level. This data may be more meaningful as it describes more specific parts of the collection (e.g., geriatrics rather than the more general medicine, or history of Portugal rather than simply history). There are over six hundred categories, though, and analysis of six hundred units is going to be more cumbersome than twenty-five. You could also use a combination of divisions and categories. If you have a large art collection, for example, you could analyze art by category (the narrower ranges) and analyze medicine by division (the broader, composite range). Your choices will depend on the size of your collection and the time you're able to devote to analysis.

If your library uses Library of Congress classification, another option is using LC subclasses. These have the advantage of being an easy way to run searches, as you won't need to type in complicated ranges. You could just limit your reports to call numbers that start with HM, for example. You can use different levels of specificity for different subjects, depending on how many books you have on that subject. Danielson (2012), whose theological seminary library is highly specialized, broke down parts of the collection by subclass or even finer subdivisions while evaluating others at the broader level. For example, his evaluation considered the entire social sciences section (letter H in the LC classification scheme) as one unit, while creating separate units of analysis for worship (BV1–510) and missions and evangelism (BV2000–3799).

As in chapters 4 and 5, you can also choose to create custom call number ranges that map to your school's programs. This has the advantage of allowing you to capture information on interdisciplinary topics or very narrowly focused programs whose data could get buried within an LC class or conspectus division. You could even create ranges that correspond to specific courses. This is very time-consuming and would not be feasible for larger schools unless the analysis covered only a small subset of courses. A disadvantage of this method is that it will probably leave gaps in the collection that aren't included in any of the ranges. The generalities section, for example (000 in the Dewey Decimal System and A in Library of Congress) probably won't fall within the call number range for any course or program. An advantage of custom ranges is that the narrow focus of the analysis can make it easier to implement action steps. The ranges are small enough that you can supplement the numbers with shelf-reading, and since the categories are tied to your own programs, it will be clear which faculty to contact for their input on what books could better serve their courses.

Since the circulation analysis will be broken down by call number, libraries that use multiple classification schemes—for example, keeping literature or biography alphabetical by author or subject while assigning classification numbers to other books—can decide to analyze these sections separately or integrate them in the analysis by using call numbers from the main classification scheme. The advantage of using standard call numbers for your analysis is that you can be more consistent when you compare circulation to interlibrary loan requests later on. The ILL data will only contain standard classification schemes, and you won't be able to separate out the materials that you would've housed in one of your subcollections. To assign standard call numbers to books that your library has cataloged using a local system, see if it is possible to print reports that pull the call number from the MARC record rather than the item record. Call numbers may already be in the MARC record even if they are not displayed to end users. If your reports only give the call numbers that are in the item record, just analyze any sections that use a different call number scheme separately. Your comparisons to ILL data will be less accurate, but you will still get useful information from both the circulation and ILL data.

There are a few situations in which you would not need to divide the collection by subject at all. This would happen mainly if you are looking at usage of your whole collection over time. You could be demonstrating that print circulation has declined as use of e-books has gone up, or providing evidence that, despite common perceptions, your patrons do still use print books. This kind of broad measurement would mainly be useful for making a case to administrators, who don't need a more detailed knowledge of what exactly is being used. For most collection development goals, analyzing the collection by subject will be useful.

What Numbers to Use for Circulation

After you've thought through what items will be included in the analysis and how to divide them by subject, there are a few more questions to ask before gathering circulation data. Decide ahead of time if you are going to count renewals as an additional circulation. Your ILS may not give you an option of separating renewals from initial checkouts, in which case the decision is made for you. Think about what years you will be using for circulation data. Circulation should be measured over several years to smooth out skewed data when a particular topic becomes popular only briefly. Academic libraries should keep in mind that many courses are offered on an every-other-year cycle, so books on certain topics will only get used every other year. Looking at circulation for an even number of years gives a fair chance to each course. Avoid making the date range too large, however. It is likely that circulation patterns in all libraries have changed a lot in the last ten years, so ten years of aggregated data won't tell you much that is relevant to your library today. Four years is more reasonable. If possible, use holdings counts based on what you owned at the end of the time period for which you are measuring circulation. If you're collecting circulation data for 2010–2013, you don't want the holdings counts to include books you bought in 2014.

It may not be possible to calculate the number of checkouts within a given time period. Knievel, Wicht, and Connaway (2006) mention that their catalog provides a date of last use and total number of uses, not the date of each checkout. If your data is the same, you can do as they did and collect data on how many books had a last-use date within your time range, but you will not know how many checkouts occurred during that period. Even the data you do have will be slightly inaccurate if some books were checked out during the time range and then again after the end of the range. These books won't get counted even if they were used within the time range. To minimize this problem, use a time range that ends recently.

Having looked at the reports available to you and decided what materials to include or exclude, how to divide your collection by subject, and what date ranges to look at, you are now ready to run the reports. Make an Excel spreadsheet that lists each segment of the collection and the call numbers that circumscribe it. Add a column for the holdings count and one for the circulation. Run the reports, filtering out your excluded materials after the fact if necessary, and fill in the numbers in your spreadsheet.

Calculating Comparative Data

Once you've collected holdings and circulation counts, you'll need to do some calculations to compare the holdings count of each section to its circulation and then compare the sections to each other. You can either compare percentages or absolute numbers. Both are shown in table 8.1, with sample data for a few departments at Arcadia

Table 8.1. Comparison of Checkouts to Holdings by Discipline

DEPARTMENT	HOLDINGS	HOLDINGS AS % OF TOTAL	CHECKOUTS	CHECKOUTS AS % OF TOTAL	CHECKOUTS TO HOLDINGS	% CHECKOUTS TO % HOLDINGS
Art	7,671	8.04%	3,163	10.60%	0.412	1.32
Chemistry	3,115	3.26%	246	0.82%	0.079	0.25
Education	4,265	4.47%	1,335	4.47%	0.313	1.00
Psychology	3,162	3.31%	1,870	6.27%	0.591	1.89
Sociology	3,960	4.15%	2,168	7.26%	0.547	1.75
Total	95,438	n/a	29,843	n/a	0.313	n/a

University. The totals in the bottom row are the totals of all holdings and checkouts, not just the counts for the departments listed in the table. The other departments were omitted from this table for the sake of brevity. If you've broken down your collection into units that don't cover the entire collection, it still makes sense to use the full totals when calculating percentages. That way you'll be showing that circulation in a certain section accounted for 20 percent of all the circulation measured by the analysis. Similarly, if your units overlap—for instance, if your call number range for medicine included psychiatry and these same books were also counted toward psychology—you can still calculate each unit's circulation as a percent of the total. In this case, the percentages will add up to more than one hundred.

Table 8.1 compares holdings and circulation to each other using a ratio. The column called Checkouts to Holdings compares how many checkouts there were in a given section to how many books are in that section. This number shows how much activity each section gets, though we don't know whether the activity was due to a few very popular books being used a lot or many books being used once each. A section with 100 books and 150 checkouts, for example, has a ratio of 1.5, regardless of whether every book was checked out or just a few were used repeatedly. The rightmost column, Percent Checkouts to Percent Holdings, shows whether the use of a particular section is higher or lower than you'd expect given the size of the section. If every section were used an even amount (for simplicity's sake, imagine each book in the collection got borrowed once), then a section that made up 10 percent of the collection would also account for 10 percent of the circulation. Dividing 10 percent by 10 percent gives a percent-checkouts-to-percent-holdings ratio of 1.

To better understand whether a lot of books in a given section are being used or just a few, you can use the count of how many books were checked out. If you're unable to get a count of how many total checkouts occurred during your time range, the number of unique books checked out may be your only measure of circulation. How you obtain this number will depend on what the reports from your ILS look like. Once you have a count of how many unique books were borrowed, you can calculate what percentage of books were borrowed by dividing the number of books borrowed by the number of books owned and multiplying by one hundred. An example of this is shown in table 8.2, using the same Arcadia University departments as the previous table. If you have numbers for both the total unique books checked out and the total number of checkouts, you can do an additional calculation of checkouts per borrowed book. Divide the total number of

Table 8.2. Unique Books Checked Out

DEPARTMENT	UNIQUE BOOKS CHECKED OUT	HOLDINGS	PERCENTAGE OF BOOKS CHECKED OUT
Art	1,917	7,671	24.99%
Chemistry	174	3,115	5.59%
Education	839	4,265	19.67%
Psychology	1,125	3,162	35.58%
Sociology	1,229	3,960	31.04%
Total	18,042	95,438	18.90%

checkouts by the number of books checked out. This shows you how many times each of the borrowed books in the section was used. If the number of books borrowed is low compared to the holdings and the checkouts per item is high, you have a few books being used a lot and others getting dusty on the shelf. If the number of books borrowed is high compared to the holdings but the checkouts per book is low, your usage is nicely distributed so that many different books are being used but none heavily.

Vendor Reports for E-Books

Many libraries are purchasing fewer print books as more books become available electronically. As the e-book market is changing quickly, so are library collections. Usage statistics can help you make decisions as you navigate these changes. Compiling statistics on e-books is hard to do comprehensively, as vendors currently sell e-books using many different models. Sometimes the library pays an upfront fee, often followed by a small annual fee, for perpetual access to e-books. Perpetual-access purchases can be for collections or for books that the library selects à la carte. Other e-books come as part of subscription packages. The library pays a yearly subscription cost and acquires access to new titles as they are added to the collection. Some larger reference works, like the Oxford English Dictionary, offer subscriptions to a single book. A popular newer model is patron-driven acquisitions (PDA). In this model, described in more detail in chapter 7, a library is given many MARC records to load into the catalog and is only charged when patrons actually use the e-books. It is sometimes possible to purchase e-books from the same company using multiple models—subscription, perpetual access, or PDA—and have the e-books housed on the same platform, yet it is also common for libraries to own or access e-books via several different platforms.

Availability of Statistics

There is no commonly accepted method for comparing e-book usage statistics across models. Although you can probably get counts of how many titles on each platform were accessed, for anything that is paid as a subscription you'll want to calculate the cost per use, and you won't have a comparable calculation for perpetual-access titles. Librarians have tried to calculate cost per use for e-books to which they have perpetual access, but with some difficulty. Lowe and Aldana (2013) describe how Frostburg State University in Maryland tried to measure cost per use across multiple purchase models by dividing the upfront purchase price by the number of years they had owned the titles. This calculation makes it look like a book is cheaper the longer it has been owned and would not help the library decide about future purchases of similar things. Due to the difficulties in comparing different models and the fact that many evaluation goals can be met by looking at one model at a time, this chapter does not propose any ways to compare the cost per use of subscriptions to perpetual-access purchases.

E-book statistics are usually available through an administrative module on the vendor's website. The vendor can give you a password for accessing the site. Some, but not all, vendors will provide statistics in COUNTER-compliant format. Project COUNTER (2012) is a standard for publishers and vendors for reporting usage statistics. It was created in 2002 with guidelines for journal and database statistics. Standards for books were added later in January 2005. The standards specify reports that a vendor

RATIOS TO HELP INTERPRET CIRCULATION STATISTICS

For all the ratios described, *checkouts* refers to the number of checkouts of the material types included in the analysis for the time period being analyzed. Similarly, *holdings* refers to holdings of the material types included in the analysis, not necessarily all the items the library owns.

Checkouts to Holdings

What It Means: If the ratio for a particular section is higher than the ratio for the entire collection, this section is heavily used compared to the rest of the collection.

How to Calculate: Number of checkouts in section divided by number of holdings in section.

Example: Psychology has 3,162 books, which were checked out a total of 1,870 times.

1,870 (checkouts) ÷ 3,162 (holdings) = .591 (checkouts-to-holdings ratio).

This is higher than the ratio for the entire collection, which table 8.1 shows is .313.

Percent Checkouts to Percent Holdings

What It Means: If every book were used an equal amount, a section that made up 16 percent of the library collection would also be responsible for 16 percent of checkouts, yielding a ratio of 1. If the ratio is higher than 1, this section accounts for more circulation activity than would be expected given the size of the section.

How to Calculate: Checkouts for this section as a percentage of the total checkouts divided by holdings for this section as a percentage of the total holdings.

Example: Chemistry books account for 3.26 percent of the total holdings, while checkouts of chemistry books are only 0.82 percent of total checkouts.

0.82% (percent checkouts) ÷ 3.26% (percent holdings) = 0.25 (percent checkouts to percent holdings).

This is much lower than one, which means that the library sees fewer chemistry books borrowed than might be expected given how many there are in the library.

Percentage of Unique Books Checked Out

What It Means: This looks at how many books within a given section were borrowed during the chosen date range. If the percentage for a particular section is lower than the percentage of the collection overall that was checked out, this section has a lot of unused books and may need to be weeded.

How to Calculate: Number of unique books borrowed divided by number of books in the section.

Example: The education section has 4,265 books, of which 839 were checked out.

839 (number of unique books borrowed) ÷ 4,265 (number of books in the section) = 19.67%.

This is slightly higher than the percentage of the entire collection that was borrowed in the same time period, which was 18.90 percent, so this section is relatively well used.

Checkouts per Borrowed Book

What It Means: This ratio includes only the books that got borrowed and shows how many times these were used. It can tell you whether certain books within a section are frequently used, even if the section as a whole may not be.

How to Calculate: Checkouts in the section divided by number of unique titles checked out.

Example: There were 1,917 art books borrowed (see table 8.2). These books were borrowed 3,163 times (see table 8.1).

3,163 (checkouts in the section) ÷ 1,917 (unique titles checked out) = 1.65 checkouts per borrowed book.

This is the same as the ratio for the collection as a whole.

needs to provide in order to be COUNTER compliant and defines the data elements included in these reports. For books, there are five reports, though the most commonly used are Book Report 1: Number of Successful Title Requests by Month and Title (BR1) and Book Report 2: Number of Successful Section Requests by Month and Title (BR2). Vendors provide BR1 if their interface offers each book as a single file and BR2 if the books are divided into a separate file for each section. A section is often a chapter, or it can be an encyclopedia entry. If you are comparing a vendor that uses BR2 to one that uses BR1, be aware that usage numbers will probably be higher for the vendor that uses BR2, as each chapter is counted separately. Other reports provide information on instances when access is denied and the number of times patrons conduct searches within the e-book collection. In accordance with COUNTER standards, all the reports are updated monthly and can be downloaded into Excel.

There are many reasons you'd want to look at usage data of your e-books. Table 8.3 lists several questions you might have and what data would answer them. For most of the questions in the table, there would be no need to compare subscription costs to perpetual-access costs or to PDA. For example, when deciding what subscriptions to renew, you would not need to collect usage on e-books that are not paid for as subscriptions. Demonstrating the usefulness of a patron-driven acquisitions program might require some comparison data, but not necessarily a comparison to subscription purchases. Although usage data is imperfect, it can still be useful for decision making.

The first question in the table refers to patron-driven acquisitions, the second to subscriptions, and the last two could apply to any model of e-book purchasing. This section provides examples of evaluations of PDA and subscriptions. For perpetual-access titles, you might have the same kinds of questions that you have about print books, namely, which subjects are popular and what kinds of e-books should you continue to buy. It will be hard to sort the data by subject, however, since COUNTER reports do not include information on the subject of the books. You can either look up the call numbers of specific books by ISBN or run a BR1 or BR2 report and glance at the titles to get an informal sense of popular topics. For subscriptions and patron-driven acquisitions, though you still might not be able to analyze usage by subject, you can do a more detailed analysis to answer other questions.

Table 8.3. E-Book Evaluation with Usage Data

WHAT YOU MIGHT WANT TO KNOW	WHAT DATA TO USE	SHORTCOMINGS OF THE DATA
Do patron-selected purchases get used again?	Report that includes owned status, as some PDA models allow libraries to use a book as a loan without purchasing.	
What subscriptions should you renew?	Report of usage by package, only of subscription-based packages. Cost per use. Requires some basis for comparison, preferably between different subscription packages.	Difficult if you have only one subscription package.
Which subjects are popular for e-books?	A report of usage by subject from all vendors. If possible, compare usage to everything that's available in your catalog, regardless of whether you own it.	COUNTER reports don't include call numbers; could look up every book by ISBN.
What publishers are popular for e-books?	Vendor report of usage by title, including publisher information, from all vendors. Compare usage to everything that's available in your catalog, regardless of whether you own it.	COUNTER reports do not list publishers.

Evaluation of Subscriptions

A common way of using usage data for e-books is for deciding whether or not to renew subscriptions. This requires taking into account not only how much use the subscriptions are getting but also what they cost. Most libraries evaluate their subscriptions, whether to e-books or to journals, based on cost per use. Use is most often measured as downloads of full-text content, whether it be a book section (as in BR2 for books that are divided into multiple files) or the entire book (as in BR1 for books that are provided in one file). Comparing multiple subscription packages to each other can help you decide what constitutes a high cost per use. If you only have one subscription package for e-books and need some point of reference, you could compare an e-book subscription to a perpetual-access purchase, maybe e-books purchased in the previous year. As you can't accurately compare cost per use of a subscription to that of a perpetual-access title, you'd just compare how often each of the titles was used during the year.

Table 8.4 shows an example of the data you'll need to compare e-book subscriptions. It compares five e-book collections on different subjects and of different kinds of materials—

Table 8.4. Comparing Usage of E-Book Subscription Packages

PACKAGE NAME	REPORT USED	PRICE 2012–2013	USAGE 2013	NUMBER OF BOOKS	COST PER USE	USE PER BOOK
A. Medical Textbooks	Non-COUNTER	$19,223.00	168,250	79	$0.11	2,129.75
B. Literary Criticism	BR2	$1,497.00	4	541	$374.25	0.01
C. Plays	Non-COUNTER	$645.84	942	1,517	$0.69	0.62
D. Forensic Science Handbooks	BR2	$3,730.00	217	472	$17.19	0.46
E. Oxford English Dictionary	BR2	$918.60	788	1	$1.17	788.00

reference, textbooks, literature, and other research materials. Although some of the vendors use COUNTER and others don't, all of the reports count how many times a section of a book has been viewed rather than how many views per book.

When comparing subscription e-book packages, you'll need to know how often each package was used and how much the package costs. You may also want to note how many books are in the package. Start by creating a spreadsheet with columns for price, usage, and number of books. Later you'll add columns in which you'll calculate cost per use and use per book. Check to see if each vendor has COUNTER reports available through the administrative module of their website. If so, use Book Report 1 or 2. If not, look for a report that counts how often each book was used within a specified time period. Ideally, you'd collect COUNTER data for a time period that matched with the subscription dates. Collecting data for the calendar year will be simpler, as COUNTER reports are organized by calendar year. If you choose to work with data from the calendar year, use prices for the subscription period that ended in that calendar year. You should have pricing information from past invoices. The total number of books in the package will probably be mentioned somewhere on the user interface. Fill in price, usage, and number of books in your spreadsheet.

After you've filled in the data that you looked up, you can do several calculations based on what you collected. Cost per use is the primary way of evaluating a subscription, though use per book may also be of interest. The latter is similar to the checkouts-to-holdings calculation used to evaluate print books.

Evaluation of Patron-Driven Acquisitions

An evaluation of e-books acquired through patron-driven acquisitions will be very different than for subscriptions or perpetual-access titles because the relationships between holdings, use, and cost are so different. Comparing holdings to use is somewhat less important for PDA than for other models, as the nature of PDA means that everything the library purchases has been used. Despite the cost-efficient nature of patron-driven acquisitions, though, librarians have many concerns about this relatively new model, and usage data can help address these issues. Price and McDonald (2009) conducted a much-cited study of patron-driven acquisitions that addressed a fear they had heard expressed by many librarians: that books chosen based on an individual patron's immediate needs would not get used by future patrons. Their study, which showed that patron-driven acquisitions in five libraries actually got used more often than purchases selected by librarians, can be replicated by other libraries that are concerned about usage of PDA titles. An example below shows how you can do this with your own library's data.

Price and McDonald (2009) compared PDA purchases to what they call "preselected" purchases using data from libraries that bought e-books from the same vendor using both purchase models. If you don't purchase in both ways on the same platform, you can compare your patron-driven acquisitions to an e-book collection on another platform, as long as both are multidisciplinary or both are in the same discipline. If you have no appropriate e-book collection to compare your PDA to, you can use print books for the comparison. E-book statistics are not really comparable to print circulation statistics, for reasons already described, but it is better to have some point of comparison than none.

Your first step is to use reports provided on each vendor's website to collect information on usage of your two sets of e-books, patron-driven and preselected. If the reports are COUNTER compliant, there will be a BR1 or BR2 report for each calendar year that lists each title that was used and how many times it was used. Reports that are not COUNTER compliant might show use differently. Choose a time period for which data is available for both vendors. If you only started your PDA program two years ago, use only two years' worth of data for the preselected e-books as well. Whatever format the usage data is in, you'll need to do some manipulation of the data so that you have one file for each vendor. Run the report for each calendar year, export to Excel, and paste the data into one report for PDA books and one for preselected. Titles will be in the list more than once if they were used in multiple years, or if your vendor report lists each title once for each time it was used. For simplicity's sake, remove all columns except the title and number of times used. The example below assumes these columns are labeled Title and Usage.

A nice trick for counting usage when titles are listed more than once in the report is to use a pivot table in Excel. To do this, highlight all your data. Then click on Insert at the top and select Pivot Table. Excel will then open a new tab in your file that includes a list of fields on the right. The field names will be taken from the column headings of your data. Drag Title down to the box for Row Labels. Then drag Usage down to the box for Values. It should default to Sum of Usage. This will add up the usage for each title. So, if the report you created by pasting multiple years of COUNTER reports together lists "*Handbook of Special Education—2*" for one year and "*Handbook of Special Education—4*" for another year, the pivot table will add these numbers and list "*Handbook of Special Education—6.*" Figure 8.1 shows a pivot table that sums the usage of various e-books. If you have a non-COUNTER report, it will be arranged differently and might list each title once per use, so the same titles are repeated over and over. In this case you don't want the Values column to

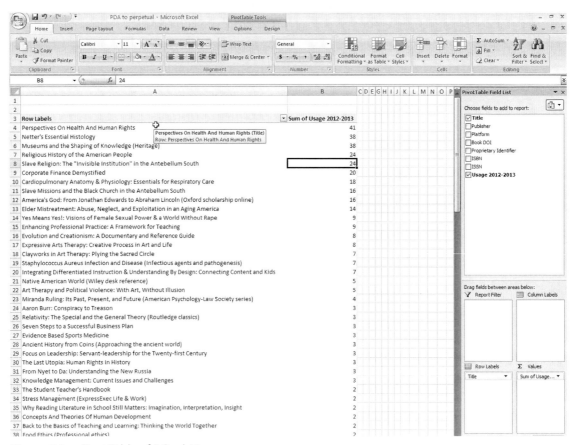

Figure 8.1. Pivot Table of E-Book Use.

be Sum of Usage. Instead, you want to count how often each title is listed. When making your pivot table, drag Title to the box for Row Labels, then drag Title again to the box for Values. It should default to Count of Titles. If not, click the little black arrow next to the field name and click on Value Field Settings. Select Count of Titles. This will create a table that lists each title once and totals how many times it was used each year. Now that you have a table with each title listed once, you can easily calculate how many total titles were used by looking at the row numbers in Excel. The bottom of the pivot table will automatically sum the total number of uses of all e-books.

You can now use the counts of how many titles were used and how many times each to answer the question about whether books purchased via PDA will be used again post-purchase. Table 8.5 shows a comparison of two collections available through the same library. Both include e-books from many different disciplines and are hosted by major e-book aggregators, making this a comparison of like to like. The major difference is that the books on one platform were purchased through patron-driven acquisitions, whereas the books on the other platform were preselected by librarians. The data set for Vendor A includes only titles that have already been purchased; many more are available in the catalog and may have been used but not purchased. This vendor allows libraries to pay a loan charge the first few times the book is used, and a purchase is triggered after a set number of uses. The way the library's settings are configured, all the titles that are purchased have already been used at least three times, so even if they show no use postpurchase, they have already been more useful than a preselected title that was purchased and never used. Initial purchases from Vendor B were done as part of a consortial purchase, so the library did not get to choose specific titles. There have been no consortial purchases in recent years, and in the last few years the library has bought 107 books that were individually selected, usually by faculty. This is obviously not a perfect comparison, as the books from Vendor B are older and were not always selected by the institution's own staff. The results are so clear, though, that it is unlikely that a cleaner comparison (books purchased during the same time period and selected by someone at the institution in question) would show a different conclusion. In addition, the differences in use between the books that did get used are noticeable.

Several of the calculations for e-books are the same as those you've done for print books. Because you'll have both the number of books used and the total number of uses, you can do several calculations. Table 8.5 shows how many of the books were used, both as an absolute number and as a percentage of all owned titles. Since this analysis is designed to answer a question about how PDA affects your library's collection, you should calculate the percentage of books used in relation to the number you've actually purchased, not all the ones you make available through the catalog. You can calculate average uses per title by dividing the total number of uses by the number of titles used. The bottom two rows in table 8.5 have some optional data that helps confirm the point that PDA books are getting more use than preselected books. To get these figures, go back to your pivot chart and sort it by the usage column. Look toward the bottom to see how many e-book titles list 1 as their number of uses. In the example in table 8.5, you can see that although the preselected books were used an average of four times each, about half of them were only used once. With PDA purchases, 36.26 percent were used only once after purchase; nearly two-thirds were used multiple times. The last number in the table, highest number of uses per book, will also be in your pivot chart. The most used e-book will be at the top of the chart, along with the number of times it was used. All of these numbers together can show you whether your patron-driven acquisitions

Table 8.5. Usage of PDA E-Books, Postpurchase, Compared to Preselected E-Books

	VENDOR A PDA BOOKS	VENDOR B PRESELECTED BOOKS
Titles Owned as of 12/31/13	271	990
Titles Used in 2012 and 2013	171 (63.10%)	108 (10.90%)
Average Uses per Title	6.77	4.09
Titles Used Only Once after Purchase	62 (36.26% of titles used)	55 (50.93% of titles used)
Highest Number of Uses per Title	101	41

program, like the one in the example and the libraries Price and McDonald studied, is helping your library to build a well-used collection.

Reshelving Counts for Print Journals

Another significant part of any library's collection is journals. Although you'll need to evaluate journals separately from books, you'll be using some of the same kinds of data. Because journals are always subscription purchases, and you need to decide every year whether or not to continue subscribing, evaluation of journal usage almost always takes cost into account. Journal evaluations are usually focused on making a renewal decision about a particular subscription rather than looking for broader patterns of how usage is distributed across subjects.

When evaluating print journals, data collection is a simple process but produces unreliable numbers. The traditional way of measuring how often print journals are being used is by counting every time your staff needs to reshelve them. To do this, you need a printout of all your journals or a spreadsheet that you'll access on a portable device such as a tablet. You could also create a form using Google Drive. Whether you use a printed chart, a spreadsheet, or a Google Drive form, list all the journals and provide a place to indicate whether the issue that was used was from the current year, two to five years old, or more than five years old. Separating usage by the age of the issue will help if you want to weed backfiles or move them to offsite storage.

Table 8.6 and figure 8.2 show two possible ways of keeping track of reshelving data. You can easily create a chart like the one in table 8.6 using Word or Excel and either print it out or use the file on a tablet or laptop. Figure 8.2 is a form that was created us-

Table 8.6. Sample Reshelving Count Table for Word or Excel

JOURNAL TITLE	CURRENT YEAR	2–5 YEARS OLD	5+ YEARS OLD
Journal of Forensic Sciences	‖‖‖ ‖‖‖ ‖	‖	
Journal of Marriage and Family	‖‖	‖‖‖‖	
Psychology of Women Quarterly	‖‖‖‖		

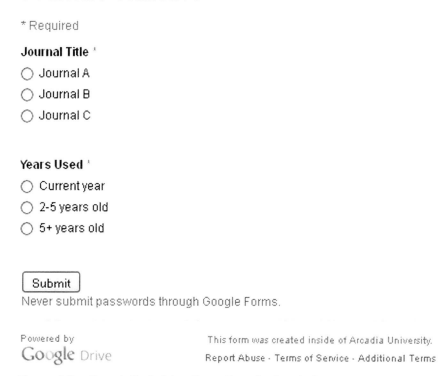

Figure 8.2. Sample Reshelving Count Form for Google Drive.

ing Google Drive. When you fill out the form and submit it, the input will automatically populate a spreadsheet, which you can look at to see everything that was submitted using the form. Whoever reshelves the print journals should bring with them either a printed chart or a tablet or laptop so they can input data as they reshelve.

A major problem with using reshelving data as a measure of usage is that some of your patrons are probably reshelving journals themselves. You can try to discourage this by creating a prominent place for patrons to leave issues that need to be reshelved and placing signs asking patrons to leave items out for reshelving. This might discourage but will probably not completely prevent users from doing their own reshelving. A way to capture some of the instances when patrons reshelve items themselves is to count as use any time your staff needs to rearrange issues that are out of order. Journal issues that are in the wrong order are an indication that a patron took something off the shelf and put it back themselves.

When preparing to collect reshelving data, there are a few other details to work out regarding what you will count. You may or may not want to count issues that were used for interlibrary loan. This will depend on whether you have a consortial obligation to keep titles for the use of other libraries. Make sure you are not counting new issues that are being shelved for the first time.

Even if you're doing the best you can to get an accurate count of when your patrons use your journals, there is only so much reshelving counts can tell you. Knowing how often someone picked up an issue of a journal is not the same as knowing how useful the issue was to them. Patrons could use multiple articles from the same issue or bound volume, and this will only register as one use. It is also possible that a professor photocopied an article and then distributed it to the whole class, or that someone glanced at an issue, decided it wasn't useful, and left it out for reshelving. In the aggregate, though, reshelving statistics will give you some sense of which journals are used and which aren't. You can review the reshelving counts yearly and use the tally along with the subscription price to calculate a cost per use for each journal.

COUNTER Reports for E-Journals and Citation Databases

Chances are good that your library subscribes to many more online journals than print ones. Since it is also common to purchase online journals as part of large bundles, this section on online journals will focus mainly on evaluating packages rather than individual subscriptions. Usage statistics for e-journal packages are similar to the measures described above for e-book packages, focusing on cost per use for the package.

There are several ways of counting usage for electronic journals, though COUNTER statistics are preferable when available. Before COUNTER reports were widespread, some libraries used their server logs to track use. This requires in-house technical expertise to arrange the transaction logs into meaningful information. Some libraries also get data from their link resolver tools, such as Serials Solutions, SFX, or EBSCO's Full Text Finder. This has the advantage of providing a single website that has data on all the journals, as opposed to COUNTER reports, which require you to go to a separate website for each platform. For most libraries, the link resolver will not be a reliable source of data, though. Your users may not go through a link resolver every time they access an online journal. If there are links in your catalog, for example, that point directly to the journal pages, then patrons who use those links to access the journal are not using the link resolver, and these uses won't get counted. If you don't provide any direct links to journal homepages but always use links that go to the link resolver, then the link resolver can work as a source of data.

Most libraries use COUNTER reports, as they capture all usage of the library's online resources, and the international standard makes it clear what the numbers are measuring. For vendors that don't have COUNTER reports, look for a report on the vendor's administrative website that contains information similar to what is in COUNTER. Because collecting data from different vendors' websites could be excessively time-consuming for online journals that you have as individual subscriptions, you may choose to use another source of data, such as the link resolver, for individual subscriptions. For packages, use what the vendor website provides, preferably a COUNTER report.

What the Reports Tell You

The COUNTER standard includes eight usage reports that relate to journals. Five of them break down usage information by journal, two provide usage at the database level, and one at the platform level. For a vendor to be considered COUNTER compliant, it must provide Journal Reports 1, 2, and 5, Database Reports 1 and 2, and Platform Report 1. These are described in table 8.7. Journal Reports 1a, 3, and 4 are optional.

The most used report for libraries is Journal Report 1 (JR1): Number of Successful Full-Text Article Requests by Month and Journal. You should use this for any database that has full text. If you're collecting statistics from a vendor that isn't COUNTER compliant, they will probably still have a report that counts article downloads that you can use instead. If you have several databases that are all on the same platform (e.g., several EBSCO databases), you can view separate JR1 reports for each one. The report really

Table 8.7. COUNTER Reports

REPORT TITLE	DESCRIPTION
Journal Report 1 (JR1)	Number of Successful Full-Text Article Requests by Month and Journal
Journal Report 2 (JR2)	Access Denied to Full-Text Articles by Month, Journal, and Category (Turnaways)
Journal Report 5 (JR5)	Number of Successful Full-Text Article Requests by Year of Publication and Journal
Database Report 1 (DB1)	Total Searches, Result Clicks, and Record Views by Month and Database
Database Report 2 (DB2)	Access Denied by Month, Database, and Category
Platform Report 1	Total Searches, Result Clicks, and Record Views by Month and Platform.

From www.ProjectCOUNTER.org

measures how often articles have been viewed, not necessarily used, as a user may have just glanced at an article and decided not to use it or could have printed out multiple copies to distribute. The use could even be from a librarian who was testing that the online access was authenticating correctly. COUNTER includes some measures to avoid overcounting usage, though. The guidelines state that a vendor should not count more than once any clicks that occur on the same link within ten seconds of each other, as this may represent a page that was loading slowly, causing the user to click on the same link again, or a user who routinely double-clicks on links instead of single-clicking.

Despite the standardization provided by COUNTER, statistics can also be inconsistent between databases due to differences in the interface. If an interface is designed so that users need to first view the full-text HTML of an article in order to get to a link for the PDF, the database will show as much as twice as many downloads as there were actual articles viewed. Bucknell (2012) suggests a simple way to compensate for this discrepancy by using a range of numbers to represent article downloads. The upper limit of the range is the total year-to-date downloads, including both HTML and PDF downloads. In theory, it's possible your users viewed each article in only one format, HTML *or* PDF, so that the total number of downloads accurately represents the number of articles that were viewed. The lower end of the range is either the HTML total or the PDF total, whichever is the larger amount. If you imagine an interface where everyone has to see the HTML of an article first in order to get to the PDF, say your users viewed eighty different articles in HTML, and forty-five times they continued clicking to download a PDF. The larger number, eighty, represents how many articles were actually viewed.

Although most libraries see JR1 as the most useful report, it is only appropriate for databases that contain full text. Some of the most well-known and reputable online databases, such as Web of Science and the Modern Language Association International Bibliography, contain abstracts and citations only. In order to know if your patrons are using these, you'll need to look at numbers on how many searches have been done. This statistic is provided in Database Report 1 (DB1): Total Searches, Result Clicks, and Record Views by Month and Database. Some libraries have observed that federated search tools or discovery tools can skew the search statistics, as each time someone does a search using a discovery tool it gets counted as a search in multiple databases. To make the statistics more accurate, the rules for DB1 state that searches done through "automated search agents" should be counted and listed separately from searches done using the database's native interface. The report lists "Regular Searches" and "Searches—federated and automated." You can use only the number of regular searches if you want to avoid the inflated numbers that you'd get from counting federated searches.

Another report you may want to use is Journal Report 2: Access Denied to Full-Text Articles by Month, Journal, and Category. This report measures turnaways, times that someone tried to access a resource and was denied. Patrons can get turned away from a database because there are already too many simultaneous users accessing it, in the case of databases that limit simultaneous users, or they can get turned away because the library only subscribes to parts of the collection. For example, if your library subscribes to three JSTOR collections, your users may be searching JSTOR and coming across articles from collections to which you don't subscribe. The turnaway report can then be a source of feedback on whether you should purchase additional user licenses or subscribe to additional full-text resources.

Collecting Data Using COUNTER Reports

Although there is a protocol, called SUSHI (Standardized Usage Statistics Harvesting Initiative), that allows for automated downloading of COUNTER reports, it is not widely used. Most libraries gather data by going to vendor websites manually and using Excel to record and organize their statistics. Keeping statistics in Excel is a way to compare data from multiple vendors and also to customize the presentation of the data so it matches the time period you want to report on. COUNTER reports only let you look at one calendar year at a time, a time frame that does not line up with most institutions' fiscal year and also differs from the academic year. By importing the data into Excel, you can rearrange the monthly numbers and add them to get a total for your fiscal year, academic year, or whatever time period you are reporting on. For example, if you want to arrange the data by academic year, you could collect the August to December statistics from one calendar year and the January to July statistics from the next calendar year and add these to get an academic year total. You do not necessarily need to rearrange the numbers to exactly match your reporting period, however. In the example below, the total number of downloads per calendar year is compared to the price for the last subscription period, even though these two time frames are not the same. The numbers still allow you to compare which databases are more heavily used than others. If you choose, you can wait to collect the data until you need it for reporting or renewal decisions, or you can collect data regularly every month. When making renewal decisions, you'll want to be able to compare usage data of one database to usage of the others, so it is a good idea to collect data on all your electronic resources on some kind of schedule, whether it is monthly or yearly, and then evaluate the subscriptions by looking at them all together.

Using the data you're able to get from the vendor websites, you will want to calculate some additional measures that take pricing into account. Table 8.8 shows an example of both the data provided by COUNTER reports and the numbers you can calculate using pricing information and COUNTER reports. The table includes a price, which is whatever was on the invoice for the subscription year ending in 2013. The article downloads are for the calendar year 2013. Keeping the data according to calendar year is probably sufficient for a cost-per-use analysis, since it is not likely that adjusting the usage data to exactly match the subscription year would change the results enough that a less-used resource would change to being highly used or vice versa. If your library uses a firm cutoff of what cost per article or cost per search is too much to pay, you'll want to be more precise about collecting usage data that exactly matches the subscription year.

Table 8.8. Comparison of Cost and Usage of Online Database Subscriptions

	PRICE FOR SUBSCRIPTION YEAR ENDING IN 2013	ARTICLE DOWNLOADS: LOWER BOUND	ARTICLE DOWNLOADS: UPPER BOUND	SEARCHES	COST PER ARTICLE	COST PER SEARCH
Database A—Business	$16,620	1,781	2,535	5,450	$9.33–$6.56	$3.05
Database B—Multidisciplinary, comes with:	$26,897	54,282	99,901	117,675	$0.48–$0.26	$0.20
i.		1,224	2,074	4,117		
ii.		686	776	7,930		
iii.		354	354	3,368		
		Total: 56,546	Total: 103,105	Total: 133,090		
Database C—History and Social Sciences	$6,550	13,616	21,531	17,445	$0.48–$0.30	$0.38
Database D—News	$5,744	5,904	5,904^	4,580	$0.97	$1.25
Database E—Psychology Index	$7,129	n/a	n/a	22,224	n/a	$0.32
Database F—Sociology Index	$1,390	n/a	n/a	4,776	n/a	$0.29
Database G—Multidisciplinary Index*	$12,850	n/a	n/a	2013	n/a	$6.38

^ Articles are only available in HTML format.

* Not COUNTER compliant

The numbers in the two rightmost columns in the table are the ones you will use to evaluate your subscriptions. These are two different measures of cost per use: cost per article download and cost per search. Cost per article is by far the most common way that libraries evaluate their online subscriptions. Here it is calculated as a range, using Bucknell's suggestion for marking a lower and upper bound of article downloads. Cost per search is another useful number, as it helps you evaluate databases without full text. The table calculates this number for all of the databases, not only the ones without full text, to give a wider basis for comparison. It is easier to see which databases are outliers in terms of very heavy or very light usage if you have more databases to look at. You'll notice that Database B in the table looks a little different from the others. This is because the subscription to the main database came with several other databases that the library would not have necessarily sought out. When calculating cost per article or cost per search, it makes sense to add together the usage of all the databases that you are getting for that price. This will give you a more accurate measure of what you are getting for your money.

While most of the time you'll be looking at usage for an entire database, occasionally you might want to look at how many times specific journals within a package are getting used. If a database is not getting much use and you are thinking of canceling it, you might want to see if a few of the journals in it are being used consistently while others get no use. If this turns out to be true, it might be cheaper to subscribe to only those journals than to the whole package. You can easily see which journals are being used by running Journal Report 1. After running the report, export it to Excel and sort by the Year-to-Date Total for article requests so the most used journals will be listed together. You can then pick a cutoff point for what you consider high usage and look up the cost of subscribing individually to any journals that had high usage in the last year or last few years. If the cost of subscribing to the high-use titles individually would be more than the package, then it is worth keeping the whole package even if its overall cost per use is high, or if you know it is padded with journals you don't want.

Reports from OCLC on Interlibrary Loan

Now that you have a good sense of which parts of your current collection are being used, you will have ideas about what to keep buying, what to renew, which sections to weed, and what subscriptions to cancel. Chapter 9 discusses specifics on using the data to make these decisions. What usage data doesn't tell you, however, is what else your users might have wanted that you don't currently offer them. To find this out, interlibrary loan (ILL) data can be useful. Some questions you can answer with ILL data are:

- What are the most requested books?
- What are the most requested journals?
- What authors are frequently requested?
- How much of each format is requested for each subject?
- What kinds or genres of materials are frequently requested—for example, research materials, textbooks, or leisure reading?

ILL data will come from the software platform that you use to manage requests. Many academic libraries, particularly larger ones, use ILLiad as their ILL management software. This is an interface to WorldShare Interlibrary Loan that provides some additional features such as the ability for users to check the status of their requests, the ability to populate the request form from databases that use Open URL linking, and customized workflow queues. Its statistics site includes reports that are geared toward answering a particular question, such as what are the most requested journals or which departments make the most ILL requests. These premade reports can be time savers, but you may want to use the raw data to create some of your own charts if you have questions that the reports don't address. WorldShare Interlibrary Loan provides access to your raw data whether you use ILLiad or WorldShare's own interface. This section will take you through the steps of turning the data into a useful report.

Health sciences libraries often use DOCLINE, an interlibrary loan system produced by the National Library of Medicine. Like ILLiad, it offers reports that answer specific questions. The relevant report for a collection evaluation is Report 1-8: Ranked List of Serial Titles Requested—Borrower. There are two versions of the report: 1-8B covers the calendar year, and 1-8A covers July through June, which is a common cycle for a fiscal year. Both versions list journal titles along with the number of successful requests for each title that were placed during the reporting period. If you work at a DOCLINE library, you can use this report to find potential journal subscriptions to add, as described in chapter 9. As DOCLINE is designed primarily for lending and borrowing journal articles, and monograph lending makes up very little of the activity in the system, there is no report of most requested monographs. Health sciences libraries that are within universities may use WorldShare for their monograph borrowing in addition to DOCLINE, in which case reports from both systems can inform collection evaluation.

If you do use WorldShare, whether by itself or in addition to DOCLINE or ILLiad, you can gather a large amount of information by manipulating the detailed list of borrower transactions. Start by downloading data from the OCLC Usage Statistics website using an administrator password. If you don't know your credentials, contact OCLC. Select OCLC WorldShare Interlibrary Loan on the left. The Borrower Resource Sharing Stats Report is the one you want. It lists every borrowing request that has come to your ILL department. As the report only shows one month at a time, you will need to run several reports, export each one to Excel, and paste them into one big report. Select a month at the top, and click Update, then Export. Repeat this for all the months you need.

Next you'll want to clean up the file a little bit to make it easier to work with. Delete the rows at the top so that the column headings are in the first row. You may want to eliminate the columns you don't need, but make sure you keep the following fields as you may use them:

- ILL Record Number
- Title
- Author
- Format
- Call Number (for LC or Dewey, whichever you use)
- ISBN
- ISSN
- Request Initiated Date

If you use any other system not described here for managing interlibrary loan, it will probably have similar fields. You can adapt these instructions using any list of transactions that you can export or copy into Excel, though you may be able to skip the next step, removing duplicate listings for the same request.

Duplicates will often show up in WorldShare if a request is placed in one month and completed the next month, as it is listed in the report for both months. To find duplicates, first sort the data by ILL record number. Then in the third row, first empty column (column J in figure 8.3), you can use the following formula to label each request as either a duplicate or unique:

$$=IF(A3=A2,"duplicate","unique")$$

The example assumes your ILL record numbers are in column A. This formula checks if the record number on the third line (in cell A3) is the same as the record number on the second line (in cell A2). If the numbers are the same, the formula will output the word "duplicate," and if not it will output the word "unique." To fill in the formula all the way down, click on the cell where you typed it. Then move the cursor to the bottom right corner of the cell and hover until you see a plus sign instead of the cursor arrow. This is shown in figure 8.3. Click and drag the cursor down the column. It will fill in the formula, incrementing the numbers on each row so that it checks whether A4=A3, A5=A4, and so on.

To remove the duplicates, you will need to sort by the field that says "unique" or "duplicate" (labeled Uniqueness in figure 8.3). However, because the field has a formula

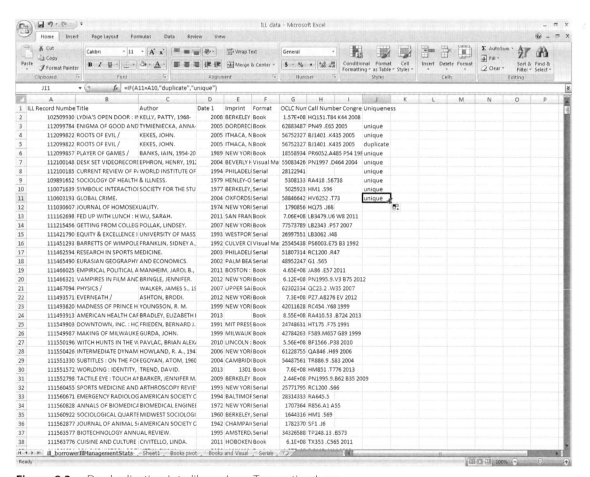

Figure 8.3. De-duplicating Interlibrary Loan Transaction Logs.

comparing one cell to the one above it, some of the values will change if you rearrange the rows. To get around this, first, copy the spreadsheet, then go to a new tab and right-click the top cell. Select Paste Special, then Values. This will paste the data including the words "unique" or "duplicate" just as they are without recalculating the formula. You can then re-sort the data on this second spreadsheet tab by uniqueness. Now delete everything with a value of "duplicate." This will be easy once the duplicates are all grouped together.

The next step is separating book requests from journal requests or requests for other formats so that you can analyze each separately. Sort the spreadsheet by Format. Copy and paste all the serials requests onto a new tab and the book requests onto another so you can analyze these separately. Make sure to name the tabs, as you'll have at least four by now. Logical names for the tabs would be Raw Data; De-duplicated: All Formats; De-duplicated: Books; and De-duplicated: Journals. You can decide if you want to include visual materials on the books tab or analyze these separately. You might not want to analyze a format that you deliberately do not collect, such as dissertations or musical scores, though it is worth a glance to see if you are getting large numbers of requests for these items, in case this influences you to change your policy.

To find out the most requested journals, books, or authors, you can use a pivot table. ILLiad users will have access to automatically generated lists of most requested journals and monographs but can use these instructions to create a list of most requested authors. Go to the tab that you want to pull the data from, either De-duplicated: Books or De-duplicated: Journals. From the menu bar, select Insert, then Pivot Table. A new tab will open, containing a chart on the right showing the fields you can use in your table, as shown earlier in figure 8.1. Select Title as the row label and Count of Title as the values. The pivot table will count how many times each title appears. You probably want to then sort the table by Count of Title so that the titles will be listed in order of most to least requested. You can create pivot tables for journal titles, book titles, and authors in the same way.

You can also sort ILL requests by call number so that you can analyze them by subject. You'll want to assign subject categorizations that match what you used when analyzing circulation statistics. Assigning subjects to the requests has to be a manual process, similar to the process explained above for circulation. You will probably only do this for books and not journals, as your local usage data for journals won't be sorted by call number. Sort the report by call number, then in a new column assign each item to one of your subject categories, using the same categories you used for the circulation data. You can then calculate how many and what percentage of ILLs are requested for each department, LC class, or conspectus division. Chapter 9 talks about how to compare ILL data to circulation to see which of your programs may be underserved by your current book collection.

Key Points

Usage statistics can be complicated because use is calculated so differently for different formats. Although you can't compare different formats to each other, you can still use usage data to tell you a lot about what subjects, formats, or specific titles your users prefer.

- Circulation data for print books can tell you where you should collect more, identify sections to weed, and possibly reveal sections in which certain books get used heavily while others are never checked out.

- Evaluating e-books is very different than evaluating print books due to the variety of ways libraries pay for e-books. You may be evaluating subscriptions to make renewal decisions, or evaluating a patron-driven acquisitions program to see how it differs from traditional acquisitions.
- When evaluating usage of any online resources, try to use COUNTER-compliant reports when possible. Journal Report 1, Database Report 1, and Book Report 2 are the most commonly used.
- When you are evaluating any kind of subscription, pricing information is relevant. You can use it to calculate a ratio of cost to the number of times someone uses the resources, usually called cost per use.
- Interlibrary loan data can supplement other usage data by telling you what your users want that you don't have.

Because there is so much usage data you could potentially collect and many different ways to manipulate the data to answer different questions, these numbers can be very helpful in making collection management decisions. Chapter 9 describes ways to use this data for decision making.

References

Bucknell, Terry. 2012. "Garbage In, Gospel Out: Twelve Reasons Why Librarians Should Not Accept Cost-Per-Download Figures at Face Value." *Serials Librarian* 64, no. 2 (August): 192–212.

Danielson, Robert. 2012. "A Dual Approach to Assessing Collection Development and Acquisitions for Academic Libraries." *Library Collections, Acquisitions, and Technical Services* 36, nos. 3–4: 84–96.

Knievel, Jennifer E., Heather Wicht, and Lynn Silipigni Connaway. 2006. "Use of Circulation Statistics and Interlibrary Loan Data in Collection Management." *College & Research Libraries* 67, no. 1 (January): 35–49.

Lowe, Randall, and Lynda Aldana. 2013. "Biz of Acq—Gathering Data: How Two USMAI Libraries Are Using Ebook Statistics." *Against the Grain* 25, no. 3 (June): 64–67, 73.

Price, Jason S., and John D. McDonald. 2009. "Beguiled by Bananas: A Retrospective Study of the Usage and Breadth of Patron vs. Librarian Acquired Ebook Collections." *Library Staff Publications and Research* 10. Claremont, CA: Claremont Colleges.

Project COUNTER. 2012. "The Counter Code of Practice for E-Resources: Release 4." http://www.projectcounter.org/r4/COPR4.pdf.

CHAPTER 9

Usage Statistics—Interpreting and Acting on the Data

Benefits and Limitations of Usage Data

LIBRARIES VERY COMMONLY RELY ON USAGE STATISTICS in making collections decisions, particularly related to renewing subscriptions. Because there are so many kinds of data you can collect relating to usage, there are also many ways to incorporate usage statistics in your ongoing collection development. Depending on your library's mission, usage might play a large or a small role in your selection decisions. Almost any library would probably say they want to provide access to the materials their patrons want. In practice, though, there are usually some limits to this goal. If your patrons want DVDs of popular TV series, and your main mission is to support teaching and research, these materials might be outside the scope of your collection. On the flip side, for archival purposes you might deliberately collect some materials that very few patrons use, such as your own students' dissertations. Before making decisions based on the usage data you've collected, spend a little time thinking about the extent of your commitment to providing materials that will be heavily used.

Making decisions based on usage means having two assumptions: patrons are the best judges of their own needs, and use is a sign of value. The first assumption does not always hold up when working with students, however. Students, particularly undergraduates, at times use journals that are not scholarly or are inappropriate for their discipline, or books that are outdated. Your students could be reading articles from trade magazines that were included in online journal packages as filler, overlooking seminal works because they are old, or citing only what they can find online and ignoring the library's print books and journals. Because students are not always skilled at choosing the best resource for their purpose, what they are using might not necessarily be the best resources for the library to buy. Walters argues that "the goal of the [academic] library is to educate students," which it can do by "guid[ing] patrons to works that . . . experts . . . have found to be most useful" (2012: 204). The educational mission of an academic library does not mean usage statistics are useless, however. By combining usage data with your usual selection criteria, you should be able to build a collection that is both high quality and relevant to user needs.

The second major assumption of usage statistics is that usage equals value. A recent pamphlet on budgeting shows how common this assumption is. Of eight librarians quoted, five mentioned usage statistics as their major way of measuring the library's value (DeCooman, 2010: 4). An alternate view is presented by Bourg (2013), assistant university librarian for public services at Stanford University, who questions whether libraries should treat usage as a measure of value. Something that is rarely used at the moment might be useful for future research, particularly if that research is historical and in-depth. The item could then become valuable to the person doing the research, although it will still have low usage. Bourg also argues that libraries have a responsibility to promote diversity of information, and that niche topics will never find their audience when libraries only purchase what is popular. Diversity is its own value, she says, distinct from popularity. Although most libraries will have financial reasons not to pay for materials they don't expect to get used, if you can articulate other values of your library, such as diversity or historical preservation, you will be able to balance these with usage statistics when making collections decisions.

In practice, almost all libraries use usage data in some way. Budget constraints make it hard to justify renewing a subscription that doesn't get used or purchasing books on topics that you have no evidence would be of interest to your patrons. Furthermore, usage can tell you a lot about what subjects and formats your patrons are using, even if some of your patron populations are not expert enough for you to trust their judgment on which specific titles are most important. The data you have collected can give you many ideas of what to purchase or what current collection habits to continue, and you can then select materials based on your existing policies and values as well as expert recommendations.

Even if your philosophy and budget lead you to rely heavily on usage data in decision making, keep in mind that usage data is not a perfect scientific measurement of how much any item actually was used. Someone could borrow an item and not read it or use something in-house and not check it out. If your checkout periods are different for different patron groups—say, if undergraduates get four weeks and graduate students get all semester—then research-level materials might have fewer checkouts because the people who needed them were able to borrow them just once without renewing. Faculty sometimes borrow books and keep them in their offices for long periods of time if there is no penalty to them for doing so, and these books will show only one checkout for the time they sit on the faculty member's shelf. If you do not allow recalls, then it is possible that more people wanted to use a given book than actually borrowed it, but they could not do so while someone else had it out. Additionally, some of your checkouts were probably for interlibrary lending, meaning these books were actually used by patrons of other libraries. As with all the data in this book, the fact that usage data is not a perfect measure does not mean you can't use it. You will be comparing some parts of your collection to other parts, and since the same factors affect your data equally across the board the comparisons are still valid. You can use the data to see general patterns and can then look more closely at specific sections of the collection to understand in more depth how they are being used.

Interpretations of Circulation Data

One of the major kinds of usage data that libraries collect is for circulation of print books. In order to evaluate your print circulation, you began by collecting counts of the holdings in each section that you wanted to analyze. It can be tempting to draw conclusions based on these numbers by themselves, particularly if it turns out you own strikingly few books on a subject and feel that just can't be enough! Although in some cases the holdings count does matter—for example, if you are doing quantitative benchmarking—when doing a usage analysis, try not to draw too many conclusions about the absolute size of any section before you've looked at whether the books are circulating. You will want to take the holdings into account when the number is especially high or low, but for the most part holdings data are useful at this point to give context to circulation numbers. Circulation rates will tell you whether you are serving patrons' needs or not.

The most important numbers for a usage evaluation are the ones you calculated using information about both holdings and circulation. Chapter 8 showed you how to make some calculations comparing holdings and circulation. These ratios, shown in table 8.1, are checkouts to holdings and percent checkouts to percent holdings. The checkouts-to-holdings ratio is the number of checkouts in each section divided by the number of items in the section. This number shows how much overall activity each section is getting. The second ratio, percent checkouts to percent holdings, is the percentage of all circulation accounted for by this section divided by the percentage of the entire circulating collection that this section accounts for. This number measures whether a section is responsible for more circulation activity than you'd expect given its size. Because both of these are measures of whether a section is heavily used, you don't need to look at both. Use whichever makes more sense to you.

There is not necessarily an ideal checkouts-to-holdings value that you are looking for. It would be nice to see that all the books in the collection had been used in the course of a few years, but this is unlikely to happen. To gauge what counts as a heavily used section, look at the total ratio of checkouts to holdings for the whole book collection. Table 8.1 lists this at the bottom: the ratio is 0.313. This ratio means that, on average, just under a third of all the books in the collection were borrowed during the time period being studied. The number doesn't tell how many books were checked out. Maybe fewer than a third of the books were borrowed, but those books got used over and over, driving up the number of checkouts. This ratio just gives you a general sense of which parts of the collection are getting a lot of activity, so you can decide which sections to target first when you go in for a closer look at usage. Heavy activity is anything above the average for your collection. In the collection that is described in the chart, you could consider anything with a ratio higher than 0.313 to be relatively highly used and sections with a lower ratio to be lightly used.

The second ratio, percent checkouts to percent holdings, is another way to see which sections are most heavily used. This measure has a built-in comparison of the usage of each section to its size. If every book in the entire collection was used once, a section that made up 5 percent of the holdings would also have 5 percent of the checkouts, and the ratio would be 1. This is the case with education, shown in table 8.1. Books on education make up 4.47 percent of the library's collection and account for 4.47 percent of all book circulation. Art, psychology, and sociology, with ratios higher than 1, are all used more than you'd expect, given the size of the collection in those areas. Chemistry, in contrast, is only used a quarter as much as you'd expect. These books are taking up 3.26 percent of the shelf space while only making up less than 1 percent of all books that are checked out, resulting in a percent-checkouts-to-percent-holdings ratio of 0.25.

Because the percent-checkouts-to-percent-holdings ratio and the checkouts-to-holdings ratio measure the same thing, the rest of this section will discuss only the checkouts-to-holdings ratio. If you have used percent checkouts to percent holdings instead, anytime this section mentions a checkouts-to-holdings ratio that is above (or below) the average for your collection, you will instead look for a percent-checkouts-to-percent-holdings ratio that is above (or below) 1.

Because neither of these two ratios actually tells you how many of the books in each section are getting used, there is one more number you should use to analyze your circulation. This is the percentage of books checked out, shown in table 8.2. It is useful to know the percentage of unique books used in your entire collection so you can compare the different sections to the overall collection. In the example given in chapter 8, 18.90 percent of all the circulating books in the library were borrowed during the four-year period being studied. In comparison to this figure, the psychology section looks very heavily used, with 35.58 percent of its books checked out, while chemistry is very lightly used, with only 5.59 percent of its books checked out.

To some extent, the percentage of each section that gets used is affected by whether or not you've recently weeded unused items. Weeding will decrease the holdings count and therefore increase the percentage of the section that is borrowed. Conversely, a section that you have not weeded in a long time might have a very small percentage of its books used even though there could be useful books in the section. It might contain some books patrons use a lot, as well as many books no one is using. To make an educated guess of whether the low percentage of books checked out is due to a lack of weeding, you can look at the holdings counts. In table 8.2, you'll see that psychology and chemistry have almost the same number of books (3,162 and 3,115, respectively), yet almost seven times as many psychology books have been borrowed. This makes a case that there is not much demand for chemistry books and more demand for psychology books, rather than that the psychology collection only looks more heavily used because it was more recently weeded.

If you were able to get enough data from your ILS that you have a checkouts-to-holdings ratio and a percentage of unique books checked out, putting together these two ratios can give you a fuller picture of each section. Table 9.1 presents four possible scenarios based on the possible combinations of findings.

Table 9.1. Scenarios for Circulation Data

CHECKOUTS-TO-HOLDINGS RATIO	WHAT IT MEANS	PERCENTAGE OF UNIQUE BOOKS CHECKED OUT	WHAT IT MEANS	PUTTING IT TOGETHER	ACTION STEPS
Higher for this section than for the collection as a whole	This section gets used a lot, relatively speaking.	More than the percentage of your whole collection that was checked out	Many books in this section are useful to your patrons.	Overall strong usage.	Keep collecting and try to get even more.
Higher for this section than for the collection as a whole	This section gets used a lot, relatively speaking.	Less than the percentage of your whole collection that was checked out	Few books in this section are useful to your patrons.	A few books are getting used a lot, but most not at all.	You may want to weed and also collect more books similar to the ones being used.
Lower for this section than for the collection as a whole	This section does not get used very much, relatively speaking.	More than the percentage of your whole collection that was checked out	Many books in this section are useful to your patrons.	A lot of books are being used, but only once or a few times each.	You're doing okay. Keep collecting in this area.
Lower for this section than for the collection as a whole	This section does not get used very much, relatively speaking.	Less than the percentage of your whole collection that was checked out	Few books in this section are useful to your patrons.	The books in this section are not useful to your patrons.	Weed unused books, if this is your policy. Also try to figure out if there is a need for other books on this subject that you don't have.

Book Selection and Deselection

Deselection

Two of the above scenarios have an action step of weeding. If you have a historic preservation mission or reason to believe that future researchers might want your older books someday, weeding might not be the best decision for you. Some libraries that for whatever reason do not discard less-used materials are instead moving them to off-site storage. Some of the decision-making strategies in this section are applicable to off-site storage as well.

As table 9.1 shows, the sections you'll probably want to weed are those in which the percentage of unique books borrowed is less than the percentage of your whole collection that was borrowed. The size of the section could also be a factor in deciding to weed. If you are concerned about space, it makes sense to start by weeding areas that have a large absolute number of unused books. Even if the percentage of books checked out is high, in a huge section this still means a lot of shelf space is taken up by items you may not want. Look at the holdings count for each section and start with where you think you'll have the most weeding to do. This could be a large section with an average percentage of unique books checked out or a medium-sized section with a low percentage of unique books checked out. You could use the same strategy to identify parts of your collection to move to off-site storage.

Before you begin weeding, you probably want to gather a little more data on the section in question. Although chapter 8 suggested collecting circulation data for a four-year time period, when it comes to picking specific books to remove from the shelves, you may want to look at circulation over a longer period. You do not necessarily want to be so harsh as to get rid of all items that were not used in the last four years, especially if they may have been used just five years ago. After using the percentage of unique books checked out to identify which sections to focus on, it will probably be helpful to run a report on these sections that lists all titles used over a somewhat longer time period. The CREW Manual (Larson, 2008) provides detailed weeding criteria specific to different subjects, noting that usage is a more important criterion for some subjects than others and that books get outdated at different rates depending on the subject. Books on computers, for example, become outdated after three years, books about current events after five years, and books about folklore or philosophy almost never. Run reports on usage of specific sections using a time range tailored to the subject. You can then take this to the shelf and pull the unused books as candidates to weed.

You will most likely not be automatically removing everything that was not checked out in your chosen time period, however. As noted in chapter 7, sometimes you'll want to leave an older or little-used book on the shelf because it is a classic. You can use authoritative lists to identify classics and then make a "do not weed" note in the online catalog (using a nonpublic field) for future librarians at your institution. Another piece of information to consider when making weeding decisions, described in chapter 5, is looking at overlap with consortial partners. You may want to keep titles that few of your consortial partners own so that the books will be available if someone needs them. If you have a collaborative arrangement with other schools that commits you to collecting in a certain area, you will need to look at the terms of the arrangement before weeding.

Another time you might decide not to weed an item with low use is if you know that faculty really wish their students would use it. You won't always know that this is the case, but if you are confused by low usage—maybe because you know there's a course on this topic or you remember someone requesting you buy this item—ask the faculty how they feel about the materials. You don't necessarily want to tell them you're weeding, as they might protest against any weeding, but you can say you noticed a particular series or subject wasn't getting much use and ask if they know why. It might be that they prefer students to use journal articles anyway, or they may tell you they encourage students to use this but have not been successful. You or an instruction librarian then can talk to them about how to encourage use, and you can also make a note not to weed these items for the time being.

Selection

As table 9.1 shows, there are times that your circulation data for a given section will tell you that you should do more purchasing. Purchasing is clearly desirable if many of the books in the section are getting borrowed and they are being borrowed frequently—that is, both the checkouts-to-holdings ratio and the percentage of unique books checked out are high. For the sections in which you want to purchase more, use your current collection strategies or the ones described in the various "Interpreting and Acting on the Data" chapters in this book. You could look for lists of core titles or best titles of the year. You could use WorldCat to identify the most widely owned books on a topic. Adjusting the collection levels on an approval plan is also a way to ensure you'll receive more on this topic in the future.

You may also want to buy more books for a section that has a low percentage of unique books checked out if certain books in the section are being used a lot (i.e., the checkouts-to-holdings ratio is high). The tricky thing in this situation is purchasing more books that are similar to the ones being used rather than to the ones that aren't being used. Looking more closely at specific titles could help you figure out what makes the borrowed books better than the unused ones. You can go to the shelf or run reports that list the titles in that section and the titles borrowed. One difference that would be obvious to spot is if the books that are getting used are newer than the unused ones. In this case, you can just buy some newer books on the subject. Some questions to ask yourself about your highly used books is what their audience is, what publishers and authors recur, and what the purpose of the books is. Are they summaries of the field, practical how-to guides, or original research? You can also ask faculty what they would like more of. They may describe books in terms you haven't thought of, giving you new ways to look at what you're collecting.

Interlibrary Loan Data as a Supplement to Circulation Data

Another way both to get ideas of what to purchase and to understand your patrons' needs is to compare the circulation data with the interlibrary loan data. Putting the two numbers together can tell you how much of you patrons' needs were met at their home library versus how much they needed to get elsewhere. There are two things to keep in mind when looking at ILL data. One is that you cannot expect to have everything your users need. This is especially true at higher levels of research, as each doctoral student or professor could be researching a different topic from the other, and you will not have specialized resources for all of them. You are not aiming to have zero ILL borrowing requests. The second point is that patrons are more likely to use materials that are in their home library than materials they need to request. If something was requested twice on ILL in a year, the same book or journal might have gotten used more than twice if you owned it. Similarly, even if something has never been requested on ILL, it still might get used if it were on hand locally. If very little is requested on ILL overall, this might mean that your users don't need anything you don't have, or it could mean they are avoiding using ILL for some reason. Nevertheless, when your patrons do use ILL, they are sending a message about their needs.

Analyzing ILL Data by Subject

As shown in chapter 8, you can analyze interlibrary loan data by subject or by looking at the specific authors and titles that were requested. Starting with the broader analysis of subjects, you can compare ILL requests for certain subjects to circulation of your own books on those subjects. If you divided up your book requests by call number range, you can divide the number of checkouts in each range to the number of ILL requests in the same range. This will produce a circulation-to-ILL ratio, which shows how often your patrons got their information needs met at their home library versus another. If your circulation-to-ILL ratio is, for instance, fourteen, this means that your patrons borrowed fourteen books from your library for every one book they needed to request through ILL. A result of one would mean patrons were using books from your own library in equal amounts to borrowing books through ILL. A result less than one means patrons are using ILL books more often than books you own. As with the other ratios, there is not a particular number that will be the target for all libraries. Certainly, you want patrons to be able to find most, or even a large majority, of what they need in your own library, but there is no absolute way to define what ratio you're looking for. You can use the average for your whole collection as a baseline. Take the total number of checkouts of your book collection over a certain time period and divide it by the number of ILL requests for books in that same period. This is the average circulation-to-ILL ratio for the collection. It is possible that you'll feel intuitively dissatisfied with the average. If this is the case, you need to improve your selection strategies in general, which you can do using many of the ideas in this book. If the average is higher than one and feels okay to you, look at each section to see if it is above or below the average. There are four possible scenarios you could find, shown in figure 9.1.

Purchasing Specific Books Based on ILL Requests

ILL data will not only tell you where you need to purchase more books, it can also provide guidance on what books to purchase. Although some people do not believe a past request for a book is necessarily an indicator of future demand, there is some evidence that patron requests make good purchases. Remember Price and McDonald's (2009) study on patron-driven acquisitions of e-books, described in the previous chapter. It compared five libraries and found that in all of them books that were purchased through the PDA model were used more times after purchase than books that were selected by librarians. Sample data from Arcadia University (table 8.5) showed the same result. If this is true

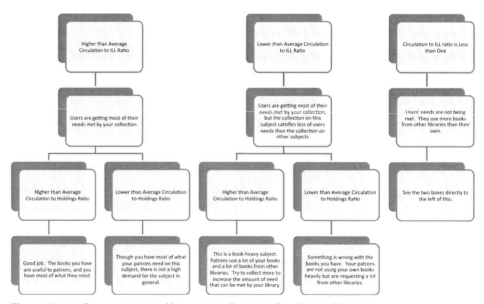

Figure 9.1. Comparing Interlibrary Loan Rates to Circulation Rates.

of e-books, there is no reason that patron requests for print books would not also be an indication that there will be repeated demand for these books.

To shorten the time lag between patrons demonstrating their needs through ILL requests and the library purchasing books to meet this need, you could implement a patron-driven acquisitions program for print books using some of the methods described in chapter 7. For ILLiad users, the Getting It System Toolkit (GIST) can facilitate this process. It allows you to add fields to the ILL request form asking requestors if they would prefer the library purchase the book. On the staff side, you can configure the form to pull in additional information to help you decide whether or not to purchase the requested book, such as which other libraries in your consortium have it, price, and availability. To make the decision process quicker, many libraries come up with basic guidelines about which requests they will route to acquisitions and which to ILL. Guidelines could be a price cap, a limit to recent publications, the scholarly nature of the material, and format. Remember that you don't have to buy everything your patrons request, even if it is recent and scholarly. Your goal is not to reduce ILL requests to zero but to build a collection that gets used and satisfies a large part, though not all, of your patrons' needs.

If you implement patron-driven acquisitions for print books, you can compare the circulation and ILL statistics again after the new procedure has been in place for at least a year. If possible, it makes sense to count the first use of the purchased books as an ILL request and further use as circulation. If this isn't possible, another way to evaluate whether the program is useful is to compare the total checkouts of preselected purchases to checkouts of items you purchased in response to an ILL request, similar to Price and McDonald's (2009) study of e-books. This will tell you whether the patron-driven acquisitions program for print is generating purchases that are getting used.

If you do not plan to implement a patron-driven print program, you can still use ILL transaction records to improve your collection. Chapter 8 showed you how to make a pivot table listing how often each book or author was requested. You'll want to find a little information on the books and authors before buying them. It is possible that a lot of the items your users request on ILL are things you don't own because it is not your policy to collect them, such as textbooks, fiction best sellers, or DVDs of popular television shows. Look up the authors to see what kinds of materials they write, and check book titles to see if they are appropriate for your library. Of the materials you decide are appropriate, you can pick which to buy based on how many times they were requested. If you're able to calculate the average number of times a book in your collection circulates (total checkouts divided by total number of books checked out), this is a good number to use as a cutoff point, ordering any ILL books that were borrowed more than your own books were. You can also use your budget as a deciding factor. Figure out how much you can spend, and start by ordering the most requested books and keep going until you've used up the money. With authors, you can also keep them in mind for future purchases, adding them to your approval plan or creating alerts to see when they've published new books.

If the data showed there was something wrong with your collection—your patrons are not borrowing your books but are requesting other ones on ILL—it can be hard to figure out what to do differently. Purchasing some of the requested books and authors should help. You can also compare used (via ILL) and unused (on your shelves) books using the ideas above concerning weeding and purchasing books.

ILL data might also prompt you to reconsider your policies about what you do and don't collect. It is quite likely that many of the items your users are requesting on ILL are things you deliberately don't buy. One type of material that libraries often exclude from their purchasing, despite high demand, is textbooks. Greiner (2012) makes a case for libraries to purchase textbooks since rising costs have made more students unable to purchase their own copies. If you are open to considering this change in policy, you can use interlibrary loan to figure out how often your students are requesting textbooks via the library. Figuring out if something is or isn't a textbook requires more detail than the statistical reports show. Look for book summaries on Amazon or Books in Print, or look at the publisher to see if they are a textbook publisher. You won't need to look up every book to get a sense of whether textbooks are a common request. You can also look for other formats that you don't currently collect, maybe audiobooks or CDs, to see if you should start buying them.

E-Book Purchasing Models

Since the e-book data described in chapter 8 was all collected with a specific goal in mind, using the data is straightforward. Most of the data on PDA is geared toward justifying the concept of buying e-books with this model. If you don't yet have PDA, you can use published studies of other libraries to make a case for starting a program at your library. If you started doing PDA with a pilot project, data on your own PDA program can be very useful. Usually the people deciding whether or not to implement PDA are inside the library, unless you are seeking additional money and need to make the case to a budget director. Either way, simply showing that books purchased through PDA get used again will send a message. For someone outside the library, you may not want to show the comparison between PDA and preselected books, as you don't know what conclusions your audience will draw from the fact that the library is buying books that don't get used. You might compare the uses per title for PDA and preselected books but leave out the information on how many preselected books actually don't get used.

For subscription e-book packages, usage data serves a very obvious purpose, as it is an important factor in the decision to renew or cancel a subscription. You can use both cost per use and use per book (both shown in table 8.4) as ways to judge the usefulness of a subscription. The table illustrates why cost per use is an important measure. You can see that Collection A has by far the highest price and the second-lowest number of books, which might have made it seem like an unwise purchase when it was new. Usage is astronomical, however. Each book is used on average over two thousand times, and the cost per use is the lowest of any of the collections, making this a very economical purchase. In the opposite scenario, the literary criticism collection, Collection B, initially looked like a desirable purchase because of its reputation and because it was requested by faculty. From a usage or monetary perspective, however, it looks less appealing. The collection was used only four times in 2013. Although four uses in a year would be low for any online resource, being able to compare this package to others makes the case stronger. Having comparative data is especially useful for subscriptions whose usage is less extreme. Collections C, D, and E all have usage patterns that would be hard to judge without a point of comparison. The chart allows you to look for outliers in both cost per use and use per book. You do not need to follow the official statistical definition of outliers; it probably is enough to just look at what numbers seem especially high or low compared to the others. In this case, Collection D is a bit of an outlier with its cost per use of $17.19, though it is much closer to the norm than Collection B's cost per use of $374.25. When deciding whether or not to cancel the outliers, ask whether a given collection supports a program that has few other resources or if it could be a classic or standard work. You might also have political reasons for deciding not to cancel something with low use. In many cases, though, you will be able to make cancellation decisions based on usage.

Comparison of E-Books to Print Books

Your e-book data can also help shed light on your print circulation, at least informally if not systematically. If you noticed earlier that circulation was low for a certain area, it might be that the patrons who read on this subject prefer e-books. Maybe they are especially comfortable reading online, or maybe they are distance learners or commuters who are not on campus enough to make checking out print books convenient. E-book data can't be compared directly to print book data, though, for several reasons. Unless your e-book vendors provide reports that include call numbers, it will be very hard to categorize your usage data by subject. Also, if you are new to collecting e-books and have only purchased them for a few subjects, you won't have e-book data for all the subjects for which you have circulation data. It is likely, however, that some of your packages, whether they are subscriptions or perpetual access, are focused on a particular subject. For the sections of your collection that had low circulation, think about whether you have an e-book collection on the same subject. If its usage is high, then the low circulation is more the result of those patrons preferring electronic resources to print than a sign that you are collecting the wrong books.

For some purposes, you will not necessarily care which titles or even which subjects are being used but will want to look more broadly at usage of online materials versus print. Your circulation data may show, for example, that overall usage of print is declining. This could be a sign that you should shift your budget to spend more on online materials, unless use of these is declining as well. Some libraries are facing outside pressure to repurpose shelf space within the library based on the assumption that print books are no longer used. Even if your users are comfortable with e-books, not every book is available to libraries in this form and your patrons may still be using print books when this is their only option or even when the same titles are available electronically. Data comparing the total number of print circulations over a number of years can demonstrate that your patrons still use print and can help your case for retaining both the budget and the space to maintain a print collection. If circulation is consistently declining, however, the data can make you more comfortable removing books and using the shelf space for another purpose.

Renewals, Cancelations, and New Subscriptions

For journals, usage statistics are also most often used to decide what to renew and what to cut. You can look at either the absolute number of uses and select a minimum that a resource needs to have in order for you to renew it, or you can look at the cost per use, or a combination of both. To some extent, your budget constraints will affect what your cutoff points are, as your decisions will be different when you need to cut rigorously than when you can afford to renew everything.

When picking a minimum amount of use, you can choose a number that seems reasonable in comparison to your library's overall patterns of journal use. If your most used journal gets forty uses a year, then keeping a journal with four uses might be reasonable, whereas if the most used journal is used three hundred times, then the four uses of the other journal will seem negligible. Anything that is online is likely to get used more than the print subscriptions, so the minimum number of uses you'll pick will probably be higher. This is both because electronic journals are more accessible and because statistics for print materials usually undercount usage due to patrons doing their own reshelving. A common minimum is five uses; this is the amount you would be able to borrow from interlibrary loan without paying copyright fees. If a journal to which you currently subscribe is currently used less than five times a year, relying on ILL will be more cost-effective than subscribing.

If you are using cost per use as the deciding factor in renewals, you can decide on a maximum cost per use by looking for outliers among your subscriptions. Another way to set the maximum is to calculate the average cost of an interlibrary loan transaction to determine if it is costing you more or less to subscribe to the journal or database than to request the needed articles on ILL. Keep in mind if you are using cost per use to make renewal decisions that journals in the natural sciences usually cost more than those in the humanities. To avoid biasing your collection against sciences, you can set a different maximum cost per use for each disciplinary area. You could also look at both the cost per use and the absolute number of uses together before making a decision. If a science journal has an unusually high cost per use but was used more than many of your cheaper journals, it is probably worth renewing.

There will be times when you won't cut the subscriptions that cost-per-use data suggests you should. Relying strictly on cost per use could lead to an imbalanced collection, so look over each journal to see if it merits an exception for some reason. You might hold onto some subscriptions that benefit very small programs. Although these journals will show low use due to the small number of students taking relevant classes, the library needs to support even the small programs to some extent, and accreditation requirements may dictate a certain amount of journal holdings. Think about how many journals you have that support each department, and don't cut to the point where you're no longer supporting them. If you compared the number of journals that serve each department with the enrollment of each department, as suggested in chapter 4, this data can help you see which departments are underserved in terms of the number of journals. Other times, you may want to cancel something but be unable to, as many packages that come from publishers include a commitment to maintain spending levels at a certain amount. Make sure to note somewhere your reasons for keeping the journals with a high cost per use so you don't need to run through the same decision-making process year after year.

Single Subscriptions

For print journals, renewal decisions will primarily involve reshelving counts. Gather the data from your tally sheet and combine it with pricing information from your subscription agent to calculate cost per use. Because of the notorious inaccuracy of reshelving counts, you'll want to collect some anecdotal feedback from users before making a cancellation. If something has a low reshelving count, you can ask relevant faculty if they use the journal. It's better to phrase the question as "Have you been using this?" than "Is it okay if we cancel this subscription?" Faculty may be opposed to canceling subscriptions to anything they might need in the future and are probably not aware of your budget details, so try to keep the decision in the library's hands while taking faculty input into account.

Single subscriptions to electronic journals are similar to print journals. You can look at the total number of uses per year or calculate a cost per use. Remember that usage will almost always be higher for electronic resources, so you might use a different cutoff point for cancelations.

Journal Packages and Citation Databases

For electronic journal packages, renewals decisions are a little more complicated, although the process is similar to the process for e-book subscriptions. You'll be looking at the cost per use for each package, with use measured in two different ways: article downloads and searches. If you used a range of numbers to represent the full-text article downloads, according to Bucknell's (2012) suggestion, calculate your cost per article as a range also. Cost per article is the most commonly used usage measure, though you'll use cost per search for those databases that do not have any full-text articles. The packages that do have full text are likely to contain many titles that you don't need, but don't worry about how many titles in the package are not being used. If the package overall has a good cost per use, then it is worth owning.

The only time renewing a highly used journal package would not be financially smart is if it would be cheaper to get the few well-used journals in it separately. If you think that very few journals in a package are being used, use JR1 to see which ones these are. For every journal whose usage exceeds your minimum for individual subscriptions, look up pricing for an individual subscription. If the total cost of subscribing to all the well-used journals as individual subscriptions exceeds the cost of the package, then it is worth continuing to subscribe to the package for the sake of those journals.

The reverse situation can also occur, where you might be able to find a package that will include journals you currently subscribe to individually and will cost less than all the individual subscriptions. A good way to check for this is to look up your individual subscriptions in CUFTS (http://cufts2.lib.sfu.ca/MaintTool/public/search). CUFTS is an open-source electronic resource management system and link resolver created by Simon Fraser University. The knowledge base associated with CUFTS is free to search online. You can look up a journal and find a listing of which databases index it and which include its content full-text. Look up all your individual subscriptions and make a spreadsheet noting which database packages include these journals. Check for embargoes so that you don't accidentally cancel a subscription that includes the current year and replace it with a package in which the current year is embargoed. Then review the spreadsheet to see which packages appear on it repeatedly, meaning they include more than one of the titles you currently subscribe to individually. Get a title list from the vendor that sells the package to double-check that it really has the titles. Title lists are often available on vendor websites, or a customer service representative can send you one. Ask the representative for a price quote as well, so you can see if the package would cost less than the individual subscriptions. Although it might contain a lot you don't need, if it also has what you do need and at a lower cost, it is a cost-effective move.

Adding Journal Subscriptions

If you have the money, you may also want to add subscriptions to journals that you expect will be used in the future. There are two ways to gather evidence on what new subscriptions would get used: interlibrary loan data and COUNTER Journal Report 2. To analyze your ILL data, use the pivot table of journal titles that you created to find the most wanted journals. DOCLINE libraries will use Report 1-8: Ranked List of

Serial Titles Requested—Borrower. You could consider subscribing to anything that was requested more than five times because of the copyright law mentioned earlier. You could also start with the most wanted journal and keep moving down the list until you run out of money. Make sure, of course, that the journals fit the library's usual collection development criteria.

COUNTER reports can provide evidence on what new subscriptions would be good to add as well. Under the current guidelines, JR2: Access Denied to Full-Text Articles by Month, Journal, and Category (the "turnaway" report) provides data on two situations. One is when a user is denied access because the number of allowed simultaneous users has been exceeded. If this happens often relative to the number of times users successfully access the resource, you should try to buy an additional license. You can choose how to define "often," whether it means users are denied access on one-quarter of their attempts, one-tenth, or some other amount.

The other situation described by JR2 is when a user is denied access to something because the library does not subscribe to the item. This is most likely to happen when the user is searching a publisher's platform and the library subscribes to some but not all of the journals on the platform. Patrons will see an article and click on a link for full text, only to be told they need to log in or pay if they want to view the article. Vendors sometimes draw libraries' attention to the turnaway reports as a sales tactic, as the report provides evidence that you should buy an additional user license to their site or subscribe to more of their journals. Turnaways are not quite as strong an indicator of patron need as interlibrary loan requests. After all, if a patron clicked on an article, found they could not view the full text, and then decided not to request the article on interlibrary loan, this person has made a decision that the article is not essential. If you are considering adding a subscription to a journal based on its appearance in the turnaway report, use a higher threshold for how many turnaways it should have than you would use as your threshold for ILL requests.

Key Points

Usage data can provide a wealth of information on how your library is meeting patron needs. It can help you identify sections of the print collection to weed and journals to cancel as well as areas where you should buy more books or new journal subscriptions you might want to start. When making decisions based on usage data, here are some things to remember.

- Balance your desire for a heavily used collection with other values such as preserving rare materials, highlighting diversity, or supporting all academic areas.
- For print books, if possible combine several measures of usage to get a better picture of the collection. Some numbers to use are the checkouts-to-holdings ratio, percentage of unique books checked out, and the circulation-to-ILL ratio.
- Focus your weeding on the sections where there is the most to weed, most likely the larger sections. Then weed the smaller sections if they have a low checkouts-to-holdings ratio.
- Try to collect more books like the ones that are being used. Consider the age, audience, and purpose of the materials.

- For subscriptions to e-books, individual journals, and journal packages, cancel if the subscription exceeds a maximum cost per use that you set, but be careful that you do not cancel in ways that leave your collection imbalanced.
- Use interlibrary loan and the journals turnaway report to find specific book or journal titles to add.

Many of the philosophical questions around using usage data are equally true when using the next, and last, method of collection evaluation, citation analysis.

References

Bourg, Chris. 2013. "Beyond Measure: Valuing Libraries." *Feral Librarian*, May 19. http://chris-bourg.wordpress.com/2013/05/19/beyond-measure-valuing-libraries/.

Bucknell, Terry. 2012. "Garbage In, Gospel Out: Twelve Reasons Why Librarians Should Not Accept Cost-Per-Download Figures at Face Value." *Serials Librarian* 64, no. 2 (August): 192–212.

DeCooman, Daria, ed. 2010. "Developing Strong Library Budgets: Information Professionals Share Best Practices." *Library Connect* 12.

Greiner, Tony. 2012. "'All Textbooks in the Library!': An Experiment with Library Reserves." *Library Philosophy and Practice* 838. http://digitalcommons.unl.edu/libphilprac/838.

Larson, Jeanette. 2008. *CREW: A Weeding Manual for Modern Libraries*. Austin: Texas State Library and Archives Commission. https://www.tsl.texas.gov/sites/default/files/public/tslac/ld/ld/pubs/crew/crewmethod12.pdf.

Price, Jason S., and John D. McDonald. 2009. "Beguiled by Bananas: A Retrospective Study of the Usage and Breadth of Patron vs. Librarian Acquired Ebook Collections." *Library Staff Publications and Research* 10. Claremont, CA: Claremont Colleges.

Walters, William H. 2012. "Patron-Driven Acquisition and the Educational Mission of the Academic Library." *Library Resources & Technical Services* 56, no. 3 (July): 199–213.

Citation Analysis— Collecting and Analyzing the Data

WHILE THE USAGE STATISTICS DESCRIBED IN THE PREVIOUS CHAPTER can tell you a lot, they provide only a general overview of what is being used, without any information on who is using the materials or to what purpose. You won't know if the books on education law that were borrowed were used by law students or people studying to be school administrators. You might wonder, is looking only at circulation of education books enough to tell you what your education students need, or might they be using some psychology books as well? Your most heavily used journal might be very popular among undergraduates and not well respected by researchers, or it might be the go-to standard for one faculty member and irrelevant to everyone else.

One way to gain a more detailed understanding of how your patrons are using library resources is through citation analysis. By looking at the bibliographies in specific people's work, you can learn what is important to users from different disciplines and at different levels of scholarship. Rather than the aggregated overview that you'd get from circulation statistics or COUNTER reports, citation analysis creates a more narrowly focused but more detailed picture. Since citation analysis only captures usage that led to a written paper, it is not necessarily representative of all the ways your collection is useful to patrons. With the amount of detail citation analysis provides, however, the process can give a wealth of information that you can use to evaluate your library collection.

History of Citation Analysis

The first citation analysis was done by Gross and Gross in 1927. It relied on citations from the *Journal of the American Chemical Society* to create a list of journals considered essential for any academic library's chemistry collection. Gross and Gross's methodology was like the technique for creating core lists discussed in chapter 6. The process described in that chapter relies on citations either in one particular journal or in all journals indexed by Web of Science to create a list of journals that are supposedly the most influential in the scholarly world at large. The analysis process explained in this chapter is a descendent of Gross and Gross's method but uses a different source of citations and serves different goals. This chapter describes how to use citations from your own patrons' written work, with the goal of discovering what will be most valuable to them. You may still end up with a core list, as did Gross and Gross, but it will be a list tailored to your own users and reflective of what resources they are currently using rather than what is important to others in their respective fields.

Since at least the 1990s, academic librarians have been analyzing students' and faculty's work to answer various questions about the use of their library collections. The evolution of citation analysis from Gross and Gross's list of recommended journal titles to a means of measuring local use of all material types came as the result of several technological changes. Feyereisen and Spoiden (2009) note that computers and online databases have made it much easier for librarians to collect, store, and analyze data. The Web of Science index, which despite its name includes citations from the social sciences, arts, and humanities as well as the sciences, has been a frequently used tool in local citation analyses. Because of its breadth and because it allows searches by author affiliation and includes the full bibliographies of articles it indexes, librarians commonly use it to collect the published work of their own faculty. Scopus, launched by Elsevier in 2004, has similar content and features to Web of Science and could also be useful for conducting a local citation analysis. With either product, academic librarians can collect bibliographies from their faculty's works to use as source material for a citation analysis that focuses on local use.

Benefits and Shortcomings of Citation Analysis

As a tool for measuring local usage, citation analysis has a few advantages over the measures described in the previous two chapters. Because the citations come from specific people and from a specific kind of work (publications or student papers), you can get a more detailed and more human picture of how resources are being used. You will know which departments are using which materials, rather than simply assuming that all psychology materials were used by the Psychology Department, and you will know what your patrons have done with the materials they used. You can also tell whether a heavily used journal is really only serving one person or is useful to many. Bibliographies capture usage that the library would otherwise be unaware of—for example, if patrons are reshelving journals themselves or faculty are consulting their personal copies of journals and books. Citation analysis is particularly useful for interdisciplinary fields whose library resources don't all fall within one call number range, as you can begin with papers by people affiliated with this field and use their citations to see the scope of the resources they are using. This technique is also useful for balancing the needs of small departments with larger ones. A small program's resources might have low usage compared to other library resources, but citations can show you what is most important to the small group of people affiliated with this program.

There are of course limitations to citation analyses as well. You don't really know if your patrons are using your library resources, even if the sources they cite are available through your library. They could be accessing another library with which they are affiliated or using a personal copy. This is not necessarily a problem, because most of the time when something is cited by more than one user, this is an indication that it is of some importance, and the library will probably want to make it accessible to people who do not have personal copies as well. Another issue is that bibliographies only capture usage that gets cited in substantial written work. Students or faculty in health professions may be using library materials in clinical settings rather than reading them as background for a paper, or faculty could be copying articles or book chapters to pass out in class. Bibliographies might not even capture all the resources that were used in writing the paper, as people sometimes use introductory works like a handbook or specialized encyclopedia to orient themselves to a topic. Citation analysis will also not tell you about your patrons' use of online databases that include only abstracts, even though these tools may have been very helpful in getting them to the resources they ended up citing. A significant difficulty is dealing with incorrect citations, which could lead to some gaps or errors in the data. You will usually be able to figure out what the person meant to cite, though verification of citations can take time.

As with usage statistics, citation analysis cannot reflect perfectly what is most useful to your patrons because of the bias toward using what is locally available. This bias is illustrated in Beile, Boote, and Killingsworth's (2004) study of doctoral dissertations at three different universities. Although the students they studied were all in the same field, at each school 59–67 percent of the resources cited were not used by students at any other school. At each school, 91–97 percent of what the students cited was available at their own library. This very high availability of materials combined with the low overlap between schools suggests that, even at the doctoral level and even when pursuing a long-term project that would presumably allow time for interlibrary loan, students prefer to cite what is easily available to them. If the students had all sought out the best journals in their field regardless of availability, they would have been more likely to use the same sources as each other.

Undergraduate work poses the largest obstacle to citation analysis, because in addition to the bias toward local resources, these students may not be citing materials that are truly reflective of what is important in their fields. Being new to their chosen disciplines, they do not necessarily know the major works or authors in the field, and the repeated appearance of an author or journal in undergraduate bibliographies may be a result of chance rather than an indicator that this is important material. They could also be citing popular magazines that their professors and the library's information literacy program have tried to dissuade them from using. If you have reason to suspect that your undergraduate work shows low information literacy skills and is not prescriptive for you about what you should be purchasing, you will not be able to use these bibliographies in all the ways described in this chapter and the next. You can still get something useful from the data, though. Chapter 11 discusses how to be circumspect with undergraduate citations while still using them to inform collection development.

Applications of Citation Analysis

Whether your citations come from published works, dissertations and theses, or undergraduate papers, there are many ways you can use the data. The questions you can answer fall into two general categories: questions about each discipline and questions about library processes. The first kind of question provides information that is descriptive of the field, program, or discipline rather than evaluative of the library collection, but it can be very useful for collection development. By calculating what percentage of citations are to journals versus books or something else, you can decide how to allocate the budget by material type. A common use of citation analysis is to make local core lists of journals, tailored to the needs and interests of your own users. These lists can help you identify journal subscriptions to cancel or new ones to add. You can also use bibliographies to identify major authors whose work you can collect in the future. Information about the years of cited materials can help with weeding, as the data will reveal at what age materials typically stop being useful. Learning what disciplines students and faculty in each program are using can help with future purchasing.

Citation analysis can be used to evaluate library processes and the collection in various ways. Almost all citation studies ask what percentage of cited resources the library owns and use this number as a measure of how well the library is meeting patron needs. Some additional data can show in what particular ways you are meeting these needs. The library catalog can tell you if you have the books your users cite in print or as e-books, giving you a sense of what format users prefer. You can also see which database packages contain the bulk of the cited articles. This can shed light on user behavior, showing you which places your patrons tend to look for information. If you have records on how specific book orders originated, you can compare which of your selection methods are most useful to your patrons. All of these evaluative measures can provide detail on how particular patron groups are using your library.

TEXTBOX 10.1.

QUESTIONS THAT CITATION ANALYSIS CAN ANSWER

- What percentage of citations are to books, journals, and so on?
- What are the most cited journals?
- What authors are popular and presumably important?
- What are the ages of the materials users are citing?
- What disciplines are used by each of the departments at your institution?
- How many of the cited resources are available via your library's catalog?
- What database packages are most useful to these patrons?
- How did the library acquire the books patrons are citing?

Data Sources

Almost any academic library will have some kind of written work it can use as a data source for an analysis of local citations. Faculty publish books and journal articles, doctoral and master's students write dissertations and theses, and undergraduates write papers as part of their course work. You can choose which kind of work to use based on how easily you can get your hands on the bibliographies and which patron group you see yourself as primarily serving. Some librarians have questioned whether the citations from any one group can be used to make generalizations about the collection. A study by Joswick and Stierman (1997) found that faculty used different journals than undergraduates; in fact, they found no overlap between the top twenty-four journals cited by faculty and by undergraduates. Studies that have compared graduate students to faculty, however, usually find that these groups cite similar sources, though this is not always the case. Because different user groups could be citing different sources, you will want to be cautious in making selection or cancelation decisions based on only one user group, though the citation data can still be part of the decision-making process. If you have access to data from multiple user groups and time to analyze it all, it could be a good idea to use bibliographies from different kinds of patrons in order to get a more comprehensive picture of usage.

Faculty publications are a common source of bibliographies for citation analysis. You can get these by searching a database that includes a field for author affiliation, such as Web of Science or Scopus. This database will probably not include all of the publications produced by your university's faculty, so search several databases that cover different disciplines. Online indexes will also not include monographs, so to find these you can contact department chairs or administrative assistants to ask for a list of recent faculty work. There may also be an office at your institution that keeps records of what scholarly work your faculty or students have published each year. When collecting faculty publications, think about whether you want to include works that were co-authored with faculty at other institutions. Information on whether or not you own the cited sources will be irrelevant for this kind of work, though the data about preferred material types and most cited journals is still useful as it probably does describe your own faculty's needs.

Graduate student work is another very common source of data. This data can be easier to obtain than faculty work. Doctoral students are usually required to submit dissertations somewhere, whether to the university's archives, an institutional repository, or ProQuest Dissertations. University libraries that keep copies of their students' dissertations or theses sometimes catalog them with a special location or item type to make them easy to find. Because each student who graduates in a given year produces one thesis or dissertation, you can verify that you have a comprehensive set of papers. This is harder to confirm with faculty work, since a faculty member could publish multiple articles or none, and you won't necessarily know if you've missed something. If you believe your graduate students are citing the same things as faculty, as some studies have found, then the overlap in citations combined with the ability to collect dissertations and theses comprehensively makes graduate work a better choice. The disadvantage to using graduate work as a data source is that you only get it at the time the students are leaving the institution, and next year's class could have different research interests.

Undergraduate work is another possibility for citation analysis, though you need to be somewhat cautious when using it. As explained earlier, this population is the most likely to be citing things that they shouldn't. Not only will undergraduates be prone to citing what is locally available (as are graduate students), but they may have low information literacy skills or a rudimentary sense of their discipline. If you are going to use undergraduate work for collection evaluation, either because this is what you have access to or because these students are your primary user group, you will need to take an additional step of determining whether their citations are appropriate enough to use to guide future collection development. Chapter 11 describes how to do this. If some of the citations are questionable, however, you can still learn from the data. Citations will give you information about popular paper topics, preferences for a particular material type, and how students are accessing library resources. It is best to use a senior culminating paper, both because its bibliography will be longer than that of other papers and because the long-term nature of the project means students had time to wait for interlibrary loan requests to arrive and were not limited to what was on hand.

If you have an institutional repository, this can be a great, easy way to collect student papers. If your students are not submitting their papers to an institutional repository, you will probably have to ask faculty to send you student papers. It is important that whoever is sending them remove students' names from the papers so that you will not need to seek IRB approval for the analysis project. Research that is done using preexisting data (i.e., information that was already collected for a purpose other than your project) and is presented in a way that the subjects cannot be identified is exempt from IRB review. All the other kinds of data mentioned above do not need the writers' names removed and are exempt from IRB review because they rely on publicly available data (i.e., from published work or material that is available through a repository).

Whichever population you are using, you probably want several years' worth of data since dissertation or paper topics can vary a lot year to year, and faculty might not publish something every year. If data from every department from multiple years is more than you can work with, it's okay to take a sample. This is preferable to shrinking the data set by only using one year's data, as the sample will be random and therefore more representative. The section on collecting data explains how to take a random sample using Excel's random number generator. To make sure all disciplines are represented, select a random set of bibliographies from within each discipline rather than compiling all the bibliographies into one list and selecting from that.

Data Collection

Inputting the Data into Excel

It is recommended that you keep a separate Excel file for each department or program so that you can easily analyze each one separately. Large universities might want to aggregate the spreadsheets by broad disciplinary area—social sciences, natural sciences, and humanities—if doing each department would be too time-consuming. If you are going to use a sample rather than all the bibliographies you have, the first step is to figure out which bibliographies you are using. Give each bibliography a unique identifier, probably a number. You will use the unique identifier later even if you are not selecting a random sample. Create an Excel document that lists all the identifiers in a column. This is shown in figure 10.1. In the column next to it, in the top cell, type the formula =RAND(). Excel will output a random number between 0 and 1. Fill in the same formula all the way down by hovering the cursor over the bottom right corner of the cell that has the formula in it, then clicking and dragging the cursor down to the bottom of the column. You will end up with a random number next to each bibliography. Next, sort the document by the random number. Depending on how many bibliographies you are able to analyze for your evaluation project, start at the top and go down the list, selecting bibliographies until you have reached your target amount.

In a new tab on your spreadsheet (this will be your first tab if you didn't do the random sampling), create columns called Bibliography ID, Department, Author 1, Author 2, Author 3, Editor, Title, Year, Material Type, Availability, and Source. Some other fields you can add, if you want to analyze these details, are Purchase Method and Call Number. The field for Purchase Method can be used to compare whether cited items were purchased through an approval plan, user request, or a firm order from a librarian. The Call Number field will help you figure out whether students and faculty within a discipline are frequently citing works outside their discipline, or can help illustrate the scope of interdisciplinary fields.

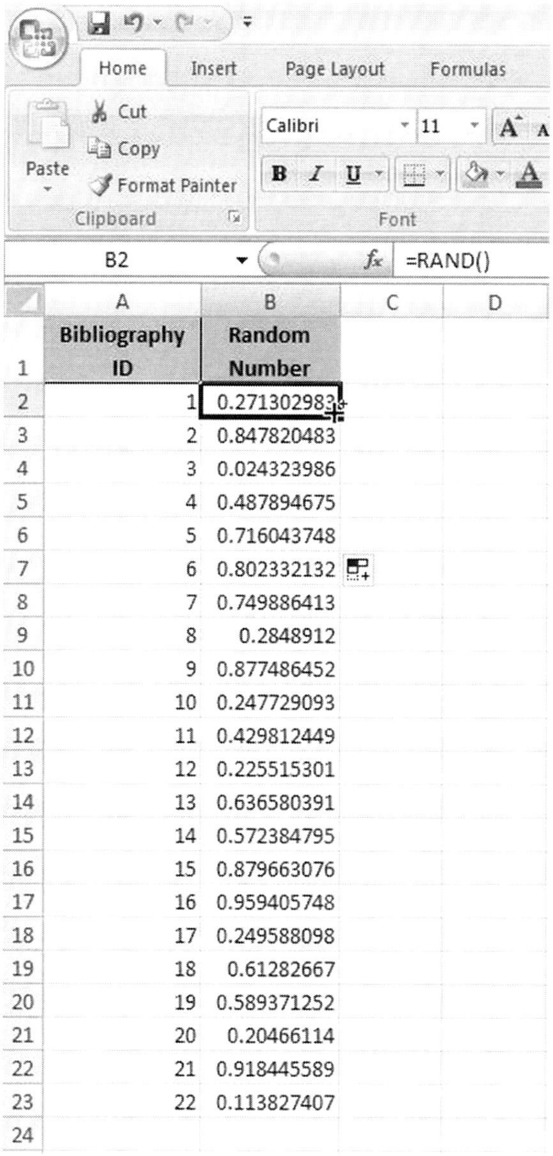

	A	B	C	D
1	Bibliography ID	Random Number		
2	1	0.271302983		
3	2	0.847820483		
4	3	0.024323986		
5	4	0.487894675		
6	5	0.716043748		
7	6	0.802332132		
8	7	0.749886413		
9	8	0.2848912		
10	9	0.877486452		
11	10	0.247729093		
12	11	0.429812449		
13	12	0.225515301		
14	13	0.636580391		
15	14	0.572384795		
16	15	0.879663076		
17	16	0.959405748		
18	17	0.249588098		
19	18	0.61282667		
20	19	0.589371252		
21	20	0.20466114		
22	21	0.918445589		
23	22	0.113827407		
24				

Figure 10.1. Using the Random Number Generator.

Begin inputting the information that you can glean just from looking at each citation. For journal articles, input the author and the title of the journal (not the article). For full books, input the author (if single-authored) or editor (if edited) and the title of the book. For book chapters, input the author, the editor, and the title of the book. The author's name will be useful when you create a top-cited authors list later, as it will tell you whose work is important in the field, whereas the editor's name is useful if you want to look up information about the book as a whole, such as its availability and call number. If multiple chapters of a book are cited in the same bibliography, it is best to count this book only once per bibliography. Include all the authors who were cited in each bibliography, though, listing them on the same line as if the repeated citations to chapters from a book were actually all one citation. Be careful when inputting authors' names, as there are many ways the same person could be listed. You won't always know whether L. Hammond is the same person as L. C. Hammond, for example, but if you do know, write the author's name the same way each time it appears. Then check for possible duplication later by sorting the list by author so that authors with the same last name are listed adjacently and seeing if any might be the same person listed in more than one way.

When inputting material types, define ahead of time what categories and terminology you will use. Categories to start with would be journal, book, conference proceedings, report, website, and other. If you find that certain types are coming up that you did not expect, maybe government documents or dissertations, you can create a new category partway through. Just make sure you go back through everything that is labeled "other" to check if it now belongs in your new category. Material type will often be clear from looking at a citation, though you may find some citations that are improperly formatted so that it is hard to tell if the reference is to a book, journal, or something else. You'll usually be able to find more detail by Googling the information you have and finding the full citation listed elsewhere, if not the work itself. This is an opportunity to catch some incorrect citations and correct them.

For the next column, Availability, you will need to check your library catalog. Some categories to use are Have, Don't Have, Have Older Years, Have Newer Years, Free Online. The options Have Older Years and Have Newer Years only apply to materials that are published serially, so you won't use these options for books. For books, only count them as Have if you have the same edition that the person cited.

The information in the Source column can help you figure out how your resources are being accessed. Citations to books will not tell you if the person accessed it electronically or in print, but your catalog will tell you which you have and can therefore provide a reasonable guess. For journals, it could be helpful to know which packages they are in. This won't necessarily tell you that users are going directly to those packages when they want to search for articles, but it will tell you which of your packages are the most useful to this group of patrons. You will probably only want to check the source for books and journals, and only for ones you own, so sort the spreadsheet by Material Type, then Availability, then Title. You'll save yourself a little time by grouping repeats of the same book or journal title together so you can look up each one just once. In this column, note print, e-book, or print and e-book next to all the cited books you have. For journal articles, record in the spreadsheet which database packages make these journals available for the year that was cited. If a journal is available in multiple packages, list all of them because you don't know which one your patron used. Repeat the packages every time the journal is listed, being careful that you only include the packages that contain the year cited.

The column for Purchase Method is only applicable to books, and only ones you have, so before collecting data on purchase methods sort the spreadsheet by Material Type, then Availability, then Title before filling in this column. (It will already be sorted this way if you just followed the instructions in the previous paragraph.) What information you put here will depend on the ordering options you have at your institution. If faculty are significantly involved in collection development, you may want to compare faculty-selected books to librarian-selected ones. If you do the bulk of your ordering through approval plans but use firms orders for special requests, you could compare approval plan titles to firm orders. If you have a formalized process for patron-driven acquisitions, you can compare PDA titles to preselected ones. This won't be possible if your PDA plan lists all requestable titles directly in the catalog, as is usually the case with e-books, since it will be unclear from the catalog whether you have actually purchased the title or not. Collect data on each book using your own acquisitions records.

The last piece of data to collect is call numbers. You can leave the document sorted as it was, or sort by Material Type and Title, ignoring the Availability field for now. If you use WorldCat to look up call numbers, you can analyze cited materials by subject regardless of whether your library has them. Another advantage of using WorldCat instead of your local catalog is that it will have call numbers for journals as well as books. Some of the material types will not be included in WorldCat, such as conference proceedings or reports. If these do not make up a significant percentage of the citations, you may want to exclude them from the rest of the analysis and only use them in the calculation of material types. For journals, you can look up each title once and copy the call number to any subsequent rows for the same journal. For books, this is an opportunity to check that you have listed each book only once per bibliography and to consolidate duplicate listings. If a book was cited by more than one user, keep it listed once for each user and repeat the call number on each listing. If WorldCat includes multiple records for the same item, take the call number from the record with the most holdings. When two call numbers are listed in the same record, choose the one that describes a narrower topic. The process of looking up books in WorldCat will also help you catch if any citations are incorrect.

After finding a call number for each book or journal, add a new column in which you will map this call number to a subject category. As before, you can use custom call number ranges that match your own programs, or conspectus divisions and categories, or subsections of a standard call number scheme. For this step, you'll save a little time if you sort the document by Call Number without separating the books from the journals. That way you'll have all the call numbers in alphabetical order so that similar numbers are grouped together when you are assigning them to categories.

Calculations

Now that you have gathered all the information that you'll need to answer your questions, you'll need to do some calculations to turn the data into answers. Keep the data for each department or program separate so that you have distinct results for each one. Don't do any calculations until you are done collecting all the basic information for that department. Each step of the collection process described above provides another chance to verify correct citations and to catch your own errors while listing multiple chapters from the same book or listing the same title twice, with a subtitle and without, or misreading journal citations as books. You don't want to have to go back and redo the calculations if you discover an error.

Descriptive Information

Some of the questions that collection evaluation answers are simply descriptive: they tell you what kinds of materials your patrons use so you can buy more of them. The first descriptive question above is what percentage of the citations are to books, journals, or other material types. This is simple to calculate. You can count how many times each material type is cited by sorting the spreadsheet by material type and then looking at the row numbers. If rows 57 to 98 are for books, for example, you know there are twenty-two citations to books. You can also use Excel formulas to count how many times each format is listed. Make a separate little table on the same spreadsheet, using a new tab if you want, that looks like table 10.1. The nonitalicized text shows what will appear in the cell (i.e., the value). The numbers will of course differ according to your data. The italics show the formula that you will type in the cell. The example assumes that Material Type is in column

H, so adjust the formula if yours is in a different column. You'll need to format the Percentage column as a percentage in order for it to display as one.

Figuring out which journals are cited the most involves using pivot tables, which are explained and shown in chapter 8. The first step to making a pivot table of journals is to sort your spreadsheet by format so that you can separate out the jour-

Table 10.1. Percentage of Citations to Each Material Type

FORMAT	COUNT	PERCENTAGE
Book	60 =COUNTIF(H:H,"=Book")	12.17% =60/493
Journal	408 =COUNTIF(H:H,"=Journal")	82.76% =408/493
Website	25 =COUNTIF(H:H,"=Website")	5.07% =25/493
Total	493 =SUM(K2:K4)	

nals. You probably want to copy the journal titles and their corresponding bibliography IDs to a new tab to make it easier to select only the data you want for the pivot table. It is important to keep the bibliography IDs linked to the journal titles so you'll be able to tell how many different bibliographies, and therefore different people, have cited each journal. Your new tab will have two columns, one for journal titles and one for bibliography IDs. Use the Insert menu at the top of the page to insert a pivot table. Make Journal Title the row labels and Bibliography ID the column labels. Make Count of Journal Title the values. Table 10.2 shows approximately what the pivot table will show you. The numbers across the top row are the bibliography IDs, and the table shows how many times each bibliography cites each journal.

The rightmost column in table 10.2 is not part of the pivot table and was added manually. To count how many different bibliographies cite each journal, you can use an Excel formula to count, for each row, how many of the columns have a number in them. In the column to the right of the total, on the first line after the column headings, type =COUNTIF(C3:L3, ">0"). This formula is shown in table 10.2 in italics. In an Excel spreadsheet, each column has a letter and each row has a number, and a letter-number

Table 10.2. Top-Cited Journals

JOURNAL NAME	BIBLIOGRAPHY ID										TOTAL	NUMBER OF BIBLIOGRAPHIES
	1	2	3	4	5	6	7	8	9	10		
Journal of Personality and Social Psychology	1			3	1				8	2	15	5 *=COUNTIF(C3:L3, ">0")*
Psychological Bulletin	1			1		1	1	2			6	5
Rehabilitation Psychology						5		3		10	18	3
Developmental Psychology		2			7						9	2
Journal of Experimental Psychology: Learning, Memory, and Cognition	7							1			8	2
Neuropsychology		1		5							6	2
Law and Human Behavior	9										9	1
American Journal of Dance Therapy		7									7	1

combination represents the cell where the column and row intersect. In the example, imagine that the box where *Journal of Personality and Social Psychology* and bibliography ID 1 intersect is column C, row 3, and the box where this same journal intersects with bibliography ID 10 is column L, row 3. C3:L3 refers to the range of cells from cell C3 to cell L3, which contains the count of how often *Journal of Personality and Social Psychology* was cited. When working with your own spreadsheet, instead of using C3:L3 in the formula, use whatever cell numbers are the first and last of the row, not including the cell that has the journal title in it. The formula will count how many cells have a number higher than zero in them. Drag this formula down so that the entire column fills with the formula. As you drag it down, it will adjust the formula so that on each line the formula is counting the numbers on its own row, such as C4:L4, C5:L5, and so on. Name this column Number of Bibliographies and sort by this column so that the journals cited by the largest number of people are at the top.

You can make a pivot table of authors the same way you made one for journals. This table can include authors of journal articles, books, or anything else. The original tab with all the citation information contains three columns for authors, so you will have the names of the first three authors of each document. To include all these authors in a pivot table, you'll want to get all the authors' names into one column without losing the link between an author and which bibliography cited that author. Copy all the authors and the corresponding bibliography IDs into a new tab. Copy the second column and the bibliography IDs and paste them below the end of the first column. Copy the third column and the bibliography IDs and paste them at the end. Then delete the second and third columns of author names, since these names are now listed in the first column. There will be a lot of rows with no author listed as not every cited source has a second or third author. Sort by author and delete all rows that have no author. You're now ready to make a pivot table. Make Authors your row labels, Bibliography ID the column labels, and Count of Author the values. Use the same formula as above to count how many bibliographies cite each author.

To learn about the ages of the materials your patrons are citing, it is useful to have both an average age and a visual representation of how the years are distributed. Copy the Years column from your main tab and paste it onto a new tab. Sort from smallest to largest (i.e., from the oldest year to the most recent). Then make a pivot table that counts how often each year appears in the bibliographies. Make Year your row labels and Count of Year the value. There is no column label this time. You can then go back to the list of all the years and calculate the average using the Excel formula =AVERAGE(). Inside the parentheses put the cell range for the list of years, for example, A2:A408. For a visual representation of how the citations are distributed by year, you can make a bar chart. Click on the pivot table, then go to the top of the screen and select Insert, then Column; pick the first 2D column. You'll now have a vertical bar chart with the years labeled across the bottom, which will look like figure 10.2. A taller bar means there were more citations from that year.

Another descriptive question concerns the disciplines cited by people in each department. During the data collection phase, you created a column that mapped the call number for each book or journal citation to a subject category, either one of the conspectus categories, an LC subclass, or a category corresponding to your own institution's programs. Now you want to calculate how often materials from each category were cited. You may want to keep information on books and journals separate. The subjects of journals are often very general as some of the most reputable journals publish a wide variety of articles (such as *Science*), whereas the call numbers for books are more specific. In addition, some journals will have call numbers representing subjects like "journalism"

Years of Citations

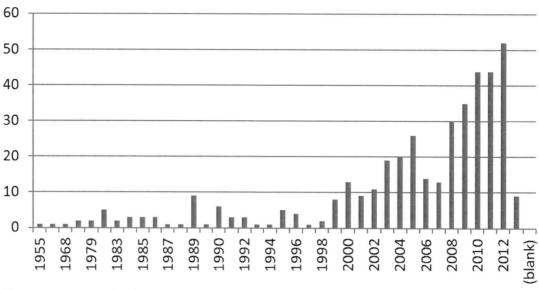

Figure 10.2. Years Cited.

or "societies" that do not reflect the content of the journal but instead mean that it simply contains journalism or is published by a society. Sort the main spreadsheet by material type to easily separate the books from the journals.

The easiest way to calculate how often each subject was cited is to sort the Excel spreadsheet by Material Type, then Subject Category, and then use the row numbers to count how often each category is listed for books and for journals. You might also want to know how the subjects are distributed across the bibliographies so you can see whether an unexpectedly high use of a certain subject is due to one person's unusual research topic or is reflective of the general interdisciplinary nature of the field. A pivot table will present this data for you clearly. If you want to have separate tables for books and journals, copy the Bibliography ID and the Subject Category columns for books onto a separate tab, then copy the journals information onto another tab. On each of these new tabs, go to the top and select Insert, then Pivot Table. Make the Subject Category the row labels, Bibliography ID the column labels, and Count of Bibliography ID the values. You can make a pie chart by clicking on the pivot table, then selecting Insert, then Pie Chart, from the top. If you want to make separate pie charts for each bibliography, follow these steps:

1. In the pivot table, click the down arrow next to Column Labels. This will bring up a list of all the column labels, which in this case are the Bibliography IDs. Uncheck the box for Select All and check off only one of the bibliography IDs. Click OK. The pivot table will now show only one bibliography, as in figure 10.3.
2. Go to the top and select Insert, then Pie Chart. This will create a pie chart for only the selected bibliography, as shown in the same figure.
3. If you select a different bibliography, the pie chart will automatically change. To save this one, click on the pie chart, right-click it, and then select Copy.
4. Go to a new tab, right-click a cell, and select Paste Special.
5. Select any one of the options for Picture and click OK. This will paste the pie chart as an image, and the image will not change if you make changes to the pivot table.

Books

Count of ID	Column Labels	
Row Labels	25	Grand Total
Constitutional History & Administration: Asia, Africa, Australia, Oceania	1	1
History of Europe	1	1
History: Southwestern Asia, Ancient Orient, Near East	1	1
International Relations	1	1
Grand Total	**4**	**4**

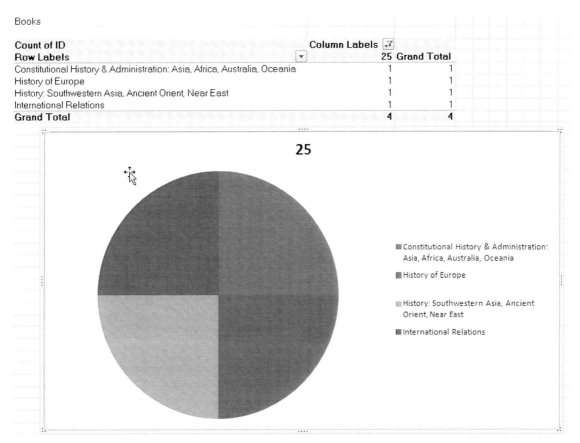

Figure 10.3. Subjects Cited in One Bibliography.

Evaluative Information

Now that you have made calculations that have taught you about your patrons' research needs, the evaluative questions can tell you how well you are meeting those needs. The most basic evaluative question is whether or not you have the materials your users are citing. First, sort the main spreadsheet by Material Type, then Availability. Count how often each availability option appears for each format. You can do this manually or by formula. To count how many books are available, imagine that on the spreadsheet the books are in rows 2 through 61, and the Availability is in column H. A formula you can use to count how many of the cited books your library has would be =COUNTIF(H2:H61, "=Have"). This counts how often the value "Have" appears in column H, rows 2 through 61. Divide this number by the total number of books and multiply by one hundred to get the percentage of cited books that your library has. Repeat this process for each format and each availability option. You'll probably want to make a small table on a new tab, which will look like table 10.3.

When you made the pivot table showing how often each journal had been cited, you probably noticed that a lot of the journals were cited only one or a handful of times. This is likely to be the case with any library's data. The 80/20 rule, which has long been a basic principle for libraries, states that 20 percent of a library collection will usually account for 80 percent of all usage of that collection (Trueswell, 1969). Transferring this rule to citations, it predicts that if you were to put the journals in order from most cited to least and go down the list to count the top 20 percent of the list, the citations to those top journals would make up 80 percent of all the citations. The remaining citations will be scattered

Table 10.3. Availability of Books and Journals

	TOTAL	HAVE	DON'T HAVE	HAVE OLDER YEARS	HAVE NEWER YEARS	HAVE OLDER & NEWER YEARS	FREE ONLINE
Books	60	20	39	n/a	n/a	n/a	1
Journals	408	328	50	7	9	2	12

a few apiece among many journals. Trueswell presented this rule as a way of identifying a core collection that a library should have in order to satisfy the vast majority of user needs. Rather than aiming to have everything your users might cite, it is more reasonable to aim to have enough journals to provide 80 percent of all the citations. Therefore, checking how many of the top 20 percent of journals are provided by your library is more meaningful than calculating a percentage of all cited journals you own.

To calculate your holdings among the top 20 percent of journals, first look at how many distinct journals were cited (not how many citations to journals) and calculate 20 percent of that number. Go to the pivot table and make sure it is sorted with the most cited journal at the top. Starting at the top, go down and highlight journals until you have hit the number representing 20 percent of the journals. Check to see if these account for roughly 80 percent of the citations by counting how many citations are in these journals and comparing it to the total number of journal articles cited. You may end up with a lot of journals that are tied with each other in the ranked list, and your 20 percent cutoff may not be a good dividing point. You can go slightly above or below 20 percent so that you don't end up excluding journals that were cited the same number of times as journals you included. If your top 20 percent of journals is not even close to 80 percent of the citations, figure out how many citations make up 80 percent and keep going down your list of journals until you have captured the full 80 percent. This is now your top tier of journals. Once you've identified this top tier, go back to the main spreadsheet to find information on whether or not your library has these journals. You can then calculate what percentage of the top journals your library has access to.

Another evaluative question relates to where your patrons are getting the materials they use. What database packages do they find the most useful, and are they using print books or e-books? Calculating the ratio of print books to e-books is easy. Sort the citations table by Format, then Availability, then Source. This will group together the books that you have, and these will be sorted by whether they are print or electronic. Count how many you have of each and calculate a percentage.

To figure out which databases were most useful, you can count how often a cited journal article was available in each database. To make counting easier, copy the section of the Source column that lists databases and paste it into its own tab. Then copy and paste the data so that there is just one column listing databases, with one database per row. Database names will repeat if they occur more than once. You can then make a pivot table to count how often each database name appears in the list. Table 10.4 shows an example of the data this pivot table can provide. You can see that the total (511) is higher than the total number of journal articles (408, shown in table 10.3) because some articles are available in more than one database.

The last evaluative question is what purchase method is best meeting your patrons' needs. Sort the spreadsheet by Material Type and then Availability so that you can easily look at only the books you have. Using whatever criteria you put in this field (e.g.,

Table 10.4. Databases in Which Cited Journal Articles Are Available

DATABASE	COUNT OF DATABASE
ABI/INFORM	28
Academic Search Premier	97
American Physical Therapy Association	1
Annual Reviews	1
Blackwell Synergy	7
Business Source Elite	12
Directory of Open Access Journals	13
Health Source	25
Informa Healthcare	1
JSTOR	3
LexisNexis	2
MD Consult	5
OMNIFile	44
Opposing Viewpoints	1
Ovid	66
Print Collection	1
PsycARTICLES	140
Sage	23
ScienceDirect	39
Taylor & Francis	1
Wiley InterScience	1
Total	511

approval plans versus firm orders, faculty selected versus librarian selected), calculate the percentages of books you have that were purchased according to each method. As above, you can look at these numbers in a table, bar graph, or pie chart.

Key Points

The above instructions should help you gather extensive information on how your patrons are using the library and how you are meeting their needs. The main ideas to keep in mind when gathering citation data are:

- Citation analysis will not capture all usage of your library collection, but it will give you an in-depth view of particular users.

- Think carefully about whose citations you are going to use, as students and faculty may cite different materials.
- Decide what information to include in your spreadsheet based on what questions you want to answer.
- At every stage of data collection, be on the lookout for incorrect citations so you can verify and fix them.
- Do not make any calculations until you have gone through all the steps of data collection and checked citations for accuracy.

The next chapter will explain how citations can give ideas for future purchasing.

References

Beile, Penny M., David N. Boote, and Elizabeth K. Killingsworth. 2004. "A Microscope or a Mirror? A Question of Study Validity regarding the Use of Dissertation Citation Analysis for Evaluating Research Collections." *Journal of Academic Librarianship* 30, no. 5 (September): 347–53.

Feyereisen, Pierre, and Anne Spoiden. 2009. "Can Local Citation Analysis of Master's and Doctoral Theses Help Decision-Making about the Management of the Collection of Periodicals? A Case Study in Psychology and Education Sciences." *Journal of Academic Librarianship* 35, no. 6 (November): 514–22.

Gross, P. L. K., and E. M. Gross. 1927. "College Libraries and Chemical Education." *Science* 66, no. 1713 (October): 385–89.

Joswick, Kathleen E., and Jeanne Koekkoek Stierman. 1997. "The Core List Mirage: A Comparison of the Journals Frequently Consulted by Faculty and Students." *College and Research Libraries* 58, no. 1 (January): 48–55.

Trueswell, Richard L. 1969. "Some Behavioral Patterns of Library Users: The 80/20 Rule." *Wilson Library Bulletin* 43, no. 5 (January): 458–61.

CHAPTER 11

Citation Analysis— Interpreting and Acting on the Data

AFTER FOLLOWING THE STEPS DESCRIBED IN THE PREVIOUS CHAPTER, you should now have data that can answer several questions about your patrons' needs and to what extent you are meeting their needs. Since many pieces of the data were collected in response to particular questions, it might at first seem obvious what the data is telling you: you are or aren't meeting patrons' needs, your users like this or that journal, or users from a certain discipline use books more than users from another discipline. Yet, because the citations don't represent all of your patrons or all the ways they use the library, you may be unsure what you can do with the information. To what extent can this particular subset of users tell you what your library ought to have? There are some decisions you can't make based on a citation analysis, but due to the depth of the information you've collected, there are still many ways you can use the analysis to improve your collection development.

Differences in User Groups

One of the benefits of citation analysis is the level of detail it provides about how resources were used. You know what discipline researchers came from, their status within the institution, and whether usage of any particular resource was due to one person or several, and you can take this information into account when making decisions. You can respond differently to the citations of a just-graduated master's student whose interests seem to differ a lot from her classmates than to those of a new faculty member who is planning to design courses around his area of specialty, or to a group of undergraduates who seem to be citing a lot from *Time* magazine. Some people's research is more representative than others' of the department's focus or of the major works within a discipline. Although this can seem like a weakness of citation analysis, the fact that you know generally who your users are can help you make careful decisions.

Several studies have looked at differences between the resources used by faculty, doctoral students, master's students, and undergraduates and have drawn different conclusions about what to do with these differences. In a study of philosophy doctoral students and faculty, Jennifer Knievel (2013) found that faculty tended to cite older materials and were also less likely to cite sources outside their discipline. She speculated that this might be because faculty work from an existing knowledge base and may be citing sources that they've used in the past. This might mean that the longer someone works in a field and the more expert they become, the more they rely on authors who are known to be significant. Knievel suggests, though, that doctoral students' citation patterns could mean that a generational change is coming in which interdisciplinarity becomes more valued. It is unclear, then, whether a university should collect materials more like what its faculty cite, which are more likely to be major works, or what its graduate students cite, which could represent the vanguard of the field.

One way to deal with differences in citation patterns and uncertainty about what they mean is simply to analyze citations from multiple groups of patrons. Both the journals that students use and the ones that faculty use are important, just to different groups of people. If it's not possible to collect citations from all your user groups, though, you might decide whose citations to use based on the mission of your institution. At a teaching-focused institution, undergraduates are considered the primary patrons, whereas a research university's mission includes supporting faculty interests as well. Also, if you have doctoral programs, faculty interests may be more in alignment with student interests, as doctoral students usually seek programs that can provide an advisor whose research focus is similar to their own. Despite the differences Knievel found, her study and others have shown that, overall, graduate research is similar to faculty research. A citation analysis of one of these groups could still lead to collection development decisions that benefit the other group.

Whether you use citations from one group of patrons or multiple, it is a good idea to adjust how you interpret the data based on its source. Although some people believe that student bibliographies are not a useful tool for collection development due to the likelihood that these patrons are not citing the best materials, this supposed flaw is not necessarily a problem if you treat the bibliographies as indicators of what is most used rather than what is most important. If you are using citations from students at any level, it is recommended that you spend some time evaluating the bibliographies to help you decide in what ways you will be able to use the data they provide.

Your own knowledge of the discipline that produced the bibliographies may be enough to allow you to make a judgment on whether the students are citing significant and appropriate materials. If you are less familiar with the field, there are many things that can clue you in that the citations are something other than they should be: popular magazines appearing high on the list of most cited journals, citations that look like they are probably textbooks, or a high ratio of websites to more formally published works. It can also be helpful to bring the data to these students' professors for feedback. Faculty might be pleased to see a certain journal at the top of the list, or they might tell you that a certain resource is heavily used because they are recommending it, and you can then feel comfortable interpreting the bibliographies as an indication of what is important. On the other hand, if they tell you that they have never heard of the top-cited authors, or that they are disappointed some important journals are low on the list of most cited, you'll need to be circumspect when using the data to make future purchasing decisions. You might still try to acquire some of the most cited journals, but only after looking at some independent measure of the quality and significance of these journals. Another way citations can be useful even if your students don't seem to be citing the best resources is in telling you what paper topics are popular so you can collect more resources on these topics. You can select resources based on your determination of their quality and relevance rather than on whether students have cited these resources in the past.

Answering Evaluative Questions: Are You Meeting Patrons' Needs?

There are several questions that a citation analysis can answer using any set of bibliographies, regardless of whether the citations are to high-quality materials. The previous chapter set out three evaluative questions: to what extent is the library meeting the needs of a particular patron group, what kinds of library resources or tools are best meeting these needs, and what purchase method is supplying the largest part of what patrons are using? The first question is measured as a percentage of cited resources available via the library's catalog. The second question has a two-part answer that you'd find by calculating whether more of the cited books were available in print or online and which databases contain the largest numbers of cited articles. The third question compares how many of the cited books you already own were purchased via approval plan, a patron's request, or selection by a librarian.

Availability of Cited Books and Journals

When looking at what percentage of cited books and materials your library provides, there are a few things to keep in mind. The most important is that a very high number, indicating you have almost everything, might not mean you are doing well but could mean instead that your patrons don't know how to use interlibrary loan or are avoiding it. A very low number, meaning you have little of what is cited, might not mean that patrons' needs are unmet, but rather that they are getting their materials from another source. Faculty usually have collections of books or journal subscriptions in their offices and may cite what they have on hand because it is already part of their knowledge base. In this case, it would be immaterial to them whether the library had the items, though you may still want to order the things you don't have. If faculty citations are an indication of the importance of the work, it could be useful to own these so they can be available to other patrons. If your library has been doing patron-driven purchasing or gets a significant number of patron requests for acquisitions, your percentage owned will be high because you now own those items that your patrons needed, even if you did not yet own them at the time of need. A PDA plan does not necessarily make your data inaccurate, though. As long as you were able to respond to requests and obtain the items quickly, it is fair to say that your local holdings do meet patrons' needs.

Given the various factors that will influence the percentage of cited items you have available, you will need to make an educated guess about whether the numbers are telling you something positive about your collection or not. As with the other evaluation methods in this book, internal comparisons can give you some sense of what is a high or low percentage of citations for the library to have. If, for example, the percentage of items you own is in the nineties for most departments but only 75 percent of citations for the Business Department, then the Business Department is not well served. There are several other ways you can look for context as you try to understand what is going on. You could refer to the interlibrary loan data collected in chapter 8. If the interlibrary loan data shows that this department is using ILL in other situations, then maybe in this case they simply didn't need it. You can also look at the data on what databases are most useful, which is described later in this section. If you find that a particular group of patrons got a lot of their articles from a database that includes the full text of some articles but not others, then it is likely that this database was helping them discover articles that your library doesn't have. Conversely, if they seem to be using a database that includes full text for every indexed article, they will only be discovering articles you have and won't need to use interlibrary loan. The general quality of the citations could be an indication of whether the students are avoiding interlibrary loan, since it might be the case that students who cite inappropriate resources are also more likely to stick with what is available locally or online. Although you will be guessing what behaviors explain the relatively high or low percentage of cited items you own, this will probably give you a good sense of what is going on if you take into account all the information you have.

Books—Online or Print?

The next questions can help fill in the picture of how your collection is being used, as they illuminate how users are accessing materials. In the calculations in the previous chapter, you noted whether you had the cited books in print or electronically and which of your databases provide the cited journals. Out of all the cited books that your library has access to, you should have a percentage that is available in print, electronically, or both. Table 11.1 shows the distribution for books cited by psychology students at Arcadia University.

Of course, if students are citing very few books in a certain format, this might be because you have very few, so in order to interpret your numbers you'll need to know what you own. You might have a general sense that your e-book collection is the same size as your print collection, or is much smaller or larger. If you want a more precise measure, and if all your e-books are in your catalog and have call numbers, you should be able to run a report to count how many e-books you have in the call number range representing this discipline and another to count your print books in the same range. Arcadia owns just over three thousand print books on psychology and has access to over ten thousand e-books. Yet from table 11.1, it seems likely that undergraduates used more print books for their papers than e-books. This might not be the case, because 30 percent of the books are available in both formats, but even if all of the books that are available in both formats

Table 11.1. Formats of Cited Books Owned by Arcadia University

FORMAT	COUNT	PERCENTAGE
Print	9	45%
E-Book	5	25%
Both	6	30%
Total	20	100%

were accessed electronically, e-books would have only a small majority. Given that the library owns three times as many e-books as print books on psychology, the fact that the numbers of each format actually used are so close suggests that patron preferences are tipping the balance toward print.

Database Packages

For journals, the question of how users accessed the material is slightly more complicated. Since most libraries' journal collections are predominantly online now anyway, the analysis goes beyond asking about format and looks at which databases or platforms patrons could have used to access each cited journal article. Many of your journals will be available through multiple platforms, so you won't necessarily know which one the patron used, but the numbers should give you some sense of your patrons' behavior. Referring back to table 10.4, you can see that the psychology undergraduates in the sample study rely the most heavily on PsycARTICLES and second most on Academic Search Premier. What a chart like this tells you depends a lot on context and on who your users are. In this case, the users are undergraduates at an institution that introduces Academic Search Premier to all first-year students in at least one required course. The fact that seniors still use it fairly heavily is probably due to their familiarity with the resource, whereas their use of PsycARTICLES is probably a result of instruction during courses for their major.

Seeing what databases patrons are using can shed some light on other parts of the analysis as well. Look at the most used databases for each department and ask whether they are discipline specific, include only scholarly work or a mix, have embargoes on recent journals, and include full text for each indexed article. Then look at the citation behavior of your users. If there is a database for their discipline that includes discipline-specific scholarly work, with full text, are these users more likely than those from other departments to stay within discipline, cite peer-reviewed journals, and cite articles the library has? If your students are relying primarily on a package that has a lot of embargoed journals, do their citations tend to be older? In the example of Arcadia's psychology students, the library had a high percentage of the journal articles students cited compared to other departments (83 percent, shown in the example table in the next chapter, table 12.2), and students were also the most likely to cite peer-reviewed articles within their discipline. The knowledge that the students relied heavily on PsycARTICLES explains this, as it is a full-text database, so every citation a student discovers through it they can access using their home library. The database also contains only psychology articles from scholarly journals. Finding connections between the tools used and citation patterns can show how the collection influences citation behavior and therefore helps you make an argument for the importance of a carefully selected collection.

What the table of databases probably will not tell you is whether you should cut any packages. If COUNTER reports show that something is being used, you wouldn't stop subscribing just because journals from this database were not frequently cited. The data from a citation analysis can help, though, with a problem that arises with COUNTER statistics, which is that a database that supports a very small department is always going to have lower usage than databases used by larger departments. If the citation analysis shows that a particular database is the most important for a particular department, then you know you should keep it despite a high cost per use or low overall usage.

Purchase Methods

The final evaluative question considers the library's selection processes rather than the collection itself. This question shifts back to books and asks about purchasing methods—namely, which methods are responsible for the largest amount of cited books. If more of the cited books are being purchased through user requests than through your approval plan, then either your approval plan is off or just-in-case purchasing is not working for you. You can adjust the approval plan using some of the descriptive information discussed in the next section. Demand-driven acquisitions is another way to make sure your purchases meet user needs, as it facilitates the process of patrons making requests and the library responding to them. You might also have compared firm orders selected by librarians to orders requested by faculty. If librarian-selected titles are not being cited as often as faculty-requested titles, you can ask the faculty if they can describe what they would like you to purchase. If they are able to provide names of authors, publishers, or series, then you as a librarian can keep on top of new materials as they are published and can purchase them before the faculty request them, so that you have the books already available when they are needed. Whether you decide to modify your approval plan or your strategies for making firm orders, the descriptive questions can provide useful information.

Answering Descriptive Questions: What Do Patrons Need?

Material Types

The descriptive part of the citation analysis can be very helpful in shaping future collection development, as it tells you about patrons' reliance on particular material types (possibly), important authors and journals, popular research topics, and the interdisciplinary scope of your patrons' research. The first descriptive question that citation analysis answers is about material type. Do the bibliographies reference more journals than books? How does this differ across disciplines? Observed preferences are likely to vary somewhat depending on whose bibliographies you are using, students or faculty, and what type of written work the citations came from. For example, dissertations will usually cite other dissertations more than books would cite these resources. Nevertheless, the data will give you an idea of whether or not research in a certain discipline relies on books heavily or is mostly journal focused.

Chapter 10 showed you how to calculate the material types cited. The example given was of psychology undergraduates, whose citations were 82.76 percent from journals, 12.17 percent from books, and 5.07 percent from websites (table 10.1). The clearest way to use these numbers is for budgeting. If you can see that people from a certain department are citing books, you'll want to make sure you are spending some money on books. If each department gets its own materials budget, then the budget should be split between books and journals in the same way that citations are split. The percentages don't need to match exactly, as this set of bibliographies is probably not perfectly representative of the department's needs as a whole. Nevertheless, if you can see a department is using books, you will know to set aside some money for book purchases, and if you know they almost entirely cite journals, you'll know to spend the bulk of your budget on journals.

If you find that your patrons are citing significant amounts of work in material types that you don't collect or that you can't collect, such as reports published online, the analysis can still provide information to help with future collection development. Look at the conference proceedings being cited to see if certain conferences show up repeatedly.

Identifying the major conferences in a field can be a good way for new selectors to learn about a field. The organization hosting the conference is probably a major organization, and it might also publish books or journals that you could buy. Keynote speakers at the conference are likely to be important people in the field, and you can buy their books in the future. Looking at the organizations that the reports are coming from can also teach new selectors about important actors in the field, and there may be some kind of publication from these organizations that you can purchase.

Most Cited Journals and Authors

After looking at what material types are cited and how often, you can look a little deeper to see which journals are cited the most often. You should have this information in a pivot table that looks like table 10.2. You might also want to look at how many different people cited a journal. Many librarians want to build a collection that meets as many different people's needs as possible and might believe that a journal that was used heavily by only one person was not necessarily an important title for the library to own. This might be more of an issue if the person citing a journal is graduating and leaving the institution, as you don't have a way of knowing whether future library patrons will use that same journal. Not everyone feels this way, but if you do you will want to order your journals according to how many people cited them, not how many times they were cited.

The list of most cited journals gives you information about what journals are important to the users who made the bibliographies. Remember that your different user groups, even within the same discipline, will value different journals. A study done by Joswick and Stierman (1997) produced lists of the top-cited journals in faculty's published articles and in papers from first-year students and found that none of the top twenty-four journals cited by faculty appeared in the bibliographies of first-year students. While faculty citations might be more representative of the discipline than those of first-year students, faculty also may have narrow research interests and rely on journals that are more specialized than the ones their students use. Nevertheless, the bibliographies you collected were from patrons you serve, and if the journal is important to them, as long as it is reputable and appropriate to cite, it is still something you'd ideally like to have. If you have a place to store information about particular journals, note that a journal was heavily cited by patron group X so you can take this information into account when doing renewals or adding new subscriptions.

In part, because of the different needs of different patron groups, you probably don't want to cut a journal based on its not being cited. A journal that comes out low on the list of student citations may be important to faculty or vice versa. Many things get used in ways other than citing in papers as well, especially if you serve health professionals who are doing clinical work. If something is being cited, you know it is being used, but if it is not cited, you do not know that it is not getting used. A study by De Groote, Blecic, and Martin (2013) supports this. They compared usage statistics they had collected from their link resolver to statistics from a citation analysis and found that some journals that were never cited still had high or even moderate use when measured in other ways. Any journal with a high number of citations, though, also had a high rank in terms of direct measures of usage. This makes the case that citation data can tell you what journals to keep but not necessarily which subscriptions to drop. Direct measures of usage, such as COUNTER reports, make a better basis for cancelation decisions.

While citation analysis does not help you make cancelations, it can tell you what journals you should try to add. When identifying journal titles to add, remember that you are not aiming to have all the journals cited by your patrons. Many journals will only be cited once or twice in your data set, and their cost per use would probably end up high enough to put them on the cut list shortly after you added them. The 80/20 rule is useful here in giving you a cutoff point for how many citations a journal needs to have before you should consider adding it. Remember that the 80/20 rule, as Trueswell (1969) described it, was intended to help libraries create a goal for a core collection, which would be one that satisfies 80 percent of user needs. Chapter 10 showed you how to identify the journals that provide 80 percent of cited articles. This should be 20 percent of the journals, although each library's numbers will be slightly different. Any journal that is in this top tier that you don't have would be a reasonable one to add. If you don't have the money to add all the journals you want, look at which departments have the lowest percentage of their citations available in-house or have the fewest journals to begin with.

Using the list of most cited authors is somewhat simpler. As with journals, you may want to put your ranked list in order by how many people cited each author rather than how many times an author's name appeared total. That way, if you don't believe you should spend much money on something that is cited a lot but only by one person, you won't end up doing so. For authors who are cited by many people, you can try to buy their works in the future. If an author is frequently cited but only publishes journal articles and not books, you may not be able to buy their work in the future as it is probably dispersed across several journals. Many people write both articles and books over the course of their careers, however, so even if the citations are to articles, the author may still publish books that the library can buy. Consider adding key authors to your approval plan or creating alerts so that you'll be notified when they publish future works. You can also check to see which of their existing books you don't already have and buy some of these. As always, keep your usual collection criteria in mind. If the authors on your most cited list write textbooks, and you don't usually buy textbooks, you probably won't buy ones by these authors either.

Age of Works Cited

The next descriptive question is about the ages of works cited. From the data you collected, you should have both an average year and a chart showing the distribution of years. In the example in figure 10.2, you can see that the bars drop off around 1999, after generally declining from 2012 until then (the data is from papers written in the spring of 2013). You could use the drop-off point as a guideline when weeding, removing anything older than that, unless it was used very recently. When you do future weeding, adjust the year that you are using as a cutoff to account for how much time has passed since you did the citation analysis. At the time of this analysis, books published in 1999 were fourteen years old. If you weed again in 2015, the cutoff should be 2001, as books published that year will now be fourteen years old. The age at which something becomes no longer useful can vary a lot by discipline, so keep track of your findings for each discipline to customize your weeding guidelines.

Data on years can also help you identify important classic titles. The chart showing years cited can help you see whether there are any very old classics cited. Go back to the main spreadsheet where you compiled all the data about each citation, before you did any calculations, to find out what titles correspond with the very old dates. If you do not recognize the titles, a blurb or review online can probably tell you whether they are classics, or you can ask experts in the discipline. Consider purchasing new copies if you don't own the books or if the copies you have are worn.

Subjects or Disciplines of Materials Cited

Besides learning about classic books and important journals and authors, citation analysis can also give you more general information about the scope of the disciplines whose citations you are analyzing. The call numbers of cited books and journals will provide this information. Figure 10.3 in the previous chapter showed an example of the subject categories used in one bibliography from international studies. In this case, the student's professor felt that the bibliographies were generally appropriate and that it was reasonable for the librarians to rely on them to learn about the discipline. The full chart from international studies, shown in table 11.2, shows that quite a few of these students are using books in the history section, covering various parts of the globe. Three different students used economics books; books on religion and social work were used by two students each. Because international studies is an interdisciplinary field, the subject classifications help

Table 11.2. Subjects of Cited Books

CONSPECTUS CATEGORY	BIBLIOGRAPHY ID										TOTAL
	1	2	3	4	5	6	7	8	9	10	
	TIMES CITED										
Constitutional History: Asia, Africa, Australia, Oceania				1			1		1		3
Economic History and Conditions	1		1		1						3
Economic Theory			1								1
Ethnology and Ethnography			1								1
History of Europe				1							1
History: Africa	1										1
History: Eastern Asia, Southeast Asia, Far East	2				6						8
History: Egypt and Sudan							8				8
History: South America				1							1
History: Southwestern Asia, Ancient Orient, Near East				1							1
International Relations			1								1
Islam									5		5
Italy						12					12
Law (General)									5		5
Public Health										3	3
Religions, Mythology, Rationalism		1							1		2
Social Work		2						4			6
Sociology		1	2				1				4
Women and Feminism									12		12
Total	4	4	6	4	7	12	10	4	24	3	78

paint a picture of which disciplines make up the field. If the bibliographies had come from a program that aligned with a particular discipline, the data would show where this discipline overlaps with others or which subfields of the discipline are a focus of the institution's research. Remember to do some evaluation of the bibliographies before deciding if you can use them in this way.

You can use the findings about the subjects of cited materials to ensure that your collection offers materials that match the range of research your users are doing. Check that the call number ranges that showed up prominently in the citations are also represented in your approval plans or in a profile for PDA records that are imported into your catalog. You can also place firm orders that include works outside the discipline you are collecting for if they fall within the related disciplines that patrons are citing. The additional information you've gained from the citation analysis will allow you to collect in ways that support the full scope of your patrons' research.

Key Points

Like all the evaluation methods described in this book, citation analysis can both help you judge how well the library is currently meeting patrons' needs and teach you about those needs so you can focus the library's purchasing in the future. Although citations will only tell about a particular group of patrons and their use of materials for a particular purpose, analysis can still be very informative. The strength of a citation analysis is the amount of detail it provides about a set of users' research behaviors. Even if there are no names attached to the data, it will show which topics are broadly popular and which are only relevant to one person, and you can see which departments or programs are using which resources. You will also learn about how the collection influences citation patterns. This method more than the others gives insight into not only what is getting used but how it is used. Some takeaways:

- The strength of citation analysis is the human view it gives you, telling you who is using what and possibly how they are accessing it.
- Review undergraduate citations carefully to see if they are a good representation of the discipline.
- Take into account how many people and which people are using a resource when deciding if you should add it.
- Look at what databases are being used most often and try to find connections with how resources are influencing user behavior.
- If something is cited heavily, you know it is being used, but if something is not cited, this does not necessarily mean it was not used. Use citation analysis more for ideas of what to add than what to cut.
- Use information you have gained about the most cited journals and authors, classic works, and the scope or interdisciplinary nature of each field to make future collections decisions.

At this point, whether you have used one of the evaluation methods described in this book or all of them, you will probably be eager to use the data to improve your collection or tell people how well you are doing. In most cases, moving from data analysis to action will require the involvement of other people, either within the library or outside, so a major next step is thinking about how to approach your colleagues, administrators, or the public. The next chapter will advise you on how to present your findings to various audiences.

References

De Groote, Sandra L., Deborah D. Blecic, and Kristin E. Martin. 2013. "Measures of Health Sciences Journal Use: A Comparison of Vendor, Link-Resolver, and Local Citation Statistics." *Journal of the Medical Library Association* 101, no. 2 (April): 110–19.

Joswick, Kathleen E., and Jeanne Koekkoek Stierman. 1997. "The Core List Mirage: A Comparison of the Journals Frequently Consulted by Faculty and Students." *College and Research Libraries* 58, no. 1 (January): 48–55.

Knievel, Jennifer. 2013. "Alignment of Citation Behaviors of Philosophy Graduate Students and Faculty." *Evidence Based Library and Information Practice* 8, no. 3: 19–33. http://ejournals.library.ualberta.ca/index.php/EBLIP/article/view/19205/15726.

Trueswell, Richard L. 1969. "Some Behavioral Patterns of Library Users: The 80/20 Rule." *Wilson Library Bulletin* 43, no. 5 (January): 458–61.

Sharing What You Found

AT THIS POINT, YOU HAVE IDENTIFIED YOUR GOALS, planned out your evaluation, gathered data, reviewed your findings, and most likely made some changes to your collection in response to what you found. You should be feeling much more aware of the state of your collection than you were at the start, and you may already have achieved your original goal. Some of your goals, however, can't be achieved unless you share the data with someone else. To request a budget increase, for example, you'll want to use the data to make your case to your provost or head of finance. To promote the library to prospective students, you might provide your admissions office with quick facts they can use in their marketing materials. Even making changes to purchasing strategies or renewing subscriptions will usually involve showing information to colleagues, unless you are responsible for all collection decisions yourself. If you are not the sole person doing collection development, you'll want to share detailed results of the evaluation project with your colleagues in the library so they can improve the sections of the collection that are their responsibility. You will also at some point need to report on your library to accrediting organizations, and if your institution receives state funding, you may need to educate legislators as well.

Even when you don't have a specific goal in mind or are not answering a request for information, sharing information about the library can be beneficial. Transparency can help you establish a reputation for being trustworthy, and when people see that you systematically collect meaningful data, they feel confident that you are making evidence-based decisions. If you need to present an unpopular action, such as cutting journals or removing outdated books, an established reputation for careful evaluation may make your decisions more acceptable. Likewise, your budget requests will be better received if the administration knows you are paying careful attention to how you are spending the collections budget, which they will know if they are aware of your evaluation and some of its findings even before budget time comes around.

In all of the above situations, the way you communicate will affect how the information is received. As you plan ways to communicate your findings, you will have to make decisions about what information to share and how to present it effectively so that both the data and your message are clear. Knowing your audience and goals is crucial when sharing information. To use a simple example, you want to give the admissions office information that makes the school look good, while the information you include in a budget request needs to show ways you could do better if you had more money. To help the communication process go smoothly and successfully, this chapter offers strategies and cautions for communicating with specific audiences such as administrators, colleagues, or prospective students. It also provides widely applicable principles on how to present data clearly and effectively that will help you plan presentations to other audiences as well.

General Advice on Sharing Information

Fears about Sharing Data

Sharing your data can be scary. The methodologies described in chapters 4 through 11 all have shortcomings, and you will rarely be able to state for sure that you know what is going on with your users. The people you are speaking with may question whether the numbers really measure what you claim they do. After all, people could be using books in the library but not checking them out, so is circulation *really* the best way to measure usage? You should be able to respond to this and similar questions, though, as you considered them when interpreting the data yourself. Remember, and tell others, that even if the data is imperfect, it still paints a generally accurate picture of your collection, and you know a lot more after collecting and reviewing this data than you did before. Act confident, while at the same time preparing for possible challenges.

Another fear you may have is that the data you're sharing could be used against you. To use a common example, if you show that print circulation is low, your administrators might suggest getting rid of books and repurposing the library space. If you can anticipate the response you might get, you can be prepared with a counterargument, and hopefully the data to support it! Maybe your print circulation is low but your students are citing a lot of books that the library doesn't own, and you plan to acquire those books rather than giving up on book purchasing altogether. You may also decide to be selective about the information you share, though it is also important not to lie, as this will cause people not to trust you.

Although you may have reasons to be cautious when sharing data, don't get overwhelmed thinking about what could go wrong. Your audience will often be grateful that you've kept them well informed and glad that you are evaluating yourselves. Although you may think of your goal as improving or marketing the library, ultimately what you are doing is strengthening the institution, either by finding ways to better serve users or by leveraging the library to promote the institution. Keeping the larger picture in mind can help you present findings in a way that will be well received.

What Information to Share

The first step of planning to share data, whether in writing, a presentation, or an informal conversation, is to think about your own goals and your audience's. You already know your own goals, but to make yourself relevant and gain the attention of your audience, you should frame the conversation in terms of their goals. Choose what information to share with each population by asking yourself, what does this person need in order to do *their* job? Except for your colleagues in the library, all of the stakeholders you will speak with will be people who do not have building a strong library as their end goal. What they may not realize, though, is that the library can help them achieve their goals, whether these are bringing in grant money, attracting students, or gaining accreditation. Your interactions with stakeholders should emphasize the connection between the library and what is important to them.

An important way to make this connection clear is to structure the story you tell in a way that starts with the purpose rather than the process. For example, you might say, "We wanted to find out how well we were supporting disability studies, so we looked at a list of core journals and books in the field and found that we have X percent. To improve our collection, we need more of the core books and journals." In this way, you are focusing on the needs of the program and how you can meet those needs. Contrast this with the following: "The library just underwent an extensive process of comparing our collection to lists of core books and journals. We found that we have X percent of the core resources for disability studies, and we need more." The second example tells a story about internal processes, and your audience may tune out due to boredom before you get to the part about their program, or they might perceive your objective to be growing the library for its own sake rather than for theirs. The shift in focus can have a significant effect on your audience's reaction. It is important to have the right structure for your story from the very beginning, so you can plan your conversation, handout, or presentation around this structure.

You will not always be the one reaching out to others and trying to gain their attention. Some stakeholders may come to you asking for information. If you feel that what they are requesting is not meaningful or you have something additional that you think would be of interest to them that they did not know to ask for, in most cases you can tactfully add some information to your response. For example, if your grants office has been maintaining a list of fast facts about the library that they can insert into grant proposals, they may ask you to keep updating it with information such as the number of volumes of bound periodicals or pieces of microfilm. Chances are they will be quite receptive if you also offer them a count of your e-book holdings. If your provost wants to know how many online databases you have, feel free to also tell him or her how many articles were downloaded from these databases in the last year. People who work outside the library don't necessarily know what information to ask for, and as long as you keep your response brief and provide information that is relevant to them, they will usually appreciate learning something they didn't know to ask about. The exception to this would be outside agencies that are compiling survey data on multiple libraries, like ARL or your local consortium, as they won't have a slot in their comparison chart to include your additional data.

Whether you have been asked for specific information or are offering it of your own initiative, you need to be careful not to take up too much of other people's time. This is common courtesy and also helps you hold the other person's attention. Stay focused and avoid extraneous information. You want to tell your audience enough to take action but not so much as to bore them. If you are not sure of the level of detail someone needs, you can always start with something brief but keep more information on hand so you can look up answers to questions that come up.

There are a variety of vehicles you can use to present information to other people. Some examples are PowerPoint, handouts, or a web page. Which form you choose will depend on how you are interacting with the people reading the information and how much time you have. Marketing materials are generally printed, so they can be included in a packet with other items. In a meeting with administrators, you might use a Power-Point presentation or, if the meeting is more informal, printouts of your charts. Because detailed tables require time and attention, reserve these for people who really need the detail in order to do their jobs, such as your own colleagues.

Considerations for Specific Audiences

In order to tailor your presentation to your audience, you need to know what the audience's goals are and also how well these people respond to different kinds of information. Table 12.1 lists some people with whom you might potentially share data, what their goals might be, and what pieces of your evaluation could help them meet these goals. The examples in the table should help you target presentations to your audience.

Administrators

When it comes to aligning your goals with those of your audience, communicating with anyone who is in a supervisory role over you presents a special situation, as their goals are tied with yours in a unique way. Although the provost, president, or trustees may not be involved with library operations, anyone above the library director in the organizational chain is technically responsible for how the library performs. Simply by letting these people know how the library is doing, you are helping them in several ways. As bosses, they depend on the people they supervise to keep them informed, and your information helps them to speak knowledgeably to others about an area that is their responsibility. In addition, demonstrating evidence-based decision making will reassure them that you are doing a good job with the resources you have, which is important since the quality of the library will reflect well or badly on anyone whose place in the reporting structure falls above it. They should want to hear what you are doing well, as long as "well" is defined in their terms: meeting the institution's strategic plan, supporting their initiatives, or making the institution competitive. None of this is to say that your supervisors will be an especially captive audience or have the time to pay close attention to your data. Rather, understanding how your bosses' goals overlap with yours can help you frame the conversation so that they see it as something useful to them. Try to see your role, at least for the duration of this conversation, as helping those above you do their jobs. This will ultimately benefit you, as part of their job is advocating for you and touting your successes.

Although all administrators have some interests in common, individuals can differ significantly in how they operate. Research studies that look at what kinds of data university administrators find meaningful have shown more variation than commonalities. Lynch and colleagues (2007) interviewed six university presidents and provosts about their attitudes toward university libraries and found that different administrators preferred different data. Most did not believe that the size of a collection in and of itself was

Table 12.1. Stakeholders and What Information Serves Their Goals

AUDIENCE	GOALS	DATA
Offices promoting the university, e.g., marketing or admissions	Talk up your strengths and uniqueness	Quantitative comparison to other institutions (only if positive) Percentage of cited items owned by library (to demonstrate you can meet needs) Comparative data showing where you collection is especially strong, possibly using authoritative lists
Prospective students	Compare your institution to others Determine if their scholarly interests or personal identity is represented	Size of collections (if you compare favorably to peers) Percentage of cited items owned by library (to demonstrate you can meet needs) Comparison to authoritative lists, or a select list of resources you provide
Trustees	Determine if money is being well spent and if more is needed	Usage statistics Circulation statistics
Legislators	Make funding decisions (for publicly funded institutions)	Quantitative comparison to other institutions Usage statistics Circulation statistics
Accrediting agencies	Determine if your resources support the programs in question	Numbers of books and journal subscriptions on a given subject Description of any major databases or reference sources you have access to
Consortia	Create comparative reports Plan for collaborative collection development	Numbers of books and journal subscriptions on various subjects
Organizations offering grant money	To decide if the library can support the proposed research to such an extent to make it successful	Numbers of books and journal subscriptions on a given subject Description of any major databases or reference sources you have access to
Provost or financial officer	Decide if funding should be allocated, based on whether current money is well managed and whether requested money is needed Educate self so as to tout the library to outsiders or request funding from trustees	Usage statistics Comparison of holdings to peer institutions, including gaps representing what you need money for
Librarians	Decide what to buy more of and what to weed Allocate current budget	Circulation statistics and interlibrary loan statistics Names of key authors from both ILL and citation analysis Comparison to authoritative lists COUNTER reports and other measures of usage of subscriptions Size of segments of collection compared to aspirational institutions, plus a title list of commonly held titles you don't own Size of segments of the collection in relation to enrollment or to usage

a measure of quality, though some thought that comparing their own library to others made the numbers more meaningful. One CEO actually saw comparison with other institutions as the only serious measure of quality. All six presidents felt that circulation was an important way to show the library's value, and all appreciated hearing feedback from library users.

Administrators will also have different preferences for numbers versus stories. In general, people with a humanities background are more likely to prefer testimonials and might be distrustful of numbers as lacking a human element. If you know or have reason to believe that your administrators feel this way, you can supplement your numbers with quotes or anecdotes. Since you will probably want to share some numbers even with those who prefer stories, present the data through graphics as much as possible. This makes it easier for nonquantitative people to interpret your numbers. Advice on visual representations of data is offered below.

There are particular considerations when presenting to people with a quantitative or natural sciences background as well. These people may argue that you have not really proven anything as you haven't been able to control for all variables that could be influencing the size and use of your collection. It can be useful to remind your audience that you are describing the situation rather than trying to prove something. In addition, quantitative researchers will likely be skeptical if you make claims about cause and effect. It is very important in quantitative research to remember that correlation does not equal causation, that is, if one variable increases at the same time as another, it does not necessarily mean that the first increase caused the second. You may encounter skepticism if you claim that, say, implementing patron-driven acquisitions caused your interlibrary loan requests to go down, even though this would intuitively make sense. Be careful not to claim that one change caused another. Just describe what happened and what steps you want to take based on what the data shows.

Despite the variations between different administrators, there are a few general guidelines that you can use. Stay away from numbers that simply describe the collection. Include comparisons, measures of use, and testimonials to make the data meaningful. Even people with a quantitative background will probably appreciate some quotes to supplement the numbers. Because all administrators are busy, be concise and to the point. Your presentation should be sensitive to their time, their background, and what they need for their jobs.

Prospective Students

At the other end of the spectrum from administrators are prospective students. Although you will probably not be giving any data directly to this population, they are often the target of marketing efforts, so offices that promote your university will be conscious of this population's concerns. Like administrators, prospective students will also vary in what is important to them. Graduate students will need to use the library more heavily than undergraduates, so they may be more interested in the size of the collection than undergraduates. Because they will already know their disciplinary focus, they may be familiar with major journals or databases and want to know if the library has access to these. Undergraduates probably have less of a sense of what they'll need and may be more interested in knowing that staff at the library will be available to help them. Members of any minority or marginalized group will want to see that their population is represented. Your publicity materials can mention area studies collections, disability studies, or LGBTQ studies. Ask your admissions office what kinds of questions they get from prospective students so you can make sure your information meets their need for answers to students' questions.

Because librarians don't often interact directly with prospective students, you'll be relying on admissions or marketing to pass along the information you've gathered. This will probably require frequent communication to ensure that these offices incorporate your information into their own materials. A glossy brochure about the university could include some facts or quotes about the library, but the office that produces the brochure might not remember to include it unless you've been in touch with them since well before the brochure was designed. Meeting with these offices early on to ask what they need not only helps you know what information to give them, it puts you on their radar when they create marketing materials. A major way that admissions offices disseminate information about the university is through tours. See if you can provide some content that will be included in the tour guide's script. Ask whoever trains the tour guides what kinds of questions they get on tours so you can provide answers to these questions. You can also ask when they train new tour guides, or whether the guides learn from a manual, so that you can suggest ways to integrate the library into their training processes.

Library Colleagues

Sharing data with your colleagues in the library is different from sharing with the public or even sharing with people who oversee the library, because your audience is somewhat captive. Unlike prospective students, administrators, or accrediting agencies, it *is* your colleagues' job to build the library, and they will be willing to spend time thinking about how to do so. If you oversee the library's selectors, in theory you can require them to look at the data, even if they are not numbers people or have not asked for the information. You probably want some degree of uniformity in how collection development decisions are made—for example, evaluating all databases according to cost per use—and therefore you might ask all selectors to take this statistic into account. You might also make reviewing certain data a required part of the training process for new selectors. Yet it rarely works to simply hand down tasks and tell people they have to do them. You still need to find some way of making selectors feel invested in the evaluation process.

The best way to make people feel invested is to include them in conversations throughout the evaluation process and allow them to give input. Henle and Cochenour (2007) provide a nice example of how this strategy worked for them when dealing with a selector who initially had no interest in statistics and did not use them. When designing an internal system for organizing and disseminating usage statistics, they involved all selectors in the design process. Although initially this particular librarian told them she did not have any input, they kept in contact with her so that she could participate in the process at a later point if she chose. When she saw one of their proposed tools for displaying the data, she asked for a modification that would be useful to her. As this anecdote illustrates, asking for people's feedback can keep them involved and allow them to feel included rather than commanded. Your colleagues will feel more eager, or at least willing, to analyze data if they do not feel that the task was imposed on them but rather that they have some say in how they'd like to work with the data.

When figuring out how to make data available to your colleagues, the issue of what data to share or how to present it is somewhat different than with other audiences, as you don't need to select data based on a particular message you want to send. Whereas you would never tell prospective students that your collection of math books was older, on average, than your psychology books, or that only 20 percent of the math books had been borrowed in the last four years, librarians need to have this information so they can weed or buy new books. Because your colleagues need detail in order to do their jobs, you can provide the data in a more raw form than you would for administrators or the public. You might want to provide data in a format that allows it to be manipulated, such as an Excel file in which selectors can highlight the numbers that stand out to them or make notes on which issues they have responded to. For this audience, you will probably have multiple spreadsheets or other documents. Well-organized and labeled folders on a shared file space are a common way to make this data accessible to the people who need it.

Budget Requests

One way, alluded to above, that you will likely use your evaluation data is for making budget requests. In addition to the advice given earlier on communicating with administrators, there are some considerations specific to this situation that merit their own in-depth discussion. The literature on library budgeting makes several points about messaging. One is that you need to demonstrate that you are doing a good job managing the money you have. Ironically, no one wants to give money to a library that says, in essence, "Look how bad we are." While you might think this statement would make the case that you're underfunded, it could inadvertently also create the impression that the library is not doing a good job building a collection and that the librarians should not be trusted with the institution's money. Likewise, do not accompany your budget request with complaints about your funding in years past. This can easily be read as a criticism of the very people whose favor you are trying to gain since some or all of them were the ones who decided your budget last year!

The message when requesting money is always that you are doing the best you can with what you have and could do even better with more money. To make this point, be prepared to offer a concrete proposal of what you will do with more money and be able to justify it. If you need funding to support your new anthropology program, bring data showing that the library owns a very small percentage of what these students are citing in their papers, that these students are borrowing more on interlibrary loan than are students from other departments, and that you have very few of the core journals in the field. If you then calculate what it would cost to add enough journal subscriptions to cover 80 percent of cited articles, you will have a very good justification for this particular funding request. Your case will be even stronger if you bring this data to the anthropology faculty. If the faculty see your analysis, they not only will know you are making a good-faith effort to support them with the money you have but can also tell the budget decision makers how funding the library will benefit them. Make clear that if you do not get this money, you can't take the positive steps you just laid out. In order to do your job well, you need funding.

The people deciding the budget will be balancing the competing requests from many units within the institution. One major way that they determine priorities is using a strategic plan. Lynch and colleagues, who studied six university presidents and provosts, remind us that "it is the functional role of the library in service to the university's mission that ultimately garners budgetary support" (2007: 213–14). You should explicitly state how the library's objectives support the institution's larger vision. If you have an official strategic plan and mission, use the language of these documents in your budget request.

Also, because the people deciding the budget will be balancing the needs of many people, it is useful to make the case that funding the library benefits other units as well. In the example above of the new anthropology program, you want the administration to see that by giving money to the library, they will make two units happy, the library and the anthropology department.

The budget request process works differently at different institutions but almost always occurs once a year and involves a written request for money. The formal process should not be the only time that decision makers learn about the library's needs, though. Library directors often have regular communication with a provost, president, or other administrator who can either make budget decisions or advocate on the library's behalf. Make sure that you or your director update these people periodically on what the library is doing. You can mention, for example, that you are dealing with serials renewals and are worried about rising prices, or that you are in the process of evaluating your holdings to make sure you can support a new program that is launching. It can also be very helpful if the administrators who decide how to allocate budgets hear from constituents outside the library who would like additional library resources. When department chairs or other faculty lobby the library to start new subscriptions in support of their programs, tell them you wish you could and redirect them to whoever decides your budget.

Presentation of Data

After deciding what information you want to share and how you want to frame it, the last remaining step before you are ready to have your conversation or make your handout is to figure out what the data is going to look like visually. Whether you want the take-away to be apparent or for people to draw their own conclusions, your findings should be shown in a way that is readable and concise. The people you'll be sharing data with will not have spent nearly as much time as you have thinking about what the numbers might mean, nor are they likely to now. Some of your stakeholders will not be good at working with numbers in general. A page full of numbers not only requires time and effort for your audience to interpret but can embarrass people who are inexperienced at reading quantitative information. Along with targeting the information toward your audience's goals, you also want to present it in a way that is helpful to them, neither wasting their time nor confusing them.

Principles of Data Presentation

A great source of guidance on data presentation is Edward Tufte's book *The Visual Display of Quantitative Information* (2001). Isabelle Meirelles's *Design for Information* (2013) is also insightful. Although many of the graphics Meirelles describes are more complicated than what you are likely to use, the principles of visual perception that she offers can make a huge difference in the clarity of the images you create.

Both authors focus on the use of images rather than simple text or tables. Tufte explains that pictures are a more efficient format for displaying data than tables are: they take up less space on a page and take less time for viewers to read. A graph can be comprehensible to those who are experienced at interpreting numbers as well as those who aren't. With a graph, you have the flexibility of a variety of ways to represent your data, and you can choose the graph that makes your point most vividly.

Not all graphs are as useful as they could be, however. You'll need some skill and practice before you can achieve what Tufte calls "graphical excellence" (2001: 51). Tufte defines an excellent graphic as one that communicates ideas clearly, efficiently, and accurately. Clarity requires an easy-to-read design that encourages comparison of whichever numbers you want your audience to compare. An efficient graphic saves both time and space: the image should take up as little space as possible and also allow viewers to grasp its message as quickly as possible. It should not arrange the data in such a way as to create a message that isn't true, however. Numbers can be accurate but still be presented in a way that distorts them, and you want your presentation to be honest.

There are several techniques that can help you achieve clarity and efficiency. To help your audience identify the message you're trying to share, experiment with different kinds of images to see if one kind makes comparisons between numbers more visually apparent. Meirelles explains that certain differences between images are easier to perceive at a glance than others. People usually have difficulty comparing the areas enclosed by different two-dimensional shapes but can distinguish more easily between the lengths of lines. This means that bar graphs are usually easier to read than pie charts, as reading a pie chart requires comparing areas of wedges while a bar chart only requires looking at the lengths of the bars. An especially clear way to represent numbers visually, Meirelles suggests, is to use a repeating image that represents a set value. For example, if one book represents one hundred checkouts, two books would represent two hundred checkouts and half a book would represent fifty. If you cannot find a way to make it visually apparent that a number has increased or decreased over time, Tufte recommends using arrows to clarify the direction of the change. You can also use words to add information to a graph, even supplementing graphs with quotes or other small blocks of text if doing so would provide important context or if stories are important to your audience.

You may also want to explicitly highlight the numbers that are striking to you. You can make a specific number or section of a graph stand out by using what Meirelles calls "preattentive features" (2013: 23). These are visual characteristics that people perceive without consciously paying attention. An observer will easily notice an image that is a different color, shade, shape, or size than what is around it or a line that differs from the others in length, orientation, weight (i.e., bold vs. normal), or curvature. Objects that are circled or have a box around them will also stand out. Meirelles cautions, however, that these differences are only easily noticeable if a small number of objects are highlighted, not if you have, say, bolded a third of the numbers on the graph.

Color can also be a powerful tool for conveying information visually. If the data you are presenting has an inherent order to it, such as highest cost-per-use databases to lowest cost per use, use shades of the same color for the different bars or lines in your image. The shading creates a ranking that will be intuitive to your audience, whereas making blue symbolize high cost per use and red symbolize low will not. If you are using color to represent value on two different graphs, the color should have the same meaning on both graphs. Figure 12.1 illustrates a consistent use of color. In both pie charts, the darkest shade of grey represents articles available via the library, the medium shade shows what is not available, and the lightest shade represents materials that are free online. Because the images are in grayscale, the three wedges are essentially three shades of the same color. Since the three wedges in the pie chart do not fall along a scale, such as least available to most available, you could just as easily use three different colors, as long as there is enough contrast to make the wedges easily distinguishable. The wedge representing articles available via the library could be peach on both pie charts, and the wedge representing articles

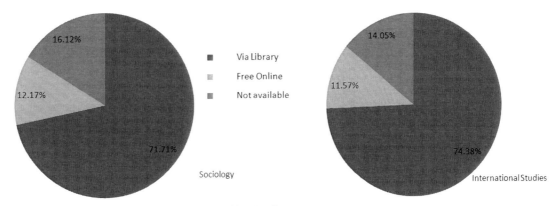

Figure 12.1. Availability of Articles Cited by Students.

freely available online could be purple on both. The important detail here is that each color means the same thing on both pie charts.

Consistency between the two charts makes comparisons easier and also allows the chart to use less ink, as it doesn't have to repeat the legend. Using minimal ink is one of Tufte's principles of graphical excellence. Note, though, that because of the principle stated earlier about the difficulty of comparing areas, it was necessary to write the exact numbers on the graph in order to compare the sizes of the wedges on one pie chart to another. A bar chart could have placed the different colored bars next to each other to make comparison possible without adding labels. This would result in a more efficient chart using less ink.

The reason for using as little ink as possible to convey as much information as possible is efficiency. A simpler image will be easier for your audience to read, and they will get its message more quickly. Note that some of the tools for drawing attention to a specific part of the graph, such as circling something or adding text, require adding ink, while others do not, such as using a different color. Sometimes you'll find it necessary to add circles, arrows, or text, but be careful that you do not add so much as to make your image look cluttered. When you try out different kinds of charts, you'll see that once you've found the format that makes comparisons most apparent, you won't need as many arrows or circles to draw attention to your findings. After you've created the graphic, as a last step erase any unnecessary lines from the image. Often the gridlines that run parallel to the x- and y-axes can be removed without any loss of information, and sometimes so can the axes themselves.

Visual Distortions

Not only does visual display affect how quickly and easily viewers can find the message in your data, it can also allow you to distort the data so that it tells an inaccurate story. Because honesty is important, you should be aware of some common errors that could lead to unintentionally skewing the message your data is sending. One possible error is having inconsistent intervals—for example, if each bar on your graph represents a year of circulation except the last one, which represents six months. Another caution is that if you are using differently sized images to represent quantities, the image sizes should be proportional to the quantities. For example, if you use an image of a book to represent the size of your history collection, and your art collection is twice the size, it should be represented either by two books or by one book of double the size. Although this sounds obvious, there have been graphs that do this incorrectly and double both the height and the width of the book, resulting in a book that is actually four times as large. The most accurate and comprehensible graphic would use a consistently sized book that repeated a different number of times to show different quantities.

Other distortions can come from excluding information that would provide important context. If your article downloads are higher in one discipline than another but you fail to explain that you actually offer more online journals in this discipline, this would be a distortion due to lack of context. It is also possible to omit context by not showing enough years in a time-series graph. Maybe checkouts are way up from last year to this year, but last year was unusually low, and even the increase this year has not brought you back up to where you were before. If your chart only shows two years, you'll be highlighting this high value and obscuring the fact that the five-year trend is actually a decline. Think about what information is necessary in order to make your data tell a true story.

Types of Graphs

With Tufte's and Meirelles's principles and cautions in mind, you can begin to experiment with different kinds of charts to display your data. There are a few different kinds of graphs you can use. One would be a time-series display, which shows increments of time across the x-axis and the value of the variable you are measuring on the y-axis. Tufte cautions that displaying how only one variable has changed across time could give the false impression that the passage of time has caused the change. Usually, you will want to show that one thing has changed in parallel with another thing, being careful not to claim causation. For instance, maybe your database downloads increased at the same time enrollment increased, or your print circulation went down when you began offering more e-books. Although you won't know for sure whether one of these changes caused the other, you can show that they are related by including both variables on the same time series graph.

Figure 12.2 is a time-series chart showing print book circulation, e-book downloads, and interlibrary borrowing requests, with a vertical bar representing each year. Each bar contains three stacked sections, one representing each kind of book use with the total

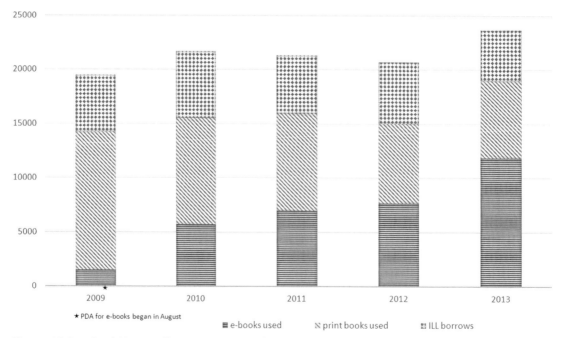

Figure 12.2. Book Usage, All Formats (Bar Graph).

height of the bar showing book use for the year. Each section is shaded with a different pattern: horizontal stripes, diagonal stripes, or diamonds. The patterns are helpful for differentiating the sections because the graph is in grayscale, but even if your presentation uses color, the patterns can make it more user-friendly for members of your audience who might be color-blind. If you are using color, avoid using red and green together, as red-green color blindness is the most common form, and use colors that have high contrast. In this example, because the bars are stacked on top of each other, it is fairly easy to see that overall book use is going up: the top of the stacked bar goes up and down but shows an overall upward trend. It is also clear that the increase in total book use is mostly due to rapidly increasing use of e-books: the segment at the bottom with horizontal lines grows significantly each year. Although e-book use is measured differently from print use and can't be directly compared, the story the image tells is accurate in a general sense: print circulation is shrinking, e-book use is growing rapidly, and the total amount of books patrons use is growing somewhat. If there is a one-time event that you believe affected your measures, such as the addition of a large e-book collection or an increased number of patrons, you can also mark this on the time-series chart with an image such as an arrow or star next to the year in which the change happened. In figure 12.2, there is a star and a note by the label for 2009 indicating that the library added a patron-driven acquisitions program in August of that year, which greatly increased the number of e-books available.

You can also make a time-series chart using lines. The value for each year is represented by a dot on the graph, and the dots connect to make a line. Figure 12.3 is a stacked line graph. This means that, like in the previous figure, the values of each type of book use are stacked on top of each other. The line for ILL borrows starts near 20,000 but does not mean that there were 20,000 interlibrary loan requests. Instead, the number of ILL requests is represented by the diamond-patterned area that lies on top of the other two areas of the graph. Because the lines connect smoothly across the graph, as opposed to the side-by-side but separate bars in the previous figure, it is much easier in figure 12.3 to see how the values are changing. Total book use is clearly increasing, with the biggest change occurring between 2012 and 2013. It is also clear that only e-book use is increasing, with the other two measures of book use decreasing. In this case, the line graph allows viewers to pick out the trend more quickly than the bar graph did. It can take a lot of trial and error to figure out which kind of graph makes your point most clearly as different graphs work best in different situations. You can experiment with making graphs using the tools in textbox 12.1, all of which are appropriate for beginners.

Although he advocates for displaying data visually, Tufte explains that there are some situations in which tables are preferable to graphs. One case would be if you find yourself adding a lot of text to your graph to explain the image. This could create a messy-looking image that might be clearer as a table. Tables are also preferable if for some reason you need to show the exact numbers rather than an overall pattern, perhaps if you are talking about how to allocate your budget. Another advantage of tables is that it is easy to conjoin several tables into one if you are describing many different variables. For example, table 12.2 compiles data on the citation patterns of students from three different departments. Because the table includes so many different characteristics of the citations—material types, age, and availability—it would be impossible to put this information all into one graph. You would need a graph for the material types, maybe a stacked column graph with a column for each department, then another column graph showing availability, and the mean ages would probably be best in a table. The large table format allows a compact

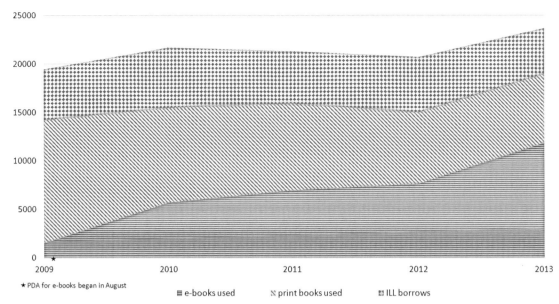

25000

20000

15000

10000

5000

0

★

2009   2010   2011   2012   2013

★ PDA for e-books began in August

▤ e-books used   ⊠ print books used   ▦ ILL borrows

Figure 12.3.   Book Usage, All Formats (Line Graph).

TEXTBOX 12.1.

TOOLS FOR CREATING VISUAL DISPLAYS OF DATA

Microsoft Excel

Available as a standard part of Microsoft Office. Highly customizable, though not intuitive to use. You may need to read the help to figure out how to make the changes you want. Does not include images like maps or pictograms (using repeat images to show quantity, e.g., a stack of book icons representing checkouts).

Many Eyes

http://www-969.ibm.com/software/analytics/manyeyes/#/. Includes standard graphs, maps, and word clouds. Does not offer as much customization as Venngage or Excel. All the data you upload is visible to other Many Eyes users.

Venngage

https://venngage.com/. Easy to customize, though you don't have as much control as in Excel. Very easy to input data and select different types of charts. You can't export to a PDF unless you're a premium user, but you can post your image to Twitter, Facebook, or Tumblr. Does not let you upload data; you need to type it in manually.

VIDI

http://www.dataviz.org/. Very easy to use and has abundant tutorials. Not very customizable. Offers only basic types of graphs—bar, chart, pie, maps. One unique type of chart it offers is a dashboard-style gauge.

Table 12.2. Data on Citations

	SOCIOLOGY		INTERNATIONAL STUDIES		PSYCHOLOGY	
	FREQUENCY	PERCENT	FREQUENCY	PERCENT	FREQUENCY	PERCENT
Material Types Cited						
Books	115	21.86%	97	30.31%	60	11.98%
Journals	304	57.79%	121	37.81%	408	81.44%
Websites	65	12.36%	43	13.44%	25	4.99%
Reports	27	5.13%	51	15.94%	3	0.60%
Personal Comm.	1	0.19%	0	0.00%	0	0.00%
Other	14	2.66%	8	2.50%	5	1.00%
N=	526	100%	320	100%	501	100%
Mean Age						
Books	1994		2003		1999	
Journals	2002		2003		2005	
Modal Age						
Books	2009		2011		2001	
Journals	2010		2011		2012	
Availability						
Books						
Via Library	39	33.91%	33	34.02%	20	33.33%
Free Online	13	11.30%	13	13.40%	1	1.67%
Not available	63	54.78%	51	52.58%	39	65.00%
N=	115	100%	97	100%	60	100%
Journal Articles						
Via Library	218	71.71%	90	74.38%	339	83.09%
Free Online	37	12.17%	14	11.57%	2	0.49%
Not available	49	16.12%	17	14.05%	67	16.42%
N=	304	100%	121	100%	408	100%
Journals cited >1x	50	22.22%	13	12.50%	64	27.47%
Citations accounted for	129	66.54%	31	25.62%	239	58.58%

presentation of the many characteristics of the citations in one place, fulfilling Tufte's imperative to use the least possible amount of ink and space.

A popular way for libraries to display data is the dashboard. The term *dashboard* does not refer to a particular kind of chart or graph but rather a web page that compiles several simple graphs in order to provide an overview of how the institution is performing. The metaphor is of a car dashboard, which uses several small displays to indicate how your car is performing. Sometimes the images on a library dashboard are modeled after a car dashboard and actually show gauges, though most often they are composed of typical charts like bar graphs or pie graphs. Some libraries have dashboards that include brief key numbers (e.g., number of books checked out in the last year) next to an illustration such as a picture of a book. This is not really a graphical display of data, as the image is only for visual interest and isn't providing any information. The examples in textbox 12.2 are all dashboards that use images to present the data rather than simply for visual interest. When you look at them, think about whether or not they provide enough context for you to judge whether the numbers indicate good performance or not. Also ask yourself how quickly you were able to notice the trends yourself when glancing at the charts.

Key Points

You are now ready to take your collection evaluation out into the larger sphere of your institution. You should be well prepared to convey information clearly and with authority in ways that will be beneficial to both the library and the institution. As you embark on this next phase:

- Anticipate possible challenges but do not be afraid to share what you've learned.
- Present information that helps your audience meet their own goals.
- When making budget requests, send the message that you are doing a good job with the resources you have and could do even better with more money.
- Present your numbers visually whenever this is feasible.
- Take the time to find the kind of graph or image that tells your story the most clearly and uses the least ink.

Collection evaluation is a complex process that requires careful planning. Nevertheless, with some attention and effort, you can complete an evaluation without having a research background or special software. While you will never be able to say for certain that you have "enough" materials or that you know exactly how your collection is being used, evaluation can nevertheless give you a wealth of information. With a rich picture of your collection and how it is being used, you can improve your library and communicate to others about its place within the larger institution.

References

Henle, Alea, and Donnice Cochenour. 2007. "Practical Considerations in the Standardization and Dissemination of Usage Statistics." In *Usage Statistics of E-Serials*, edited by David C. Fowler, 5–23. Binghamton, NY: Haworth Press.

Lynch, Beverly P., Catherine Murray-Rust, Susan E. Parker, et al. 2007. "Attitudes of Presidents and Provosts on the University Library." *College & Research Libraries* 68, no. 3 (May): 213–27.

Meirelles, Isabel. 2013. *Design for Information: An Introduction to the Histories, Theories, and Best Practices behind Effective Information Visualizations*. Beverly, MA: Rockport Publishers.

Tufte, Edward R. 2001. *The Visual Display of Quantitative Information*. 2nd edition. Cheshire, CT: Graphics Press.

Index

About the Author

Karen C. Kohn is assistant professor and collection development manager at Arcadia University's Landman Library. She holds an MS in library and information science from the University of Illinois at Urbana–Champaign and an MA in sociology from Temple University. She has published articles about collection evaluation in *College & Research Libraries* and *Collection Management* and has presented at the Acquisitions Institute at Timberline Lodge and the Charleston Conference: Issues in Book and Serials Acquisitions.